PERSONAL FREEDOM
AND THE LAW
IN TANZANIA

PERSONAL FREEDOM AND THE LAW IN TANZANIA

A Study of Socialist State Administration

ROBERT MARTIN

NAIROBI 1974
OXFORD UNIVERSITY PRESS
DAR ES SALAAM LUSAKA ADDIS ABABA

Oxford University Press, Ely House, London W.1

GLASGOW   NEW YORK   TORONTO   MELBOURNE   WELLINGTON
CAPE TOWN   IBADAN   NAIROBI   DAR ES SALAAM   LUSAKA
ADDIS ABABA   DELHI   BOMBAY   CALCUTTA   MADRAS   KARACHI
LAHORE   DACCA   KUALA LUMPUR   SINGAPORE   HONG KONG   TOKYO

Oxford University Press, P.O. Box 72532, Nairobi, Kenya

Made and printed in East Africa

To my parents
IVAN HAROLD MARTIN
and
ANNETTE JOYCE LATHAM

This book has been published with the help of a grant from the Social Science Research Council of Canada, using funds provided by the Canada Council.

ACKNOWLEDGEMENTS

I wish it were possible to express my gratitude more fully than through a formal acknowledgement, to a number of organizations and individuals who assisted me in the preparation of this book.

I am especially grateful to Hosea Talwa, then Director of the Institute of Administration, University of Dar es Salaam, for his support and encouragement during the earlier stages in the writing of this work. I would like to thank Gill Boehringer, Kevin Carey, Yash Ghai, Steve Huber, Daudi Mwakawago, John Saul and Bob Seidman, who all took part in educating me.

The Canada Council most kindly provided funds to enable me to return to Tanzania for further research. Similar assistance was received with gratitude from the University of Toronto Tanzania Project.

Patrick McAuslan read the manuscript and made many useful comments and Jim Read was a constant source of information and suggestions.

The Social Science Research Council of Canada very generously provided a grant to cover part of the costs of publication.

Carolyn McRae helped with the typing and Liz Jackson prepared the index.

It is customary for the writer to thank his wife for support, encouragement and understanding. This I readily do. However, I must thank my wife, Barbara Simpson, for much more. She typed several drafts of the manuscript. She edited early drafts and helped to clarify the analysis of many points. Her scholarly approach and her wide knowledge of East Africa were invaluable. Without her collaboration, the book simply could not have been written.

Permission to use material is gratefully acknowledged to the following:

Makerere Institute of Social Research, Kampala, 'Prolegomenon to the Rule of Law in East Africa' by J. P. W. B. McAuslan, in East African Institute of Social Science, *Proceedings*, 1964.

Faculty of Law, Makerere University, Kampala, 'The Law and the Citizen in Uganda' by G. Kanyeihamba, in University of East Africa Social Science Council Conference, *Proceedings*, Kampala, 1968. 'Developments in Criminology in East Africa' by G. H. Boehringer, op. cit.

Messrs Sweet and Maxwell, London, *Criminal Procedure in Uganda and Kenya* by Douglas Brown.

Faculty of Law, University of Dar es Salaam, *Issa s/o Amri* v. *R.* [1968] H.C.D. n. 195 in *High Court Digest*.

The Nationalist, Dar es Salaam, 'Editorial', 24 June 1969.

East Africa Journal, Nairobi, May 1966, 'Machinery of Justice in a

Developing Society' by M. D. Bomani.

Messrs East African Publishing House, Nairobi, 'The Court in the Tanzania One-Party State' by P. T. Georges, in G. F. A. Sawyerr (ed.), *East African Law and Social Change*.

The Speaker, National Assembly, Dar es Salaam, Parliamentary *Debates*, 22 February 1966, speech by the Hon. R. M. Kawawa.

Journal of Modern African Studies, London, vol. IV, no. 4 (1966), 'Constitutional Innovation and Political Stability in Tanzania' by J. P. W. B. McAuslan and Y. P. Ghai.

The Editor, *East African Law Reports*, for various cases.

His Excellency, President Julius K. Nyerere, *Freedom and Unity* and *Freedom and Socialism* (Oxford University Press, Dar es Salaam).

Attorney-General of Tanzania, Attorney-General's Chambers, Dar es Salaam, for various extracts from Tanzanian Statutes.

The Government Printer, United Republic of Tanzania, Dar es Salaam, Government Paper no. 1 of 1962; *Report of the Presidential Commission on the Establishment of a Democratic One-Party State, 1965; Annual Report* of the Permanent Commission of Enquiry of 1966-7 and 1967-8 and *Primary Courts Manual, 1964.*

CONTENTS

TABLE OF CASES

Note: Where the page number appears in bold, this indicates that an extract from the case is presented.

Abbreviations

A.C.	Appeal Cases
All E.R.	All England Law Reports
All N.L.R.	All Nigeria Law Reports
E.A.	East African Law Reports
E.A.C.A.	Court of Appeal for Eastern Africa Reports
E.A.L.R.	East Africa Protectorate Law Reports
H.C.D.	Tanzania High Court Digest
K.B.	King's Bench Reports
K.L.R.	Kenya Law Reports
Q.B.	Queen's Bench Reports
S.C.R.	Supreme Court Reports (Canada)
T.L.R. (R)	Tanganyika Law Reports (Revised)
W.L.R.	Weekly Law Reports
Z.L.R.	Zanzibar Law Reports

TABLE OF TANZANIAN STATUTES

Note: Pre-Independence enactments are styled 'Ordinances' while post-Independence enactments are styled 'Acts'. The chapter numbers refer to the 1965 Revision of the Laws.

INTRODUCTION

This book is concerned with the legal aspects of the relationship between the state and its subjects in a socialist African state, and covers three main fields. First, the provisions of the law of Tanzania which relate to personal freedom are described. Secondly, the way in which these provisions are actually applied in practice is investigated, and finally a framework is suggested within which the law and its practice may be analysed.

In setting out the law concerning personal freedom, the question immediately arises, 'What is personal freedom?' and the difficulty in defining the word 'freedom' becomes apparent. Both the word freedom and the reality which it represents have suffered greatly in recent years, and one must recognize the risk of absurdity involved in writing about freedom in an era when countries such as Portugal, Spain, Greece, and the Republic of South Africa are all subsumed within the classification, 'free world'.

The choice of the term 'personal freedom' is arbitrary. To writers on constitutional law, personal freedom normally means the specific right not to be incarcerated. Here, it is used in a somewhat wider, and, perhaps, existential sense: that is the degree to which human beings are permitted to live and develop within organized society, free from coercion, harassment, and intimidation. Personal freedom, then, becomes not simply a summation of various categories of rights claimed by isolated individuals against other isolated individuals, but a function of the ordering of society as a whole. A comprehensive study of personal freedom would require an analysis of a great variety of relationships—political, economic, social, cultural, legal, familial, sexual, educational, religious—within a given state. In this book the central concern is with legal relationships, and only with those between the state and its subjects. This kind of limitation inevitably leads to a degree of distortion, but this distortion can be minimized if one continually bears in mind that personal freedom is a total societal phenomenon and not simply a legal one. The material is presented in what may appear to be a random fashion, but an understanding of the problems involved in the legal relationships may be best achieved by building up a generalized view of structures and institutions rather than by a linear description of 'freedom of speech', 'freedom of movement', etc.

The material presented is, as far as possible, Tanzanian. Non-Tanzanian sources have been used in two situations: first, where socialists from other countries have formulated theories which seem appropriate to Tanzania, and, secondly, to illustrate the way in which other socialist states or other African nations have attempted to deal with situations similar to those which arise in Tanzania.

The bulk of the material presented is extracted from statutes, case reports, essays, speeches, and monographs, supplemented by original text. The book is intended primarily for non-law students who are concerned with the relationship between the state and the individual in Tanzania, i.e. students of political science, history, and public administration, as well as lay magistrates and administrators. The lengthy statutory and case material has been included in order to assist these readers to understand legal reasoning and techniques. It is also hoped that this book may provide a useful reference work for the magistrate or administrator on the job, and for lawyers and law students for whom extensive references to additional legal material have been included. Finally, because the book is intended primarily for Tanzanian readers, no explanations of local terms and phenomena are given.

Although the word Tanzania appears in the title of this book, the material refers to Tanzania mainland; it was not possible to obtain sufficient information about Zanzibar for a meaningful study to be made.

To see law as other than a collection of disconnected abstractions, more is required than a simple presentation of rules. Discussion is, of course, desirable, but much discussion often takes place only within the definitional confines of the rules themselves. To be fully understood, rules of law must be presented and analysed within their operational context. Even so, distortion may result unless these rules and their operation are seen in their proper place within an articulated view of society as a whole. It is also necessary to recognize that a broader view requires the integration of concepts of public law within a generalized approach to political economy.

An attempt is made to utilize this kind of approach to questions involving the state and the individual in Tanzania by presenting detailed incidents which illustrate the actual operation of particular institutions or rules of law. These generally take the form of Notes which are interspersed with the text and readings contained in the book. Besides suggesting the way in which rules and institutions operate, these notes may stimulate a continuing analysis of broader questions of policy.

In analysing public law and its operation in any society, it is necessary to use a theoretical approach based on the objective conditions of that society and ideologically and culturally relevant to its goals and priorities. The study of public law in Africa has suffered, until recently, from a failure to develop such an approach. Two traditional approaches to public law in Africa may be discerned. The first may be called the nostalgic approach:

It is to be noted that the idea of individual freedom under the law was, at independence, already well established as part and parcel of the legal system inherited from Britain by the several African states.[1]

1 T. O. Elias, 'The Commonwealth in Africa', *Modern Law Review*, vol. XXXI, 1968, p. 290.

Here it is assumed that a developed liberal democracy of the English type was introduced into Commonwealth Africa along with colonialism, that such a constitutional form is the only suitable one for Africa (or anywhere else for that matter), and that the period since independence can be characterized for public law purposes as a progressive rejection, resulting from incompetence or bad faith or both, of this precious heritage. This approach tends to be favoured by English writers on constitutional law in Africa. It can be seen quite clearly in the one book written on Tanzanian public law.[2]

The second approach may be termed the objectivity approach. Here the commentator is more understanding, appreciates the contradictions in the colonial legal system, and notes many of the problems facing the post-colonial state. The method used is comparative, objective and pragmatic, and is favoured by North American commentators. The polite conclusion is nonetheless reached that unless a state possesses all the functioning institutions of western liberal-democratic theory, it is inevitably tyrannical.[3]

A more recent and more relevant approach can be found in Ghai and McAuslan,[4] where public law in a particular African state is analysed within the historical context of that state. The only standard by which the public law of a given state is to be assessed is that of its relevance to the objective requirements of that state. A similar approach has been adopted in this book.

The analytical framework suggested in this book has a strong ideological bias. 'Objectivity' as practised by bourgeois scholars is rejected as being, in reality, a deliberate obfuscation of aggressively ideological writing. Inherent in their work is an implicit acceptance of all the values of western capitalism. Thus, explicit value judgements and all criticism of imperialism or its works can be dismissed as 'unobjective'.[5]

A socialist bias has been adopted because of the need to establish a framework within which contradictions between actual practice and institutional theory in Tanzanian state administration can be noted and analysed. The practice of politics and the operations of the machinery of state and party largely reflect a theory of socialism related to Tanzania's needs. Yet key institutions, notably the courts and Parliament, reflect a different theory of the nature of politics and the role of the state. One task of the academic study of public law should be to indicate these contradictions and suggest possible

[2] J. S. R. Cole and W. N. Denison, *Tanganyika: The Development of Its Laws and Constitution*, Stevens and Son, London, 1964.
[3] For examples of this approach see Harvey, *Law and Social Change in Ghana*, Princeton University Press, Princeton, 1966 and Franck, *Comparative Constitutional Process*, Sweet and Maxwell, London, 1968.
[4] *Public Law and Political Change in Kenya*, Oxford University Press, Nairobi, 1970.
[5] For a general discussion of this point, see 'Objectivity and Liberal Scholarship' in Noam Chomsky, *American Power and the New Mandarins*, Penguin Books, London, 1969; for a discussion of an aspect of this issue in a Tanzanian context, see John Saul, 'High Level Manpower for Socialism' in I. N. Resnick (ed.), *Tanzania: Revolution by Education*, Longmans, Arusha, 1968.

ways in which they might be resolved. A traditional analysis of institutions rooted in a theory of political economy which has been rejected in Tanzania is worse than meaningless; it serves to perpetuate mystification and a misunderstanding of the way the polity works. In a country where the whole structure of the state was imposed from outside, it is of small value, in attempting to assess the usefulness and relevance of that structure, to adopt the standards and analytical techniques of those who fashioned and imposed it.

While accepting an ideological bias, one must at the same time be wary of certain pitfalls. Ideology should be used as a basis both for intellectual analysis and the informing of consciousness. Improperly used, it becomes mere rhetoric which is manipulated by those in power to legitimate their own acts and to so mesmerize the mass of the people that rational analysis of these acts is inhibited.

Basically, this book is an attempt to raise questions about an issue which remains the 'Achilles heel' of socialism—the exercise of state power within a society attempting to build socialism.[6] How should state power be exercised, through what institutions, according to what standards? What controls should be placed on its exercise, what limits? One might argue that to place any limits on the power of the state is to place limits on the power of the people, and that to do this is to strike at the very roots of socialism. This argument neatly evades a number of crucial issues. First, state power, or certain aspects of it, must be delegated if the state is to be able to operate. To assume that every policeman, ministry clerk, tax collector, schoolmaster, prison warder, and produce inspector is at all times a functioning repository of the people's will is absurd. Secondly, not every contradiction which arises between the state or one of its servants and an individual citizen will contain a political element, nor will the interests of the mass of the people always be totally on one side. Thirdly, and most important, this argument distorts the essential point of socialism. While the dominant policy approach of any state attempting to build socialism must be the transformation of the economic base, the ultimate aim of such transformation must never be lost sight of. This aim must be, to use Fanon's words, to set afoot 'a new man'. Clearly, in order to permit the creation of this new man, a socialist state must promote economic development, dismantle its existing class structure, prevent the formation of new exploiting classes, and protect itself against imperialist predators. All these functions will require an appropriately aggressive exercise of state power, but the central goal must not be forgotten. This requires a realization that the form the legal and constitutional superstructure takes is crucial to the whole process. A state superstructure which is not

[6] See Ralph Miliband, 'The State and Revolution', *Monthly Review*, vol. XXI, no. 11, 1970, p. 77.

consistent with the ultimate aims of socialist development will impede and ultimately frustrate the transformation of the economic base.[7]

The creation of the new man is an awesome and demanding task, and shortcomings are inevitable. Where these shortcomings are noted and criticisms are made, the author is fully aware of the humiliating results which would occur '. . . if one of the leaders of one of the new African countries could take time off from the terrible problems in his own country and become a critic of the European left'.[8] Indeed, this collection of readings and essays is presented with full knowledge of its presumptuousness, but in the hope that it may make some contribution towards promoting an analysis of the meaning and mechanics of socialist state administration in Tanzania.

[7] See Engels, 'Letter to J. Bloch', Marx and Engels, *Selected Works in One Volume*, Lawrence and Wishart, London, 1970, p. 682.
[8] Amilcar Cabral, *Revolution in Guinea*, Stage 1, London, 1969, p. 60.

CHAPTER ONE

PERSONAL FREEDOM AND THE SOCIALIST STATE: SOME THEORETICAL ISSUES

The main part of this book is concerned with the operations of certain institutions within the Tanzanian political economy and the way in which they are related to personal freedom. An investigation is made of the institutions through which the power of the state is exercised, and of the institutions through which the individual can control or limit the exercise of that power. Inevitably, an investigation of this kind must be made in the context of some general theory about the nature of the state and the purpose of government. This chapter therefore outlines certain important theoretical issues surrounding the exercise of state power in Tanzania, and provides a rough framework within which this phenomenon can be analysed. If such a framework is to be of analytical value, it must arise from the objective conditions of Tanzania itself, although some valid contributions may be found in countries which are experiencing, or have experienced, a somewhat similar history.

A relevant theory about the state in Tanzania must recognize also that there are many different meanings for words like 'freedom' and 'democracy', and that not all of these meanings are appropriate. For example, the liberal-democratic theory of politics, with its emphasis on the individual and on political freedom, may be of little value in a society where intense poverty and economic inequality are the essential national problems. In fact, in such a society, a state apparatus which dedicated itself to the preservation of the 'individual rights' of liberal democracy would be the opposite of democratic. By putting the needs of individuals above the needs for independence and development of the mass of the people, a government would forfeit the right to be called democratic.

The readings that follow question the place of personal freedom in a poor country, and discuss the governmental legacy of colonialism, socialist theories of the state, the problem of the response of organized society to disagreement or deviance, and the relationship between freedom and development.[1]

A · PRIORITIES

The following two extracts, one from a speech by the President of Tanzania

[1] For discussions of 'freedom' and 'democracy', see C. B. Macpherson, *The Real World of Democracy*, Oxford University Press, London, 1966; Herbert Aptheker, *The Nature of Democracy, Freedom and Revolution*, International Publishers, New

and the other from a speech by the Attorney-General of Tanzania, attempt to put the protection of personal freedom into the context of the many economic and social problems facing Tanzania and to suggest a meaning that could be given to personal freedom in that context.

J. K. Nyerere
SPEECH GIVEN AT THE OPENING OF
THE UNIVERSITY COLLEGE CAMPUS[2]

● The people and the Government of the United Republic are aiming to build a just society of free and equal citizens, who live in healthy conditions, who control their own destiny, and who co-operate together and with other people in a spirit of human brotherhood for mutual benefit. This is the goal. It is certainly not a description of our present society, and this is the problem—how to move most quickly from the situation of gross inequality, of widespread undernourishment, and complete lack of opportunity to grow mentally.

Obviously there are certain principles of action which are essential both for the goal, and the path to it. We all know them—the Rule of Law; Freedom of speech, publication, and writing; Freedom of association for peaceful purposes; Freedom from hunger; Freedom to develop ourselves to the full through educational and other opportunities; Freedom from discrimination and imposed humiliation; human equality. The list is a long one, and to them we have to add one more— the safety and integrity of our United Republic.

If, for example, one person uses his freedom of speech and organization in a manner which will greatly reduce our prospect of economic development, or endanger our national security, what is the Government to do? Freedom of speech, freedom of movement and association, are valuable things which we want to secure for all our people. But at the same time we must secure, urgently, freedom from hunger, and from ignorance and disease, for everyone. Can we allow the abuse of
● one freedom to sabotage our national search for another freedom?

NOTE   President Kaunda made a similar point in an article written just prior to Zambia's independence: '... democracy is of little benefit to the people if they are to remain uneducated and the number of illiterates remains high'. ('The Future of Democracy in Africa' in *Transition*, no. 15, 1964, p. 37.) Nyerere himself amplified the point when he said in a speech given in Toronto in October 1969:

York City, 1967; and Paolo Freire, *The Pedagogy of the Oppressed*, Herder and Herder, New York City, 1970.
[2] *Freedom and Unity*, Oxford University Press, Dar es Salaam, 1966, pp. 311-12.

What freedom has our subsistence farmer ? He scratches a bare living from the soil provided the rains do not fail; his children work at his side without schooling, medical care, or even good feeding. Certainly he has freedom to vote, and to speak as he wishes. But these freedoms are much less real to him than his freedom to be exploited. Only as his poverty is reduced will his existing political freedom become properly meaningful and his right to human dignity become a fact of human dignity. (*Stability and Change in Africa*, Government Printer, Dar es Salaam, 1969, p. 3.)

NOTE The extract from Nyerere's speech suggests that freedom, or any particular aspect of it, can never be an absolute. The extent to which an individual will be able to act freely will ultimately depend on the nature of his acts and the context in which they take place. This principle can be illustrated by looking at two aspects of personal freedom mentioned by the President, freedom of movement and freedom of speech, in specific contexts.

Tanzania's commitment to the liberation of southern Africa has brought her into increasingly hostile confrontation with Portugal and other imperialist states, and the country has suffered through aggressive acts on the part of these states. (See, for example, *The Times*, London, 3 December 1966, and *The Standard*, 27 December 1969.) As a result of this situation, it was felt necessary to protect certain areas, largely in the southern part of the country, which were deemed vital to national security. In order to do this, freedom of movement in and out of specified areas has been restricted. Once a place is declared protected within the meaning of the Protected Places and Areas Act, 1969 (Act No. 38 of 1969), only persons with permits may enter it. When any person is found within such a place without a permit, he bears the burden of proving that he was there lawfully. (See also, *The Nationalist*, 22 October 1969.)

In another context, where national security was not involved, freedom of speech was strongly in evidence and officially encouraged. *Government Paper No. 1 of 1969*, containing the Government's proposals on a uniform law concerning marriage, divorce, and custody of children, was made public in September. Considerable controversy arose over these proposals and a lively public discussion ensued in the press, at public meetings, in various organizations, and finally in Parliament. Discussion was free and wide-ranging and much criticism was voiced. As a result of public criticism, the Government altered several of its proposals. (For aspects of this public discussion, see *The Nationalist* and *The Standard*, October and November 1969; for a comment on the proposals, see F. M. Kassam in *Eastern Africa Law Review*, vol. II, no. 3, 1969, p. 329.)

M. D. Bomani
MACHINERY OF JUSTICE IN A DEVELOPING SOCIETY[3]

● What do I mean by the 'Machinery of Justice' ? I mean the judge or magistrate, the prosecuting attorney, the private practitioner and the academician or the law teacher. These are people who are directly or

[3] *East Africa Journal*, May 1966, p. 19.

indirectly involved in the application or maintenance of the principle of legality or, if I may use more familiar parlance, the Rule of Law. It may be asked, why the machinery of justice in a developing society? Yes, because I believe the roles of the aids I have just listed are not quite the same in a developing society as those in a country whose society is more or less static, whose institutions have crystallized and which takes the necessities of life for granted. I shall illustrate this point. At a Congress of Jurists mostly from Europe, held in Athens in 1955, the Rule of Law was described as springing 'from the rights of the individual developed through history in the age-old struggle of mankind for freedom; which rights include freedom of speech, press, worship, assembly and association and the right to free elections to the end that laws are enacted by the duly elected representatives of the people and afford equal protection to all'. Here the emphasis is on the individual, his age-old struggle for freedom and his protection. There is no mention of the interests of society as a whole. In fact implicit in this description is the assumption that there is a necessary conflict between the interests of the individual and those of society as a whole. This definition of the Rule of Law reflects the preoccupation of the legal profession in these countries.

At a Congress of Jurists with substantial attendance from Asia, held in New Delhi in 1959, it was recognized that 'the Rule of Law is a dynamic concept for the expansion and fulfilment of which jurists are primarily responsible and which should be employed not only to safeguard and advance the civil and political rights of the individual but also to establish social, economic, educational and cultural conditions under which his legitimate aspirations and dignity may be realized'. Here a positive element is attributed to the Rule of Law and that is the establishment of social, economic and educational conditions which would lead to the realization of man's dignity and aspirations. It is no longer merely a negative function of protecting his individualistic interests. The machinery of justice in a developing society is therefore called upon to serve a much wider scope than that traditionally
● attributed to it.

NOTE   The first definition quoted for the Rule of Law is from the Act of Athens of 1955; the second is from the Declaration of Delhi of 1959. In 1961, the Law of Lagos attempted an African definition of the Rule of Law. See African Conference on the Rule of Law, *Report*, International Commission of Jurists, Geneva, 1961.

NOTE   Another lawyer, Mr O. E. C. Chirwa, Q.C., presently a civil servant in Tanzania, made the point very succinctly in a paper given to the November 1968 Judges' and Magistrates' Conference in Dar es Salaam: 'Justice must help and serve and not hinder political, social and economic progress.' ('Justice in Tanzania', quoted in *The Nationalist*, 20 November 1968.)

NOTE In this extract, the Attorney-General is pointing to an important distinction between the meaning of freedom in liberal-democratic theory and that which is accepted in other political theories. In English constitutional theory, freedom is conceptualized in an essentially negative way. Its totality is determined by adding up those areas of individual conduct with which the state is not permitted to interfere. Thus freedom is defined with reference to the individual and means that the state may not limit freedom of expression, freedom of movement, etc. Socialist political theory looks at freedom in a more positive sense. Under this approach, it becomes the duty of the state to guarantee the economic, political and cultural rights of the mass of the people. In one sense, the distinction may be said to be between a theory of 'freedom from the state' and one of 'freedom within the state'. In another sense, socialists would say that it is absurd to talk about the political freedom of liberal democracy, when gross economic and cultural differences exist within society. Further, in the socialist state, as the political power and participation of the people increases and the organs of the state increasingly express the will of the people, the contradiction between the state and the individual disappears. (For a discussion of these points, see Macpherson, op. cit. and Peter Schmidt, 'The Citizens' Freedoms' in Jozsef Halasz (ed.), *Socialist Concept of Human Rights*, Akademiai Kiado, Budapest, 1966.)

B · THE COLONIAL BACKGROUND

J. P. W. B. McAuslan

'PROLEGOMENON TO THE RULE OF LAW IN EAST AFRICA'[4]

● It is of course a truism that we must have some knowledge of the past in order to be able to understand the present, but it is necessary to make the point here because it does not seem to have been made before. Equally, when the past is referred to by those who discuss the Rule of Law, it is not portrayed in entirely accurate colours and it becomes necessary therefore to make a preliminary examination of it. There is much cant about the beneficial effects of British Colonialism and nowhere is this more evident than in the sphere of the Rule of Law. In an obscure but subtle way it is suggested that before the British came, there was no Rule of Law in East Africa, while they were here as the rulers there was, and when they cease to be rulers, East Africa will quickly revert to having no Rule of Law again. Rule of Law in this context means more than imposing law and order; it refers to justice and fairness and it is in the context of that meaning that we will examine

[4] East African Institute of Social Research Conference, *Proceedings*, Kampala, 1964.

the claim. Few things could be further from the truth than this claim. Even the brief examination of certain aspects of legal and constitutional history which I will proceed to make will be sufficient, I think, to show that in some respects the reverse of the claim would be more accurate; that a system of government, conceived initially in, and characterized for the greater part of its existence by, a spirit of disregard for the law and justice, has been slowly forced, under pressure from nationalist leaders, to become more fair and democratic, although even at independence it bears many of the marks of an autocratic régime. I will take one or two concrete instances:

(i)   *The system of Courts and the appointment of Judges*

Until 1957 judges of the superior courts in the colonies were appointed during the pleasure of Her Majesty, i.e. they could be removed without cause at any time. In that year their term of office was changed and thereafter they could and can only be removed for good cause after a judicial tribunal has met and considered the matter. Although the Bow Group, a collection of rather muddled English Conservatives, like to claim the credit for this move, it would perhaps be more realistic to remember that 1957 was the year Ghana obtained independence and it may have been thought impolitic to provide for one system of judicial appointments for Ghana and another for the rest of (dependent) Africa.[5] The judges of the superior courts have never however had very much contact with the vast bulk of the population of any African country—for them other courts were more important. As we are all aware, the Courts which administered what passed for justice to the majority of the population were courts staffed or directly controlled by administrative officers. It has not been until Africans have obtained control of governments in East Africa that this iniquitous practice has begun to be abolished. It must be made quite clear that this combining of the functions of the judge and the administrator was a deliberate and conscious policy designed to maintain law and order in the country at the expense of justice to the individual. If anybody doubts that, let him read the Report on the Administration of Criminal Justice in East Africa, 1934, where a commission composed primarily of lawyers was extremely critical of the system because it seemed to rely overmuch on administrative knowledge about people and not enough on evidence

---

[5] This statement is not factually correct. The tenure of judges in the Gold Coast was secured in 1954. See Harvey, *Law and Social Change in Ghana*, p. 216. For a somewhat biased account of the colonial position, see Roberts-Wray, 'The Independence of the Judiciary in Commonwealth Countries' in J. N. D. Anderson (ed.), *Changing Law in Developing Countries*, George Allen and Unwin, London, 1963. See also, *Terrell* v. *Secretary of State for the Colonies* [1953] 2 Q.B. 482.

produced at a trial. 'Rough and ready justice which too often became rough and ready injustice', was the way the Report put it, only to be met with cries of injured dignity from senior administrators in East Africa who could not conceive of a better system since the administrator 'knew the native' better than a lawyer would. The Corfield Report with its petulant complaints about the magistrates and judges who upset convictions on technicalities during the Emergency in Kenya and thus made the job of the District Officer harder would doubtless agree with the remark of the Chief Native Commissioner of Kenya in 1934 who said that the Commission had failed to understand that the conception of justice administered in Kenya was deliberately different from that in England. Now that East Africa is independent, we have Judicial Service Commissions in all three countries and the separation of executive and judiciary is nearing formal completion; if the practice does not yet go quite as far as we think desirable, let us remember that it is a good deal better than anything which has preceded it.

(*ii*) *Aspects of Constitutional Law*
(*a*) *The defence of Act of State.* An Act of State has been judicially defined as an 'exercise of sovereign power which cannot be challenged, controlled or interfered with by municipal courts. Its sanction is not that of law but that of sovereign power and whatever it be, municipal courts must accept it, as it is without question'. The area of operation in which an Act of State is mainly pleaded as a defence is foreign affairs; that is action taken against foreign countries and non-British subjects or aliens by the British government. The defence was therefore open to the colonial governments in respect of their actions taken against the inhabitants of Uganda for the whole of its period as a dependency; Kenya Colony between 1895-1920 when it was a Protectorate; and Kenya Protectorate and Tanganyika for the whole of their existence as dependencies, for Protectorates and Mandates were foreign countries and their inhabitants aliens, though aliens of a special kind, being classified, with a touch of sardonic humour, as British Protected Persons. It is customary to read about the Act of State in textbooks on British constitutional law; it would be more accurate to see it as a supreme example of British constitutional lawlessness. Colonial governments were not slow to take advantage of this blanket defence to their more discreditable activities. All over Africa there is a trail of broken treaties, agreements and pledges entered into solemnly by British colonial governments with all the trappings usually associated with legally binding agreements, yet cynically broken when it was expedient to. In East Africa the two best examples are the Masai Agreement of

1904-1911 and the whole history of the Buganda Agreements from 1900 onwards. In three leading cases on these agreements, the last of which was not finally decided until 1961, the courts came to the conclusion that they had no jurisdiction over any question arising out of them since the whole business of the agreements was an Act of State. It is this sort of background and attitude to solemn agreements which politicians have inherited and apply to modern constitutional problems; see, for instance, the KANU attitude this year to the 'Lancaster House Agreement' of 1962, and of which we must be aware, though they will have to go a long way before they arrive at the standards of the British Colonial Rule of Law in this field.

(b)　*Bills of Rights and allied topics.* I am no great believer in Bills of Rights; they are not panaceas and I think they will remain only so long as it is convenient to keep them. However, it is permissible to point out that there was nothing remotely resembling a Bill of Rights in any country in East Africa for the greater period of colonial rule. Bills of Rights have only begun to appear as these countries neared independence and one may be forgiven some cynicism as one contemplates the spectacle of colonial officials earnestly impressing on African leaders the necessity to limit the powers of the Executive, in a manner which they themselves would never have tolerated. No doubt every derogation, however slight, from the Bills of Rights in Kenya and Uganda will be hailed as proof of imminent dictatorship, but again, it will be a long haul to reach the standards of the colonial régimes.

One piece of legislation, however, which has disturbed people and which has been taken to be evidence of a departure from fair government is the Preventive Detention Act, 1962 of Tanganyika. It is not perhaps realized how closely interwoven into the public life and the practices of government in East Africa are preventive detention and similar laws and practices. Leaving aside the German period with which I am not familiar, preventive detention first appeared in British East Africa in 1897 in section 77 of the Native Court Regulations of the East Africa Protectorate which empowered the Commissioner of the Protectorate to intern anybody whom he was satisfied was disaffected with the government. There was no appeal from such a decision. In one way or another preventive detention has existed in Kenya from that time onwards. In Tanganyika, less than a year after administration under the Mandate commenced, the Deportation Ordinance, 1921 was promulgated. This empowered the Governor, when it was shown to his satisfaction that any person was conducting himself so as to be dangerous to the peace and good order of the

Territory, to order that that person be deported from one part of the Territory to any other part, and there be confined. No appeal may be made from such an order. The similarity between the Deportation Ordinance and the Preventive Detention Act, both as regards powers and the words used to describe those powers is most marked. Another Tanganyika statute I must mention is the Expulsion of Undesirables Ordinance, 1930. This gave the Governor in Council power to expel a person, *inter alia*, if it was deemed 'to be conducive to the public good and advisable in the interests of public morals' that such an order be made. There were more safeguards over this power because, of course, it would be used mainly against Europeans even if they would be those who had offended against the canons of colonial public morals. What is most revealing about this Ordinance, however, is the debate in the Legislative Council which preceded its enactment. Three people spoke; the Attorney General who justified it on the grounds that it was an expression of the inherent right of every civilized country to expel persons who are considered undesirable for one reason or another, and two unofficial members both of whom stated that it was an excellent bill but feared that it was not wide enough to catch those who had suffered no conviction yet ought to be expelled. When we compare that debate with the debate last year on the Preventive Detention Bill, which was criticized at the time for being too short and casual, there can be no question but that there was a far greater awareness of the drastic powers being given to government in the latter debate; this is not in itself a justification for preventive detention, but the point is worth making since it helps place the Act in its proper perspective in Tanganyika legal and constitutional history. Indeed I would go so far as to say that preventive detention and similar practices are part of the normal practices of government in East Africa; and just as we might dislike or even deplore normal practices elsewhere as being unfair without at the same time seeing them as evidence of a wholesale departure from the Rule of Law so we ought perhaps to see these practices in the same light. I do not think we should minimize the practice of preventive detention on the other hand, it does represent a departure from the ideal system that no one should be deprived of his freedom without having had a fair trial, but it is not a departure which heralds dictatorship in Tanganyika nor, when seen against the perspective of the past and present, does it even represent a return to the autocratic system of government which existed in the colonial era. The Preventive Detention Bill was debated in a freely elected National Assembly; the Deportation Bill was promulgated by the Governor since there was no legislature in existence at that time.

(c) *Land.* I will briefly mention land since it has been transposed into the area of public law by having provisions relating to it incorporated into the constitution of both Uganda and Kenya. These governments are required to pay 'adequate' or full compensation when they compulsorily acquire land in the public interest; this is considered to be a fundamental right for the individual. It suffices to say that both these governments would have to expropriate land for purely private purposes before they even equalled—and they could never surpass—the methods whereby colonial governments obtained control of the land in the first place.

I have stressed the historical factor considerably and I think from the evidence produced (and it is not exhaustive) we have a better idea of the background of government of which we must be aware when discussing and making judgements about the Rule of Law in East Africa. The picture which seems to emerge, and I put this forward as a tentative conclusion, is that in many respects East Africa is continually evolving towards a fairer and more democratic system of government and thus towards greater acceptance of the principles of the Rule of Law. This conclusion turns most thinking on this topic on its head and no doubt there will be incidents—indeed there have already been incidents over the past two years—which will be cited to show that it cannot stand, but the overall picture of legislation and governmental practice will, I think, bear it out. If the picture and the conclusion drawn therefrom are accepted, a re-orientation of thought and value judgements about the Rule of Law in East Africa will have to take place.

NOTE   For a detailed expansion of the points made above, see Ghai and McAuslan, *Public Law and Political Change in Kenya*, pp. 3-174.

NOTE   Two interesting monographs which illustrate some general tendencies in the administration of the law in East Africa under colonial rule are: Montagu Slater, *The Trial of Jomo Kenyatta*, Martin, Secker, and Warburg, London, 1955; and Earle Seaton and Kirilo Japhet, *The Meru Land Case*, EAPH, Nairobi, 1967. Slater's book is a journalistic account, based mainly on the actual transcript, of the Alice-in-Wonderland trial of Kenyatta and others on charges of organizing 'Mau Mau'. The book provides us with a convincing illustration of the fact that, as McAuslan has indicated above, the formalities of British justice were no protection for those who ran foul of the colonial ruling class. We see clearly the extent to which this ruling class was willing to pervert its own 'civilized' standards in order to achieve its political aims. The second book deals with the expropriation of Meru homesteads by the colonial government of Tanganyika in order to assist the expansion and development of settler farming. Again, the interests of the ruling class were able to override even the most perfunctory or ritualistic observance of basic standards of justice. (On the Meru Land Case, see, also, Anton Nelson, *The Freemen of Meru*, Oxford University Press, Nairobi, 1967 and Paul Purritt, 'The Meru Land Case' in *Tanzania Notes and Records*, no. 69, 1968, p. 53.)

An interesting article on this same general theme is Professor Seidman's, 'The Reception of English Law in Africa Revisited' (*Eastern Africa Law Review*, vol. II, no. 1, 1969, p. 47). He argues that in the process of its exportation to the colonies, English law lost most of the safeguards and control mechanisms which, in theory at least, it possessed in England. Thus, '. . . whatever may have been the "democratic" component of English law, it was plainly excised during its transportation overseas' (p. 78). He concludes that, '. . . the English law which was the "basic" or "general" law of the colonies in Africa was a truncated, narrow law whose juristic theme was Contract unrestrained by either Welfare State legislation or democratic institutions' (p. 85). It is true that some English lawyers had misgivings about certain aspects of colonial rule but, in the earlier days at least, there were many convenient rationalizations available with which they assuaged their legal consciences. Seidman makes reference to *The King* v. *The Earl of Crewe; ex parte Sekgome* ([1910] 2 K.B. 576). In this application for habeas corpus, the petitioner, a Tswana Chief, had been detained by the order of the High Commissioner for South Africa. The King's Bench were somewhat concerned about the case, but ultimately saw their way clear to upholding Sekgome's detention:

> The idea that there may be an established system of law to which a man owes obedience, and that at any moment he may be deprived of the protection of that law, is an idea not easily accepted by English lawyers . . . It is made less difficult if one remembers that the Protectorate is over a country in which a few dominant civilised men have to control a great multitude of semi-barbarous.

C · THE STATE

V. I. Lenin

THE STATE AND REVOLUTION[6]

● Summing up his historical analysis, Engels says:

> The state is, therefore, by no means a power forced on society from without; just as little is it the reality of the ethical idea, the image and reality of reason, as Hegel maintains. Rather, it is a product of society at a certain stage of development; it is the admission that this society has become entangled in an insoluble contradiction with itself, that it is cleft into irreconcilable antagonisms which it is powerless to dispel. But in order that these antagonisms, classes with conflicting economic interests, might not consume themselves and society in sterile struggle, a power seemingly standing above society became necessary for the purpose of moderating the conflict, of keeping it within the bounds of order; and this power, arisen out of society, but placing itself above it, and increasingly alienating itself from it, is the state.

6 Foreign Languages Publishing House, Moscow, pp. 11-26.

This expresses with perfect clarity the basic idea of Marxism on the question of the historical role and the meaning of the state. The state is the product and the manifestation of the *irreconcilability* of class antagonisms. The state arises when, where, and to the extent that class antagonisms objectively cannot be reconciled. And, conversely, the existence of the state proves that the class antagonisms are irreconcilable.

It is precisely on this most important and fundamental point that the distortion of Marxism, proceeding along two main lines, begins.

On the one hand, the bourgeois and particularly the petit-bourgeois ideologists, compelled under the weight of indisputable historical facts to admit that the state only exists where there are class antagonisms and the class struggle, 'correct' Marx in such a way as to make it appear that the state is an organ for the reconciliation of classes. According to Marx, the state could neither arise nor maintain itself if it were possible to reconcile classes. According to the petit-bourgeois and philistine professors and publicists, it appears—very frequently they benignantly refer to Marx to prove this—that the state does reconcile classes. According to Marx, the state is an organ of class rule, an organ for the oppression of one class by another; it is the creation of 'order' which legalizes and perpetuates this oppression by moderating the conflict between the classes. In the opinion of the petit-bourgeois politicians, order means precisely the reconciliation of classes, and not the oppression of one class by another; to moderate the conflict means reconciling classes and not depriving the oppressed classes of definite means and methods of struggle to overthrow the oppressors.

For instance, when, in the Revolution of 1917, the question of the significance and role of the state arose in all its magnitude as a practical question demanding immediate action on a mass scale, all the Socialist-Revolutionaries and Mensheviks immediately and completely sank to the petit-bourgeois theory that the 'state' 'reconciles' classes. Innumerable resolutions and articles by politicians of both these parties are thoroughly saturated with this petit-bourgeois and philistine 're-conciliation' theory. That the state is an organ of the rule of a definite class which cannot be reconciled with its antipode (the class opposite to it), is something the petit-bourgeois democrats will never be able to understand. Their attitude towards the state is one of the most striking manifestations of the fact that our Socialist-Revolutionaries and Mensheviks are not Socialists at all (a point that we Bolsheviks have always maintained), but petit-bourgeois democrats with near-socialist phraseology.

On the other hand, the 'Kautskyite' distortion of Marxism is far more subtle. 'Theoretically', it is not denied that the state is an organ of class rule, or that class antagonisms are irreconcilable. But what is lost sight of or glossed over is this: if the state is the product of the irreconcilability of class antagonisms, if it is a power standing above society and 'increasingly alienating itself from it', then it is obvious that the liberation of the oppressed class is impossible not only without a violent revolution, but also without the destruction of the apparatus of state power which was created by the ruling class and which is the embodiment of this 'alienation'. As we shall see later, Marx very definitely drew this theoretically self-evident conclusion as a result of a concrete historical analysis of the tasks of the revolution. And—as we shall show in detail further on—it is precisely this conclusion which Kautsky . . . has 'forgotten' and distorted.

Engels continues:

. . . In contradistinction to the old gentile (tribal or clan) organization, the state, first, divides its subjects according to territory . . . Such a division seems 'natural' to us, but it cost a prolonged struggle against the old form of tribal or gentile society.

. . . The second distinguishing feature is the establishment of a public power which no longer directly coincided with the population organizing itself as an armed force. This special public power is necessary, because a self-acting armed organization of the population has become impossible since the cleavage into classes . . . This public power exists in every state; it consists not merely of armed people but also of material adjuncts, prisons and institutions of coercion of all kinds, of which gentile (clan) society knew nothing . . .

Engels further elucidates the concept of the 'power' which is termed the state—a power which arose from society, but places itself above it and alienates itself more and more from it. What does this power mainly consist of? It consists of special bodies of armed men which have prisons, etc., at their command.

We are justified in speaking of special bodies of armed men, because the public power which is an attribute of every state 'does not directly coincide' with the armed population, with its 'self-acting armed organization'.

Like all great revolutionary thinkers, Engels tries to draw the attention of the class-conscious workers to the very fact which prevailing philistinism regards as least worthy of attention, as the most habitual and sanctified not only by firmly rooted, but one might say by petrified prejudices. A standing army and police are the chief instruments of state power. But can it be otherwise?

From the viewpoint of the vast majority of Europeans of the end of the nineteenth century whom Engels was addressing, and who had not lived through or closely observed a single great revolution, it could not be otherwise. They completely failed to understand what a 'self-acting armed organization of the population' was. To the question, whence arose the need for special bodies of armed men, placed above society and alienating themselves from it (police and standing army), the West-European and Russian philistines are inclined to answer with a few phrases borrowed from Spencer or Mikhailovsky, by referring to the growing complexity of social life, the differentiation of functions, and so forth.

Such a reference seems 'scientific', and effectively dulls the senses of the man in the street by obscuring the most important and basic fact, namely, the cleavage of society into irreconcilably antagonistic classes.

Were it not for this cleavage, the 'self-acting armed organization of the population' would differ from the primitive organization of a stick-wielding herd of monkeys, or of primitive men, or of men united in clans, by its complexity, its high technique, and so forth; but such an organization would still be possible.

It is impossible, because civilized society is split into antagonistic and, moreover, irreconcilably antagonistic classes, the 'self-acting' arming of which would lead to an armed struggle between them. A state arises, a special power is created, special bodies of armed men, and every revolution, by destroying the state apparatus, clearly demonstrates to us how the ruling class strives to restore the special bodies of armed men which serve it, and how the oppressed class strives to create a new organization of this kind, capable of serving not the exploiters but the exploited.

In the above argument, Engels raises theoretically the very same question which every great revolution raises before us in practice, palpably and, what is more, on a scale of mass action, namely, the question of the relation between 'special' bodies of armed men and the 'self-acting armed organization of the population'.

But let us return to Engels' exposition. He points out that sometimes, for example, in certain parts of North America, this public power is weak (he has in mind a rare exception in capitalist society, and those parts of North America in its pre-imperialist days where the free colonist predominated), but that, generally speaking, it grows stronger:

. . . The public power grows stronger, however, in proportion as class antagonisms within the state become more acute, and as adjacent states become larger and more populated. We have only to look at our present-day Europe, where class struggle and rivalry in conquest have screwed up the public power to such a pitch that it threatens to devour the whole of society and even the state . . .

For the maintenance of the special public power standing above society, taxes and state loans are needed.

In possession of the public power and of the right to levy taxes, the officials . . . as organs of society, now stand above society. The free, voluntary respect that was accorded to the organs of the gentile (clan) constitution does not satisfy them, even if they could gain it . . . Special laws are enacted proclaiming the sanctity and immunity of the officials. 'The shabbiest police servant' has more 'authority' than the representatives of the clan, but even the head of the military power of a civilized state may well envy an elder of a clan the 'un-coerced respect' of society.

Here the problem of the privileged position of the officials as organs of state power is raised. The main question indicated is: what is it that places them above society? We shall see how this theoretical question was answered in practice by the Paris Commune in 1871 and how it was slurred over in a reactionary manner by Kautsky in 1912.

. . . As the state arose from the need to hold class antagonisms in check, but as it arose, at the same time, in the midst of the conflict of these classes, it is, as a rule, the state of the most powerful, economically dominant class, which, through the medium of the state, becomes also the politically dominant class, and thus acquires new means of holding down and exploiting the oppressed class . . .

Not only were the ancient and feudal states organs for the exploitation of the slaves and serfs but,

. . . the modern representative state is an instrument of exploitation of wage labour by capital. By way of exception, however, periods occur in which the warring classes balance each other so nearly that the state power, as ostensible mediator, acquires, for the moment, a certain degree of independence of both . . .

Such were the absolute monarchies of the seventeenth and eighteenth centuries, the Bonapartism of the First and Second Empires in France, and the Bismarck régime in Germany.

Engels gives a general summary of his views in the most popular of his works in the following words:

The state then, has not existed from all eternity. There have been societies that did without it, that had no conception of the state and state power. At a certain stage of economic development, which was necessarily bound up with the cleavage of society into classes, the state became a necessity owing to this cleavage. We are now rapidly approaching a stage in the development of production at which the existence of these classes not only will have ceased to be a necessity, but will become a positive hindrance to production. They will fall as inevitably as they arose at an earlier stage. Along with them the state will inevitably fall. The society that will organize production on the basis of a free and equal association of the producers will put the whole machinery of state where it will then belong: into the Museum of Antiquities, by the side of the spinning wheel and the bronze axe.

We do not often come across this passage in the propagandist and agitational literature of present-day Social-Democracy. But even when we do come across it, it is mostly quoted in the same manner as one bows before an icon, i.e. it is done to show official respect for Engels, and no attempt is made to gauge the breadth and depth of the revolution that this relegating of 'the whole state machine to the Museum of Antiquities' presupposes. In most cases we do not even find an
● understanding of what Engels calls the state machine.

NOTE *Kautskyite:* Kautsky was the leader of the German Social Democrats and a major figure in the Second International. Lenin broke with him completely after Kautsky's party agreed to support the German government in 1914. Lenin came to use 'Kautskyite' as a general term referring to anyone he believed to be a mere opportunist.

Menshevik: In 1903, the Russian Social Democrat party split into the Bolshevik and Menshevik wings as a result of the disagreement between Lenin and Martov over the vanguard role of a revolutionary party. In 1917, the Mensheviks formed the moderate wing of the revolution. They wished to continue the war, but were ousted by the Bolsheviks under Lenin in October and later suppressed.

Socialist Revolutionaries: This party believed in agrarian revolution, a more decentralized organization of the state, and were regarded by the Bolsheviks as the romantic wing of the October Revolution. They entered into coalition with the Bolsheviks, but were later suppressed.

NOTE See also, V. I. Lenin, *The State*, Foreign Languages Press, Peking, 1965. On the occasion of Lenin's centenary, President Nyerere noted: '. . . V. I. Lenin does not belong only to the Soviet Union; his work and his ideas are part of mankind's heritage and are relevant to us all.' (*The Standard*, 21 April 1970.) *Per contra*, Okot p'Bitek has written, 'And Lenin, was he born at Arusha?' (*Song of Ocol*, East African Publishing House, Nairobi, 1970, p. 84.)

NOTE For a stimulating exposition of Lenin's analysis of the state, see Georg Lukacs, *Lenin*, New Left Books, London, 1970, ch. V.

NOTE Lenin's formulation of the nature of the state finds many unexpected, and unsuspecting, supporters among people who would be strongly disinclined to call themselves Marxists. A collection of writings by the English judge, Lord Devlin, is illustrative. In his book, *The Enforcement of Morals* (O.U.P. London, 1965) he clearly suggests that the state, through its instrument of the law, has the right and the duty to enforce the social and cultural norms established by the ruling class. This enforcement is achieved through suppressing forms of behaviour unacceptable to the ruling class. Inadvertently, his analysis provides a clearly Marxist (and clearly valid) exposition of the purposes underlying the administration of criminal law in England. Another English judge, Lord Simonds, was of a similar view when he spoke of ' . . . the supreme and fundamental purpose of the law, to conserve not only the safety and order, but also the moral welfare of the state'. (*Shaw* v. *D.P.P.* [1962] A.C. 220.) Of interest also is Lord Lugard's remark: 'The law has force at its back in every country, however civilized' (*Political Memoranda* (3rd ed.), Cass, London, 1970, p. 249).

NOTE Lenin's concept of the state is as a 'special instrument for the suppression of a particular class'. A striking illustration of this theory can be found by examining the colonial state. The fundamental reason for the existence of the colonial state was the contradiction between the capital-owning class in the metropole and the mass of the people in the colony. As local administrative and entrepreneurial classes developed, this contradiction acquired additional facets and complications, but the essentially opposed forces remained the same. State power existed in order to guarantee and facilitate the exploitation of the colony and its people. An irreconcilable conflict existed between the economic interests of the colonizers and those of the colonized, and therefore, police, prisons, and a standing army were called into being by the colonizers to ensure the supremacy of their interests. Thus, the nature of the state apparatus was determined not only by its class content but also by the specific demands of colonial rule. The colonial state, then, was not simply a bourgeois state, it was a stunted, non-liberal bourgeois state, characterized by highly centralized, autocratic organization. (The literature on this subject is extensive. Of special interest are Fanon, *The Wretched of the Earth*, Grove Press, New York City, 1965; and Jack Woddis, *An Introduction to Neo-Colonialism*, International Publishers, New York City, 1967, ch. I. For a legal analysis, see Seidman, 'The Reception of English Law in Colonial Africa Revisited', op. cit.)

Since Independence, and particularly since the Arusha Declaration, it has been argued that a new class—the workers and peasants—has come to power. Whether this is in fact true is a matter for debate for what is clear is that the struggle continues with equal intensity. The essential contradiction remains, although its resolution must now be seen on two distinct, albeit related, planes.

At the national or internal level the attainment of political independence was the signal for a process of devolving power to a national bourgeoisic, which would, it was assumed, continue to function in the interests of overseas capital. Relying on its mass base, TANU has struggled against this neo-colonial scenario, and has achieved notable victories, the most significant being the Arusha Declaration. According to one writer, the purpose of the Arusha Declaration was to ensure that '... the bureaucratic and political factions of the nation are to be denied the opportunity of further development along lines that would entrench them as an exploiting social class, as is happening elsewhere in Africa'. (Walter Rodney, 'Declaration: Implementation Problems', *Mbioni*, vol. IV, no. 3, 1967, p. 29.) In order to appreciate the dimensions of the contradiction more fully it may be useful to look briefly at the composition of Tanzania's national bourgeoisie and the way in which its various elements have been affected by the struggle. Tanzania does not have a bourgeoisie in the classical sense, that is, a capital-owning class. However, this does not, and has not, prevented the emergence of a locally-based class which represents the interests of the foreign owners of the national capital. In this note we will adopt Ledda's formulation and investigate three constituent elements of the national bourgeoisie. (See Romano Ledda, 'Social Classes and Political Struggle in Africa', *International Socialist Journal*, August, 1967, p. 560, reprinted by New England Free Press, Boston, Massachusetts.) These are the comprador bourgeoisie, the rural bourgeoisie, and the bureaucratic bourgeoisie. The comprador bourgeoisie encompasses both local entrepreneurs and all those who operate as middlemen or functionaries for foreign capital. With the nationalization of financial institutions, the import-export business, wholesale and retail trade, and the legal profession, and such measures as the Acquisition of Buildings Act, 1971, one may be fairly confident that this class will disappear. Included in the rural bourgeoisie would be large landowners, employers of agricultural labour, and the beneficiaries of proto-feudal systems of land tenure. Although the emergence of this class is creating problems in certain areas of the country, a relatively enlightened colonial policy prevented the development of an entrenched landowner class, and it is doubtful if this group presents a serious threat to socialist development. (See Issa G. Shivji, *Tanzania: The Silent Class Struggle*, Cheche Publications, Dar es Salaam, 1970, p. ii.) The bureaucratic bourgeoisie, though still not fully conscious of itself as a class, is the largest and most significant of the three groups. Because its self-consciousness is not yet fully formed, any attempt to define this group must be tentative. Clearly, however, the most important criterion of potential membership is the occupation of an executive, administrative, or professional post in one of the departments of the central government, the security forces, the educational system, and the various parastatal organizations established to control the nationalized sectors of the economy. Beginning its existence as the successor to the colonial administration, the bureaucratic bourgeoisie has grown as more areas of national life have come under state control. Strongly influenced by western bourgeois values, and the exaggerated system of privileges it inherited, it gravitates towards a system of bureaucratic capitalism. This tendency is reinforced through contact with an expatriate class which is culturally, and, by and large, intellectually ultra-bourgeois. For the purposes of this study, the existence of the bureaucratic bourgeoisie is particularly important, because it is this sub-class which has potentially the greatest interest in the maintenance of a colonial state structure. With its attempts at politicizing the civil service and the leadership provisions of the Arusha Declaration, TANU has had some successes in controlling the bureaucratic bourgeoisie, but the final issue is still far from certain. (On the problems of the national bourgeoisie, see Shivji's excellent analysis, op.cit.; Glyn Hughes, 'Preconditions of Socialist Development', *Monthly Review*, vol. XXII, no. 1, 1970, p. 11; K.W. Post, *The New States of West Africa* (2nd ed.), Penguin Books, London, 1968, p. 42 et seq.; Samir Amin, 'The Class Struggle in Africa', *Revolution*, vol. I, no. 9, 1964, reprinted by Africa Research Group, Cambridge, Massachusetts; Osei Duah, 'How Classless is Africa?' (mimeo), Southern Africa Project, London, 1970; Ledda, op. cit.; Basil Davidson, *Which Way Africa?* (3rd ed.), Penguin Books, London, 1971; and Ruth First, *The Barrel of a Gun*, Allen Lane, London, 1970. Leonard Barnes has described the members of this sub-class as 'spare parts Kleptrocrats'. See his *Africa in Eclipse*, Gollancz, London, 1971.)

Internationally, or externally, the struggle against imperialism is also pursued, and with equal effects on the administration of the state in Tanzania. In its most generalized way the whole process of development is a form of class struggle for it represents an attempt to eradicate what are the inevitable economic, social, and cultural consequences of imperialism. Any nation which shows signs of achieving too much success in this process must be wary of subversion or even invasion, for ultimately the elimination of 'under-development' means the elimination of imperialism. (See *The Standard*, 3 June 1971.) In a more particular sense, Tanzania by its clear support of revolutionary war in southern Africa, is involved in the resolution on the international level of the contradiction between the interests of imperialism and those of the mass of her people. (See Davidson, op. cit.; Lin Piao, *Long Live the Victory of People's War*, Foreign Languages Press, Peking, 1965; Michael Dawn, 'Toward an International Strategy', *Monthly Review*, vol. XIX, no. 11, 1968, p. 28; and Robert I. Rhodes (ed.), *Imperialism and Underdevelopment*, Monthly Review Press, New York, 1970.)

Only when this basic contradiction has been resolved and the struggle arising from it decisively determined in the interests of common people everywhere, can true human freedom begin to develop. As President Nyerere has said in connection with the struggle in southern Africa, '. . . we can only give top priority to those questions of developing individual freedom and individual dignity when all of Africa is free'. (*Stability and Change in Africa*, op. cit., p. 15.) States will continue to exist while class struggle exists, and the degree of freedom permitted by the ruling class of any particular state will depend largely on how intensely the class struggle threatens the position of that ruling class. Where the ruling class represents interests opposed to the mass of the people it will fall back increasingly on naked oppression, as is the case today in most of the capitalist world. Where the ruling class represents or personifies the workers and peasants, it will take stringent measures to protect the gains which have been won, but at the same time it will attempt to ensure the security of the embryonic socialist society by involving the people more and more in the construction and defence of what is now their own state. This appears to be one of the aims of the TANU Guidelines (Mwongozo). (Government Printer, Dar es Salaam, 1971. An English version can be found in *The African Review*, vol. 1, no. 4, 1972, p. 1.)

Shortly after the people had achieved state power in China, Mao Tse-Tung commented:

> Don't you want to abolish state power? Yes, we do, but not right now; we cannot do it yet. Why? Because imperialism still exists, because domestic reaction still exists, because classes still exist in our country. Our present task is to strengthen the people's state apparatus—mainly the people's army, the people's police, and the people's courts—in order to consolidate national defence and protect the people's interests. ('On the People's Democratic Dictatorship', *Selected Works*, vol. IV, Foreign Languages Press, Peking, 1967, p. 418.)

NOTE An important question concerns the kind of state structure which is congruent with the exercise of socialist power. (See Ralph Miliband, 'The State and Revolution', *Monthly Review*, vol. XXI, no. 11, 1970, p. 87.) As we have seen, the colonial state was established to facilitate imperial domination. Its structure and its style were an expression of this basic aim. The result was that one found '. . . bureaucracy as a substitute for government', or to put it slightly differently, '. . . administration [took] the place of politics'. (Hannah Arendt, *Imperialism*, Harcourt, Brace and Co., New York City, 1968, ch. III; Peter Worsley, *The Third World* (2nd ed.), Wiedenfeld and Nicholson, London, 1967, p. 191.) (For an analysis of the structure of colonial government, see J. P. W. B. McAuslan, 'Administrative Law in Kenya—A General Survey', *East African Law Today*, Stevens and Son, London, 1966.) The issue is then one of determining how a post-colonial régime is to establish a socialist and democratic state structure. For Lenin the answer was clear: 'Revolution consists not in the new class commanding, governing with the aid of the old state machine, but in this class smashing this machine and commanding, governing with the aid of a new machine.' (From the essay, 'The Proletarian Revolution and the Renegade Kautsky', quoted in Miliband, op. cit., p. 79.) The key to the creation of this new machine is the transfer of power from the bureaucracy to the masses. 'We can fight bureaucracy to the bitter end, to complete victory, only when the whole population participates in the work of government.' (Address to the Eighth Party Congress, 1919, quoted in George Thomson, 'From Lenin to Mao Tse-Tung', *Monthly Review*, vol. XXI, no. 11, 1970, p. 121.) One aim of a socialist state administration, then, should be '. . . the diffusion of power from artificial hierarchies into the minds and hands of actual people'. (David Cooper (ed.), *The Dialectics of Liberation*, Penguin Books, London, 1968, p. 10.) Unfortunately, as Lenin himself was to discover, '. . . bureaucratic rule, once entrenched, is extremely resistant to change'. (Leo Huberman and Paul Sweezy, *Socialism in Cuba*, Monthly Review Press, New York City, 1969, p. 22.)

If the people themselves are to play the central role in the struggle against bureaucracy, they must be led by a party which is ideologically and structurally adapted to the performance of such a role. The TANU Guidelines (Mwongozo) reveals that the Party is moving, ideologically at any rate, in such direction. The Mwongozo recognizes the need for theoretical clarity and a more tightly organized party, and the crucial importance of raising the people's consciousness to the level where they are active participants in all aspects of the nation's political life. (For an analysis of the Party's post-Independence problems, see H. Bienen, 'The Party and the No-Party State', *Transition*, no. 13, 1964, p. 25.)

The problem of bureaucracy and authoritarian administration is one that has bedevilled many nations attempting to build socialism. Compare, for example, the following statements. The first one is about Ghana under Nkrumah, while the second concerns Cuba in 1969.

Transfer of power was viewed not in terms of its democratization, but of its Africanization. The system of colonial administration was designed to exclude as much as possible both traditional and modern elements of democracy. The distant objective of self-government meant no more than that the system would finally be administered by Africans. African self-government was, in short, colonial administration by Africans. (Jitendra Mohan, 'Nkrumah and Nkrumahism', *The Socialist Register, 1967*, Merlin Press, London, 1967, p. 191.)

[The revolutionary government might have attempted] the difficult feat of bringing the people more directly into the governing process, forging institutions of popular participation and control and encouraging the masses to use them, to assume increasing responsibility, to share in the making of the great decisions which shape their lives. In practice, however, the relation between government and people continued to be a paternalistic one, with Fidel Castro increasingly playing the crucial role of interpreting the people's needs and wants, translating them into government policy and continuously explaining what had to be done, and what obstacles remained to be overcome. (Huberman and Sweezy, op. cit., p. 204.)

The African Independence Party of Guinea and Cape Verde Islands (PAIGC) has clearly recognized the contradiction inherent in a revolutionary party attempting to govern through a colonial state structure. Article V (6) of its programme calls for: 'Total elimination of the colonial administrative structure and establishment of a national and democratic structure for the internal administration of the country.' (Amilcar Cabral, *Revolution in Guinea, Stage 1*, London, 1969, p. 137.) (One of the clear aims of the Great Proletarian Cultural Revolution in China was to wrest power from the bureaucratic class. See, *Decision of the Central Committee of the Chinese Communist Party Concerning the Great Proletarian Cultural Revolution*, Foreign Languages Press, Peking, 1966; and, for a comment on this document see, *Monthly Review*, vol. XVII, no. 8, 1967, p. 1. See also, J. K. Nyerere, *Freedom and Development*, Government Printer, Dar es Salaam, 1968.)

NOTE   One of the consequences of the colonial system is an administrative style appropriate to that sytem, a style characterized by authoritarianism, arrogance toward the public, and a reliance on form, often to the point of ignoring content. It results in the individual bureaucrat confusing purpose and function, generally with the result that the emphasis in job performance is placed on function. V. S. Naipaul has described this situation as it existed in the colonial West Indies:

> In the colonial days the civil servant, his way blocked by the expatriate who was sometimes his inferior and occasionally corrupt as well, expended all his creative energies on petty . . . intrigue and worked off his aggression on the public. His duties were those of a clerk; he was never required to be efficient; he never had to make a decision. (*The Middle Passage*, Penguin Books, London, 1969, p. 80.)

This heritage of colonialism is compounded by two additional factors in an ex-colonial state attempting revolutionary change. The first, which has been noted by Sekou Touré, is the tendency of some leaders and officials to confuse authoritarianism with revolutionary dedication. (*The Doctrine and Methods of the Democratic Party of Guinea*, part I (no date), pp. 160-3.) The second is a similar and related tendency to over-use the danger of imperialist aggression or subversion to justify authoritarian methods. The question here is probably a matter of degree. The imperialist attack on Guinea in November 1970 and the Uganda coup of January 1971 indicate that many drastic measures may be necessary to guard the security of the state.

These problems of administrative style can be solved by means of a re-orientation of the bureaucracy towards an ethos of service. President Nyerere emphasized this point in a 1970 speech (*Arusha Declaration Parliament*, Government Printer, Dar es Salaam, 1970, p. 8):

We must work until all our people are able to rely on enjoying the respect and freedom within the law which is due to them as citizens of our country. This will be achieved only when every officer of Government, Local Government, and Party, and every Judge and Magistrate, acts consistently as an intelligent and humane servant of the community.

(See also, Touré, op. cit., part II, pp. 39-47. Also worth remembering is Mao's stricture, 'We should be modest and prudent, guard against arrogance and rashness, and serve the Chinese people heart and soul . . .', 'China's Two Destinies', *Selected Works*, vol. III, Foreign Languages Press, Peking, 1966, p. 253. On the additional barrier to serving the people created by a culturally alien governmental structure, see A. B. Lyall, 'Anomy Theory and Deviant Response With Special Reference to Socialist States', *Eastern Africa Law Review*, vol. III, no. 1, 1970, p. 43.)

NOTE Lenin emphasizes that the police and the standing army are the essence of state power. The Tanzanian Army Mutiny of 1964 revealed serious weaknesses in these organs. More precisely, the mutiny revealed the lack of force which the government possessed to counter organized threats to its existence, and the general inability of the government to assert its authority throughout the country. Changes effected since 1964 have been designed to achieve three purposes: (1) to expand the security forces generally; (2) to increase the influence of TANU within the security forces; and, (3) to create countervailing security forces which could check each other in the event that one proved unreliable. Thus, the police and the specially-created TPDF were expanded, political education in both forces was emphasized, a high-ranking officer was appointed to the TPDF to function as a political commissar, and a para-military branch of the police, the Field Force Unit, was created and trained in security duties. (H. Bienen, 'Public Order and the Military in Africa', in H. Bienen (ed.), *The Military Intervenes*, Russell Sage Foundation, New York City, 1968, pp. 59-61.) The policy of creating countervailing forces can be seen in the multiplicity of para-military forces in existence. In this category we should also note the Prisons Service, the National Service, the TANU Youth League, and the projected people's militia. Still, Tanzania has extremely small security forces. For example, the total number of full-time police is about 11,200. The ratio of citizens to police is about 1,100 to 1, as compared to 400 to 1 in most western countries and 600 to 1 in Kenya. In July 1968, the Minister for Home Affairs announced plans to increase the number of police by 2,730, but this increase did not take place. (*The Standard*, 16 July 1968.) In April 1969, the Minister stated that due to lack of funds there were 900 vacancies in the Police. (*The Nationalist*, 12 April 1969.) The Inspector-General of Police announced plans in February 1970 to recruit 600 policemen (*The Standard*, 26 February 1970) but it appears that this was not carried out. Speaking in the National Assembly in July 1970, the Minister for Home Affairs announced that the strength of the police was roughly what it had been in 1968. He said, however, that it was hoped to bring in an additional 780 recruits by the end of 1970. (*The Standard*, 10 July 1970.) In the rural areas most police work is carried out by members of the TYL. In April 1970, a programme was commenced in Dar es Salaam whereby members of the TYL would be given special training by the Police. (*Sunday News*, 5 April 1970.)

In an article entitled, 'Police/Public Relations in the Enforcement of Law' (*Tanzania Police Journal*, vol. II, no. 2, 1966, p. 31) the author, 'Law Student from the Hill', discusses the basic changes in orientation of the Tanzanian state as a result of independence, and argues that, '. . . the true image of law enforcement has come to be unfairly distorted at times because of the fact that the profession was, during the days of colonial government, an instrument of policy'. Can the law enforcement profession ever be anything other than 'an instrument of policy'?

QUESTIONS 1. Are there any similarities between the state as described by Lenin and the political organizations which existed in traditional African society? Consider the following statement: '. . . I have always been skeptical of the proposition that the democratic procedures and other attributes of the small face-to-face society can with any ease be translated into the political systems of larger post-colonial states.' (Rupert Emerson, 'African States and the Burdens They Bear', *African Studies Bulletin*, vol. X, no. 1, 1967, p. 1.)

2. In *Public Law and Political Change in Kenya*, Ghai and McAuslan sum up their criticisms of the present Government of Kenya as follows: 'The law is seen solely as being a tool of the wielders of power who use it as they think fit, legalizing their own illegal exercises of power, and attempting to prevent the acquisition of power by, and the development of, the powerless' (p. 509). Implicit in this criticism is the suggestion that the law can be conceived as something other than 'a tool of the wielders of power'. There is clearly a contradiction between this conception and the Leninist conception. How might this contradiction be resolved?

The critical factor in a socialist analysis of any state is that state's class content. Depending on which class is actually exercising state power, there should be significant variations in the organization and structure of the state. Thus one would expect a socialist legal system to be different from a bourgeois legal system. The following passage indicates what some of those differences might be.

THE NATIONALIST: COMMENT ON THE SALES TAX
(PREVENTION OF PRICE INCREASES) BILL[7]

● One way by which makers of bourgeois societies strive to maintain themselves in power is through the legacy of mystification of the 'laws' that they enact from time to time to 'regulate' the conduct of the societies they control.

In such societies the so-called laws that exist are nothing but codified secrets; able to be understood only by the 'learned', the 'wise' or 'gentlemen of higher learning'. Although in such societies, the laws are supposed to be followed by all, they are not yet known to all. They are not understood by all and this practice is deliberately en-

[7] 24 June 1969. No. 6 of 1969, which was designed to prevent the effects of a sales tax being passed on to the consumer through price increases.

couraged by the bourgeoisie. Thus in such a society, an ordinary man never knows what a particular law means until someone interprets it for him after he has appeared in court charged with an offence under that particular law!

This is understandable. The bourgeoisie makes its own laws. These laws are both its property and an instrument for maintaining it in power. This is also perfectly understandable in terms of the realities of bourgeois societies which necessarily must exist above the people. Those who exist above the people must have their laws exist above the people. It is the people that must serve and obey bourgeois laws. It is not bourgeois laws that must serve the people. This is so because in the final analysis bourgeois laws are made to protect the interests of the bourgeoisie. Mystification of the law is therefore a necessary weapon with which the bourgeoisie can 'handle' or 'deal' with the people.

In a socialist society things are different. All laws are made to serve the masses and not vice versa. This being the case, the law makers— people's representatives—as well as other people's institutions strive as much as possible to educate the people on various points of law that fall within their spheres of activity. In this way pitfalls of making administration of the law difficult and cumbersome are avoided and no chance is left to anyone to make a myth of the laws for his own individual benefit.

Socialists are judged among other things, by the way they make their laws—whether they persist in making bourgeois laws and feed them to the people or whether they unequivocally commit themselves to the making of truly socialist laws. Socialists are also judged by the efforts they put up to educate the masses on the socialist laws that they enact to serve the people.

NOTE Of special interest as a 'truly socialist law' is the Acquisition of Buildings Act, 1971 (Act No. 13 of 1971). Under this Act the President is given the power, where he believes it to be in the public interest to do so, to acquire any building the value of which exceeds Sh. 100,000 and which is not occupied by its owner. 'Occupied' is defined as occupied for residential, commercial, or industrial purposes, and 'owner' includes a natural person and a body corporate. Where a building is partly occupied by its owner, the entire building may be acquired and the owner will become a tenant of the state in that portion of the building which he occupies. The office of Registrar of Buildings is established and the holder thereof is made generally responsible for the administration of the Act. Compensation is computed by dividing the 'cost of construction' of a building into 120 units and deducting one of these units from the value of the building for each month elapsed since its completion. Thus, no compensation would be payable in respect of a ten year old building. An Appeals Tribunal is set up to review both acquisition notices and decisions concerning compensation. The courts are precluded from reviewing or enquiring into any decisions made by the President, the Registrar of Buildings, or the Appeals Tribunal. The Act became law on 22 April 1971, and the acquisition of buildings began immediately. By the end of May 1971, over 2,300 had been taken over. It appears that the operation was carried out with considerable zeal for on 30 May 1971 President Nyerere announced that certain buildings taken over would be given back to their previous owners. These included buildings belonging to individual owners where the effect of the acquisition had been to make the owner homeless, and buildings belonging to cooperative institutions and religious bodies. (See the *Daily Nation*, Nairobi, 31 May 1971. For a lucid comment on the Act, see *The Nationalist*, 17 May 1971; and for a truly despicable piece of British 'journalism', see the *Daily Telegraph*, London, 26 April 1971.) What distinguishes the Acquisition of Buildings Act as socialist legislation is its explicit class nature. The Act is no mere piece of reformist tinkering, rather it is a clear weapon of class struggle aimed at the suppression of an exploiting landlord class through the removal of its economic base. As another example of class-oriented legislation, see the Customary Leaseholds (Enfranchisement Act), 1968 (Act No. 47 of 1968) which abolished a proto-feudal system of land tenure in West Lake Region.

NOTE Engels perceived that 'in a modern state, law must not only correspond to the general economic condition and be its expression, but must also be an *internally coherent* expression'. (Italics in the original, 'Letter to C. Schmidt', *Selected Works in One Volume*, op. cit., p. 686.) Thus, to the extent that the law becomes a unified whole, its attempts to achieve internal consistency and rationality alter its nature. The need for consistency may then lead to results which appear anomalous if the law is viewed solely as a weapon in the class struggle. However, where the struggle is particularly intense, the needs of the ruling class will demand the elimination of such anomalies and the class constituent of the legal system will again become dominant. This can be seen clearly in the context of colonial Africa. Rules which protected the 'liberty of the subject' in the law as applied in England were disregarded in the interest of maintaining the imperial authority. (*R. v. Earl of Crewe; ex parte Sekgome* [1910] 2 K.B. 576; *Wallace-Johnson v. R.* [1940] A.C. 231 (PC).)

From another point of view, the impetus towards internal coherence in a highly abstract bourgeois legal system can lead to the kind of mystification noted in the extract above. Those who manipulate the law find themselves turning inwards away from the law's social basis in order to construct the rationalizations necessary to allow the system to maintain its facade of consistency. The result is that the law becomes meaningless to all but the initiated, and what appears rational to those inside the legal charmed circle is totally irrational to those outside. Among lawyers, judges and clerks, the law is seen as the highest expression of human reason; to the layman caught up in its toils, it is random, capricious, and absurd. As the extract suggests, this is a pitfall that a socialist legal system must avoid. Many western writers have commented on the absurdity of the legal systems they were subjected to. Dickens's 'The law is a ass', is undoubtedly the most succinct analysis, while Kafka's *The Trial* (Penguin Books, London, 1953) is perhaps the most disturbing.

NOTE   Few changes have taken place in Tanzania's formal legal norms, either since the attainment of Independence or the adoption of the Arusha Declaration. Speaking to a conference of Judges and Magistrates in November 1968, the Second Vice-President, Mr Kawawa, said, '. . . we have yet to take critical review of the various laws that are in use in Tanzania to see whether they are in line with our circumstances and aspirations or not'. There is also the problem of attempting to make the laws culturally relevant; that is, to ensure that Tanzania has a system of laws based on socialist principles and firmly rooted in African culture. This problem has been particularly acute in the area of family law. Since their independence, several African countries, notably Uganda, Ghana, and Kenya, have established commissions charged with attempting the revision and unification of family law. An important task of all these commissions has been to devise means whereby all forms of marriage can enjoy equal legal status. At the same time the reports of the various commissions indicate a movement away from traditional marriage towards a more individualistic relationship, based on a nuclear family rather than an extended family. The Kenya Commission has recommended that the substantive changes it suggests in family law be enforced through a combination of administrative methods and penal sanctions. What are appropriate means for bringing about social change through law in a socialist state? See J. S. Read, 'When Is a Wife Not a Wife?', *Journal of the Denning Law Society*, vol. I, no. 2, 1964, p. 46; Commission on the Law of Marriage and Divorce (Kenya), *Report*, Government Printer, Nairobi, 1968; *Alai* v. *Uganda* [1967] E.A. 596 (U); *Government Paper No. 1 of 1969* (Tanzania); and, the Law of Marriage Act, 1971, Act No. 5 of 1971. For the problems involved in translating socialist programmes into legislation, see B. Rahim, 'Legislative Implementation of the Arusha Declaration', *East African Law Journal*, vol. IV, no. 4, 1968, p. 183. On designing a socialist legal system, see G. Eorsi, 'Some Problems of Making the Law', *East African Law Journal*, vol. III, no. 4, 1967, p. 272.

NOTE   In the speech he gave on 30 June 1960 to mark the Independence of the Congo, Patrice Lumumba stated:

> We are going to re-examine all former laws, and make new ones which will be just and noble. We are going to put an end to suppression of free thought and make it possible for all citizens fully to enjoy the fundamental liberties set down in the declaration of the Rights of Man. (Quoted in Hans Kohn and Wallace Sokolsky (eds.), *African Nationalism in the Twentieth Century*, Van Nostrand, New York City, 1965, p. 120.)

NOTE   Before leaving this discussion of the nature of the state, consider the following comment:

> In my opinion most political talk is much too ambitious. People expect to use political power to accomplish some grandeur or excellence. It cannot. What it can do, sometimes, is to guarantee a situation of minimum decency in which maybe something good will occur. From this point of view the good societies in the world at present are certainly small ones, perhaps Denmark, Tanzania, or so. (Paul Goodman, 'Objective Values', *The Dialectics of Liberation*, op. cit., p. 117.)

(For a classic exposition of a political theory totally opposed to the existence of the state, see Kropotkin, *The State*, Freedom Press, London, 1969.)

D · CONTRADICTIONS

If everyone always thought and acted precisely as his rulers wished him to, then difficulties between the state and the individual would never occur. Since no one would indulge in prohibited behaviour, the problem of how the state should respond to different kinds of such behaviour would not arise. Since this is clearly not the situation, it is necessary to establish some theoretical framework within which the state should respond when people deviate from established standards of conduct. For example, it is possible to hold that anyone who disagrees with any policy or breaks any rule, no matter how trivial, is an enemy of the state, and should be eliminated or subject to severe criminal penalties.[8] Other approaches might be more permissive or might rely on less stringent sanctions.

The question, then, is two-fold, involving a decision as to the kinds of behaviour which will be tolerated and the appropriate responses of the state to such behaviour. It becomes much easier to deal with individual cases that arise if a general theory exists for dealing with all cases.

Mao Tse-Tung

THE CORRECT HANDLING OF CONTRADICTIONS
AMONG THE PEOPLE[9]

● We are confronted by two types of social contradictions—those between ourselves and the enemy and those among the people themselves. The two are totally different in their nature.

To understand these two different types of contradictions correctly, we must first be clear on what is meant by 'the people' and what is meant by 'the enemy'. . . . At the present stage, the period of building socialism, the classes, strata and social groups which favour, support and work for the cause of socialist construction all come within the category of the people, while the social forces and groups which resist the socialist revolution and are hostile to or sabotage socialist construction are all enemies of the people.

In the conditions prevailing in China today, the contradictions among the people comprise the contradictions within the working class, the contradictions within the peasantry, the contradictions between the working class and the peasantry, the contradictions between the workers and peasants on the one hand and the intellectuals on

---

[8] For example, s. 148 of the Law of Marriage Act, 1971 provides that any person who attends a purported ceremony of marriage where either of the parties is below the statutory minimum age for marriage may be punished by up to two years' imprisonment.

[9] *Quotations From Chairman Mao Tse-Tung*, Foreign Languages Press, Peking, 1966, pp. 45-57.

the other, the contradictions between the working class and other sections of the working people on the one hand and the national bourgeoisie on the other, the contradictions within the national bourgeoisie, and so on. Our People's Government is one that genuinely represents the people's interests, it is a government that serves the people. Nevertheless, there are still certain contradictions between the government and the people. These include contradictions among the interests of the state, the interests of the collective and the interests of the individual; between democracy and centralism; between the leadership and the led; and the contradiction arising from the bureaucratic style of work of certain government workers in their relations with the masses. All these are also contradictions among the people. Generally speaking, the people's basic identity of interests underlies the contradictions among the people.

Contradictions between ourselves and the enemy are antagonistic contradictions. Within the ranks of the people, the contradictions among the working people are non-antagonistic, while those between the exploited and the exploiting classes have a non-antagonistic aspect in addition to an antagonistic aspect.

In the political life of our people, how should right be distinguished from wrong in one's words and actions? On the basis of the principles of our Constitution, the will of the overwhelming majority of our people and the common political positions which have been proclaimed on various occasions by our political parties and groups, we consider that, broadly speaking, the criteria should be as follows:

1. Words and actions should help to unite, and not divide, the people of our various nationalities.
2. They should be beneficial, and not harmful, to socialist transformation and socialist construction.
3. They should help to consolidate, and not undermine or weaken, the people's democratic dictatorship.
4. They should help to consolidate, and not undermine or weaken, democratic centralism.
5. They should help to strengthen, and not discard or weaken, the leadership of the Communist Party.
6. They should be beneficial, and not harmful, to international socialist unity and the unity of the peace-loving people of the world.

Of these six criteria, the most important are the socialist path and the leadership of the Party.

The question of suppressing counter-revolutionaries is one of a struggle between ourselves and the enemy, a contradiction between ourselves and the enemy. Among the people, there are some who see this question in a somewhat different light. Two kinds of persons hold views different from ours. Those with a Rightist way of thinking make no distinction between ourselves and the enemy and take the enemy for our own people. They regard as friends the very persons whom the broad masses regard as enemies. Those with a 'Left' way of thinking magnify contradictions between ourselves and the enemy to such an extent that they take certain contradictions among the people for contradictions with the enemy and regard as counter-revolutionaries persons who are not really counter-revolutionaries. Both these views are wrong. Neither can lead to the correct handling of the question of suppressing counter-revolutionaries or to a correct assessment of this work.

Qualitatively different contradictions can only be resolved by qualitatively different methods. For instance, the contradiction between the proletariat and the bourgeoisie is resolved by the method of socialist revolution; the contradiction between the great masses of the people and the feudal system is resolved by the method of democratic revolution; the contradiction between the colonies and imperialism is resolved by the method of national revolutionary war; the contradiction between the working class and the peasant class in socialist society is resolved by the method of collectivization and mechanization in agriculture; contradiction within the Communist Party is resolved by the method of criticism and self-criticism; the contradiction between society and nature is resolved by the method of developing the productive forces. . . . The principle of using different methods to resolve different contradictions is one which Marxist-Leninists must strictly observe.

Since they are different in nature, the contradictions between ourselves and the enemy and the contradictions among the people must be resolved by different methods. To put it briefly, the former are a matter of drawing a clear distinction between ourselves and the enemy, and the latter a matter of drawing a clear distinction between right and wrong. It is, of course, true that the distinction between ourselves and the enemy is also a matter of right and wrong. For example, the question of who is in the right, we or the domestic and foreign reactionaries, the imperialists, the feudalists and bureaucrat-capitalists, is also a matter of right and wrong, but it is in a different category from questions of right and wrong among the people.

The only way to settle questions of an ideological nature or controversial issues among the people is by the democratic method, the method of discussion, of criticism, of persuasion and education, and not by the method of coercion or repression.

To be able to carry on their production and studies effectively and to arrange their lives properly, the people want their government and those in charge of production and of cultural and educational organizations to issue appropriate orders of an obligatory nature. It is common sense that the maintenance of public order would be impossible without such administrative regulations. Administrative orders and the method of persuasion and education complement each other in resolving contradictions among the people. Even administrative regulations for the maintenance of public order must be accompanied by persuasion and education, for in many cases regulations alone will not work.

Inevitably, the bourgeoisie and petit bourgeoisie will give expression to their own ideologies. Inevitably, they will stubbornly express themselves on political and ideological questions by every possible means. You cannot expect them to do otherwise. We should not use the method of suppression and prevent them from expressing themselves, but should allow them to do so and at the same time argue with them and direct appropriate criticism at them. We must undoubtedly criticize wrong ideas of every description. It certainly would not be right to refrain from criticism, look on while wrong ideas spread unchecked and allow them to monopolize the field. Mistakes must be criticized and poisonous weeds fought wherever they crop up. However, such criticism should not be dogmatic, and the metaphysical method should not be used, but efforts should be made to apply the dialectical method. What is needed is scientific analysis and convincing argument.

To criticize the people's shortcomings is necessary, . . . but in doing so we must truly take the stand of the people and speak out of whole-hearted eagerness to protect and educate them. To treat comrades like enemies is to go over to the stand of the enemy.

Contradiction and struggle are universal and absolute, but the methods of resolving contradictions, that is, the forms of struggle, differ according to the differences in the nature of the contradictions. Some contradictions are characterized by open antagonism, others are not. In accordance with the concrete development of things, some contradictions which were originally non-antagonistic develop into antagonistic ones, while others which were originally antagonistic develop into non-antagonistic ones.

In ordinary circumstances, contradictions among the people are not antagonistic. But if they are not handled properly, or if we relax our vigilance and lower our guard, antagonism may arise. In a socialist country, a development of this kind is usually only a localized and temporary phenomenon. The reason is that the system of exploitation of man by man has been abolished and the interests of the people are basically the same.

In our country, the contradiction between the working class and the national bourgeoisie belongs to the category of contradictions among the people. By and large, the class struggle between the two is a class struggle within the ranks of the people, because the Chinese national bourgeoisie has a dual character. In the period of the bourgeois-democratic revolution, it had both a revolutionary and a conciliationist side to its character. In the period of the socialist revolution, exploitation of the working class for profit constitutes one side of the character of the national bourgeoisie, while its support of the Constitution and its willingness to accept socialist transformation constitute the other. The national bourgeoisie differs from the imperialists, the landlords and the bureaucrat-capitalists. The contradiction between the national bourgeoisie and the working class is one between the exploiter and the exploited, and is by nature antagonistic. But in the concrete conditions of China, this antagonistic class contradiction can, if properly handled, be transformed into a non-antagonistic one and be resolved by peaceful methods. However, it will change into a contradiction between ourselves and the enemy if we do not handle it properly and do not follow the policy of uniting with, criticizing and educating the national bourgeoisie, or if the national bourgeoisie does ● not accept this policy of ours.

NOTE This extract is an abridged version of Mao's essay, 'On the Correct Handling of Contradictions Among the People', and also contains passages from another essay, 'On Contradiction'.

NOTE By focusing on the class nature of particular anti-social acts, Mao's theory of the way the state should respond to such acts is fundamentally different from that of liberal-democracy. The latter theory posits a code of rules which apply to all people equally, regardless of class. The result in, for example, eighteenth-century England, was, to paraphrase Anatole France, that rich and poor alike were hanged if found guilty of stealing bread. The Maoist theory finds adherents of many shades of political persuasion. One surprising (and all unwitting) advocate is Sir Ivor Jennings, who has asserted, 'The task of statesmanship is to produce a nice combination of persuasion and force, persuasion of the law-abiding citizens and force against those who are potential law-breakers.' (*Democracy in Africa*, Cambridge University Press, London, 1963, p. 49.)

Less surprising is the advocacy found in the PAIGC Programme:

ARTICLE V (2) Establishment of fundamental freedoms, respect for the rights of man and guarantees for the exercise of these freedoms and rights.
(4) All individuals or groups of individuals who by their

action or behaviour favour imperialism, colonialism, or the destruction of the unity of the people will be deprived by every available means of fundamental freedoms. (Cabral, op. cit., p. 137.)

NOTE The relationship between the state and the individual in China is based on the theory of the correct handling of contradictions among the people. During the course of the Great Proletarian Cultural Revolution, considerable stress was placed on the development and application of this theory. This was emphasized by the Central Committee of the Party:

A strict distinction must be made between the two different types of contradictions: those among the people and those between ourselves and the enemy. Contradictions among the people must not be made into contradictions between ourselves and the enemy; nor must contradictions between ourselves and the enemy be regarded as contradictions among the people.

It is normal for the masses to hold different views. Contention between different views is unavoidable, necessary and beneficial. In the course of normal and full debate, the masses will affirm what is right, correct what is wrong and gradually reach unanimity.

The method to be used in debates is to present the facts, reason things out and persuade through reasoning. Any method of forcing a minority holding different views to submit is impermissible. The minority should be protected, because sometimes the truth is with the minority. Even if the minority is wrong, they should still be allowed to argue their case and reserve their views.

When there is a debate, it should be conducted by reasoning, not by coercion or force. (*Decision of the Central Committee of the Chinese Communist Party Concerning the Great Proletarian Cultural Revolution*, op. cit., p. 6.)

NOTE The question of deciding whether a particular contradiction exists among the people or between the people and the enemies of the people is obviously crucial to any discussion of the relationship between the individual and a socialist state. Speaking to the National Executive Committee of TANU on 17 October 1968 at Tanga, President Nyerere indicated a possible Tanzanian definition of contradictions between the people and the enemies of the people when he declared that, '. . . all troublemakers who oppose the nation's chosen path of development and impede the progress of the people will be dealt with'. (*The Nationalist*, 23 October 1968.)

Consider the following example of the difficulties involved in appreciating the true nature of a particular contradiction: On 16 June 1969 approximately 150 workers at a shirt factory in Dar es Salaam walked out of work and staged a demonstration to protest against the methods being used by the production manager at the factory. The Police Field Force Unit was called to the scene and arrived at the factory wearing steel helmets and armed with semi-automatic rifles with bayonets fixed. They immediately arrested the workers and herded them into trucks. The workers were then carried to the Central Police Station in Dar es Salaam, '. . . where they were marched with hands overhead into custody'. The arrests were made on the grounds that the workers had engaged in conduct which, under Tanzania's labour laws, amounted to an illegal strike. The Second Vice-President, Mr Kawawa, then intervened. He ordered the release of the arrested 'strikers' and called a meeting to be held the next day at the shirt factory. At this meeting he ordered the dismissal of the production manager and warned the firm not to mistreat the workers. He also warned the firm not to take advantage of laws designed to inhibit strikes and seemed to disavow the action of the police. (*The Nationalist*, 17 June 1969, and 18 June 1969.) *The Nationalist*, the official organ of TANU, carried an editorial on 18 June which was severely critical of the police action and pointed out that in this case the enemies of the people were not the 'striking' workers, as the action of the police seemed to indicate, but the capitalist owners of the factory.

QUESTION What methods can be used to ensure that those who control the coercive powers of the state are able to correctly evaluate contradictions as they arise and therefore use those coercive powers only when they are necessary to protect the interests of the people?

E · FREEDOM AND DEVELOPMENT

As indicated at the beginning of this chapter, questions concerning the relationship between the state and the individual can only be accurately analysed in the context of Tanzania's objective conditions. The most important of these conditions is the country's extreme poverty, for it largely defines the meaning to be given to freedom, and also indicates the practical importance of freedom. President Nyerere has written:

> Freedom and development are as completely linked together as chickens and eggs. Without chickens, you get no eggs; and without eggs you soon have no chickens. Similarly, without freedom you get no development, and without development you very soon lose your freedom.[10]

Thus, human freedom is not simply a morally desirable goal, but also an issue of great practical significance. Development is more than a self-justifying materialistic goal; it is a process of human liberation and human growth. Clearly such development can only take place when it involves free human beings. Unless freedom and development proceed together, development degenerates into the sterile obsession with technological advance characteristic of western society today, or it does not take place at all.[11]

In his paper, *Freedom and Development*, originally delivered at a TANU N.E.C. meeting in October 1968, President Nyerere argued that authoritarian methods can only inhibit development. Although a cursory examination of the economic history of the developed capitalist states reveals that they relied considerably on slave labour for their development, such a course is

---

[10] *Freedom and Development*, Government Printer, Dar es Salaam, 1968, p. 1. See also, Nyerere's address to the Preparatory Meeting of the Non-Aligned Conference, Dar es Salaam, 13 April 1970, as reported in *The Standard*, 14 April 1970.
[11] For a stimulating discussion of the hollowness of 'development' viewed as an end in itself, see George M. Grant, *Technology and Empire*, House of Anansi Press, Toronto, 1969.

emphatically rejected by Nyerere. Moral imperatives aside, a highly authoritarian approach would be impractical in Tanzania because of the small size of the state's coercive forces. In fact, it is likely that in most Third World countries, mobilization, rather than coercion, will have to be the operational approach to development. (This point is made clear in the TANU Guidelines (Mwongozo).) There is, indeed, evidence that authoritarian methods have had a seriously inhibiting effect on development in Cuba.[12]

Nyerere outlines the practical relationship between freedom and development through a series of propositions about how the people can be mobilized. First, 'if the purpose of development is the greater freedom and well-being of the people, it cannot result from force.'[13] If force is rejected, then the only approaches through which the people can be caused to undertake their own development are 'leadership through education' and 'democracy in decision-making'.[14] Leadership then comes to mean 'talking and discussing' and 'explaining and persuading' rather than 'shouting', 'abusing' or 'ordering'.[15] Democracy in decision-making involves two elements: that everyone be allowed to speak freely and be listened to, and that once a decision is reached it is accepted as the decision of all and carried out as such.[16]

The President stressed the particular relevance of these principles to ujamaa villages, the cornerstone of the nation's rural development programme. He said that 'Ujamaa villages are intended to be socialist organizations created by the people, and governed by those who live and work in them. They cannot be created from outside, nor governed from outside.'[17] The essence of an ujamaa village is, therefore, its self-reliance, its autonomy, and the democratic nature of its control. All these attributes find their common root in the principle of the Arusha Declaration that the people must develop themselves.

The basic theory of the ujamaa village, as opposed to the earlier settlement scheme type village, grew largely out of the experience and practice of the Ruvuma Development Association. This association was founded in Litowa in 1963 and spread to parts of the surrounding area. One of the founders of the Association was sent to TANU Headquarters in 1969, where he was put in charge of the Party's ujamaa village programme. Officials of the ujamaa village sections in the Ministry of Economic Affairs and Development Planning, and in the Office of the President, used the Ruvuma Development Association as their model. In addition, the theory of ujamaa village develop-

---

[12] See, for example, Huberman and Sweezy, *Socialism in Cuba*, op. cit.; and Richard Gott in *The Guardian*, London, 14 October 1970.
[13] *Freedom and Development*, p. 3.
[14] loc. cit.
[15] loc. cit.
[16] ibid., p. 4.
[17] ibid., p. 7.

ment as taught at Kivukoni College was based on the ideas and approaches of the Ruvuma Development Association.

The essence of the Ruvuma Development Association was its communal democracy. Power in the Association and in the villages that formed it originated with the farmers themselves. In Mateteraka village, for example, control rested with the twice-weekly village meeting. An elected Manager and Secretary were the delegates from this village to the Association. Since the people were governing themselves, they also began to plan and participate in their own development. Along with the emphasis on democratic control went great stress on the development of attitudes of self-reliance. This was particularly true in the Association's school at Litowa where self-reliance became a dynamic expression of the socialist initiative of both students and teachers.

One can easily romanticize the Ruvuma Development Association and its achievements. Considerable problems existed, however, for the new man is not created overnight. Still, a significant beginning had been made in the struggle to develop the consciousness, the leadership, and the technical skills required for socialist agricultural development.[18]

On 2 October 1969, the President, exercising his powers under ss.6(1)(a) and 6(1)(b) of the Societies Ordinance (Cap. 337) declared the Ruvuma Development Association to be an illegal society and ordered it wound up.[19] In so doing, he was carrying out a decision made by the TANU Central Committee during the previous week. While foreign involvement, in terms of capital and manpower assistance, was among the reasons given for the disbandment of the Association, it is clear that the main reason was a desire on the part of the Party to bring all important institutions in the nation under its control. Thus, at the same meeting, the Central Committee placed all ujamaa villages under Party control. (The proximity of the villages of the RDA to the Mozambique border was undoubtedly also a factor in the Central Committee's decision.)

From this discussion of freedom and development, we can draw several conclusions which are generally relevant to an analysis of freedom in Tanzania. First, Tanzania does not intend to have a totalitarian state administration, even if it possessed the practical requirements for doing so. Secondly, as indicated by the Party's action in respect of the Ruvuma Development Association, and certain aspects of the administration of the frontal approach

---

[18] On the Ruvuma Development Association, see S. Toroka, 'Education for Self-Reliance: The Litowa Experiment', *Mbioni*, vol. IV, no. 11, 1968, p. 2; R. Lewin 'Mateteraka: An Ujamaa Village in Ruvuma Region', *Mbioni*, vol. V, no. 3, 1969, p. 13; and 'Socialist Land Reform in Tanzania', *The African Communist*, no. 45, 1971-p. 71. For a superb study of the development of one village during the Chinese Revolution, see William Hinton, *Fanshen: A Documentary of Revolution in a Chinese Village,* Monthly Review Press, New York City, 1966.

[19] G.N. No. 254 of 1969.

in Dodoma Region in the latter half of 1970, and generally by the very fact that the President found it necessary to write his paper on *Freedom and Development*, there is a tendency towards authoritarianism. This tendency, as suggested earlier, is inevitable in the context of Tanzania's historical experience. Thirdly, the central political institution in Tanzania is the Party, and no activities of any significance, either in national or local terms, will take place outside its auspices.[20] Finally, within the limits indicated, the emphasis will be on national development through free discussion and democratic leadership.

[20] See, for example, speeches of the President and Second Vice-President in November 1969 to Church leaders and Girl Guides, respectively, urging that all social, religious, educational, and cultural organizations follow the policies of TANU. *The Standard*, 1 December 1969.

CHAPTER TWO
THE CONSTITUTION AND THE COURTS

In this chapter we discuss certain aspects of constitutional law and practice in Tanzania, and we examine in particular those institutions which traditionally have been important in British constitutional history as devices for protecting the individual from the state. When we speak of the state in this context we mean the executive power (ultimately, the police, prisons, and standing army) while the legislative and judicial branches of government are, in the broadest sense, protective institutions. In the ideal structure of liberal democracy these two branches of government are intended to be independent of the executive arm and to act as checks on its presumed tendencies towards authoritarianism. However, it should be noted that the socialist analysis of the nature of the state is much different from that of liberal democracy. If the state exists as an instrument of class rule, the theory of checks and balances and independent branches of government becomes meaningless. The validity of the liberal-democratic theory might be usefully tested in the context of colonial Tanganyika by examining the effectiveness of the colonial courts and legislature in their control of the executive.

Constitutional development in Tanzania has drawn heavily on the liberal-democratic theory of the state with its emphasis on the role of the legislative and judicial branches. The Independence Constitution of 1961, a piece of British executive legislation,[1] introduced parliamentary democracy into Tanzania. The National Assembly was the central institution of government, and control over important aspects of state administration was denied to the executive branch of government. This constitution was short-lived because it did not take into account the two essential facts of Tanzanian politics: the need for strong executive government if the country's social and economic problems are to be dealt with, and the supremacy and ubiquity of the Party. At the risk of oversimplification, it could be said that the Republican Constitution of 1962[2] solved the first of these problems, while the One-Party State Constitution of 1965[3] dealt with the second.

Despite these changes from the original Westminster-model constitution, distinct legislative and judicial institutions still exist in Tanzania. To what extent are they performing their traditional functions? How successful are they in reacting to new demands? The answer to this last question will ultimately determine whether these institutions are to survive.

[1] S.I. 1961 No. 2274.
[2] C.A. Act No. 1; Cap. 499.
[3] Act No. 43 of 1965.

In the liberal-democratic theory of government, the function of the legislative and judicial branches is essentially negative. That is, they are seen as brakes or checks on the executive. But in a state where the prime emphasis is on the political, cultural, and economic development of the people, institutions which perform a negative, or perhaps reactionary, role can have little validity. Though Lester Pearson may have believed that Tanzania was not '. . . a parliamentary democracy in our sense of the word',[4] there is far more to true democracy than a system of checks and balances and the ritual of Westminster. As Peter Worsley has pointed out, the absence in any state of what are considered, in the West at any rate, to be democratic *institutions*, does not necessarily mean that that state is not administered according to democratic *principles*.[5] Former Chief Justice Georges made the point clearly when he said:

> There is often a tendency to identify the preservation of the freedom of the individual through the rule of law with the particular institutions which have been set up to achieve that particular purpose. This process is not at all difficult because to the extent that the institutions do succeed, they acquire a sanctity which earns for them respect in the society even apart from the role which they fulfil . . . *It is tacitly assumed that since the institution is not there, the work which it is intended to do is not in fact being done.*[6]

A · BILLS OF RIGHTS

Many countries which have written constitutions have sections in their constitutions which purport to guarantee basic freedoms or 'rights'. Such guarantees attempt to put absolute limits on the power of the state to interfere with the freedom of the individual. Normally it is the responsibility of the courts to interpret the meaning of these absolute guarantees which are often referred to collectively as a Bill of Rights. As a corollary to this right to interpret, the courts may overrule or disallow any act, executive or legislative, which they consider to be in conflict with the provisions of the Bill of Rights. For example, if a Bill of Rights prohibits racial discrimination, and the legislature enacts legislation which has this effect, the courts would have the power to disallow such legislation, at least to the extent that it was discriminatory.

While no colonial administration would have accepted such limitations on its powers, Bills of Rights became very popular with the Colonial Office

[4] *Daily Star*, Toronto, 27 February 1970.
[5] *The Third World*, op. cit., p. 181.
[6] 'The Rule of Law in Tanzania', address to the East African Academy of Arts and Sciences at the University College, Dar es Salaam, 20 September 1965. Emphasis added. For a review of constitutional change in Tanzania since Independence, see J. P. W. B. McAuslan, 'The Evolution of Public Law in East Africa in the 1960's', *Public Law*, 1970, p. 5 of part 1, and p. 153 of part 2.

during the decade of African political independence. This was probably for two reasons. First, the provision of Bills of Rights in independence constitutions fitted in with a general pattern of denying, as far as possible, effective executive power to the post-colonial government. Secondly, the ideas of the International Commission of Jurists appeared to have gained a currency they lack today.

QUESTIONS 1. Given our definition of the state, can a Bill of Rights make any difference in the way a particular state is administered?
2. Can a state which is attempting to transform itself from an under-developed, capitalist-oriented and capitalist-controlled state into a developed, socialist state afford to have any *absolute* freedoms which it cannot limit?

The Interim Constitution of Tanzania does not contain a Bill of Rights, although the subject has been raised at different stages in the country's constitutional history.

PROPOSALS FOR A REPUBLIC
GOVERNMENT PAPER NO. I OF 1962[7]

● The Government believes that the Rule of Law is best preserved not
by formal guarantees in a Bill of Rights which invites conflict between
the executive and the judiciary, but by independent judges administer-
● ing justice free from political pressure.

QUESTION Why should guarantees in a Bill of Rights invite conflict between the executive and the judiciary? When are such conflicts likely to arise? In any case, as Park has commented on the guarantees in the Nigerian Bill of Rights: 'In court they tended to have very little effect, because the judges interpreted the rights strictly and the exceptions quite liberally.' ('The Independence Constitution of Nigeria in Retrospect', Institute of Commonwealth Studies, *Post-Independence Constitutional Changes*, London, 1968, p. 61.)

REPORT OF THE PRESIDENTIAL COMMISSION
ON THE ESTABLISHMENT OF
A DEMOCRATIC ONE-PARTY STATE[8]

● *Rights of the Individual in the One-Party State*
The President in his statement on the National Ethic and his guide to
the Commission places great emphasis on the rights of the individual.
The concern for human liberty and individual freedom which was a
prominent feature of Tanganyika's struggle for independence continues
to be one of its major preoccupations today. This is shown in our

[7] Government Printer, Dar es Salaam, 1962, p. 6.
[8] Government Printer, Dar es Salaam, 1965, pp. 30-32.

policy towards South Africa, Southern Rhodesia and the Portuguese colonies. In making our recommendations on the institutions of government appropriate to a One-Party State we have had constantly in mind the need to ensure that any new arrangements we propose will not unnecessarily encroach on the freedom of the individual. This concern reflects our basic approach to the task set by our Terms of Reference. The formal establishment of One-Party government in Tanganyika is not a way of imposing bureaucratic restraint on a mass of unwilling citizens. It is rather for us an opportunity to devise new constitutional forms which will enable the ordinary man to participate more fully in the process of government.

A Bill of Rights

There are many ways in which the rights of the individual may be protected within the framework of the law. In recent years a good deal of attention has been focused on the idea of writing into the constitution a Bill of Rights which the aggrieved citizen may himself enforce by action in the Courts. A number of independent countries in Africa have constitutional provisions of this kind. In Tanganyika a Bill of Rights was considered by Government immediately before independence and again when the Constitution for the Republic was under discussion. On both occasions the idea was rejected. However, in view of the importance we attach to providing adequate safeguards for the individual we have thought it right to re-examine once again this possibility.

The provision of a Bill of Rights involves taking a number of ethical propositions about the business of government and reducing them to the cold print of a lawyer's draft. In any society this is a difficult task if the lawyers are to avoid substituting the letter for the spirit. For a young nation we believe it to be a task fraught with danger. Democratic government cannot be practised nor individual rights protected in a society torn by internal disorder. For a young nation, public order is precious but it is also fragile. In his speech at the opening of the University College Campus, Mwalimu Julius K. Nyerere, discussing the question of Preventive Detention, said this:

Our nation has neither the long tradition of nationhood nor the strong physical means of national security which older countries take for granted. While the vast mass of the people give full and active support to their country and its Government, a handful of individuals can still put our nation into jeopardy and reduce to ashes the efforts of millions.

A Bill of Rights limits in advance of events the measures which Government may take to protect the nation from the threat of subversion and disorder. However, the course of events cannot always be foreseen and constitutional guarantees for the individual will defeat their own purpose if they serve to protect those whose object is to subvert and destroy democracy itself. It is, of course, possible to draft a Bill of Rights in which the statements of principle are so hedged about with provisos and qualifications that Government retains in large measure its freedom of action. This technique (followed in a number of constitutions seen by the Commission) has the effect of divorcing the provisions of the law from the ethical principles on which they should be based. A Bill of Rights in this form provides little by way of protection for the individual and induces in the ordinary citizen a mood of cynicism about the whole process of Government.

The Commission is also conscious of the danger that a Bill of Rights would invite conflict between the Judiciary and the Executive and Legislature. If a Bill of Rights were written into the Constitution it would have overriding legislative effect. This means that the Courts could be asked to declare invalid any law passed by Parliament if it were inconsistent with a provision contained in the Bill of Rights. By requiring the courts to stand in judgement on the legislature, the Commission feels that the Judiciary would be drawn into the area of political controversy. This would make more difficult the task of the Judges in administering the law impartially. At the time of independence, the Judiciary in Tanganyika was of almost entirely expatriate origin. Although this situation is rapidly changing it is likely to be some years before the Judiciary is accepted by the public as an entirely indigenous institution. In this transitional period the maintenance of the rule of law, to which we attach the greatest importance, requires particular care that occasions for conflict between the Judges and the Executive and Legislature should be reduced to a minimum.

There is a further aspect to this matter. Tanganyika has dynamic plans for economic development. These cannot be implemented without revolutionary changes in the social structure. In considering a Bill of Rights in this context we have had in mind the bitter conflict which arose in the United States between the President and the Supreme Court as a result of the radical measures enacted by the Roosevelt Administration to deal with the economic depression in the 1930s. Decisions concerning the extent to which individual rights must give way to the wider considerations of social progress are not properly judicial decisions. They are political decisions best taken by political leaders responsible to the electorate.

For all these reasons members of the Commission are unanimous in reaching the conclusion that an attempt to protect individual freedom by a Bill of Rights would in the circumstances of Tanganyika today be neither prudent nor effective. Behind this decision is our belief that the rights of the individual in any society depend more on the ethical sense of the people than on formal guarantees in the law. The process of Government in the United Kingdom provides a striking example of the force of a national ethic in controlling the exercise of political power. A government in Britain with a majority of one seat in Parliament could legislate to abolish elections, detain political opponents without trial and establish a censorship of the press, radio, and television. Indeed most of these things were done by Parliament when the British people stood on the brink of disaster in the Second World War. They are not done in peace time; not because there is anything in the law to prevent a Government acting in this way but because they are unthinkable. In other words there is a consensus between the people and their leaders about how the process of Government should be carried on. It is on this that the traditional freedoms of the British people depend.

The Commission believes that the basis of such a consensus already exists in Tanganyika. However, we do not have behind us a long tradition of constitutional government and positive steps are needed to entrench the national ethic in the moral imagination of the people. We therefore recommend that a statement of the ethical principles which bind together leaders and people should be included in the new constitution in the form of a preamble. Thereafter everything possible should be done to win for these principles a strong commitment from the citizens of the United Republic.

NOTE   When the Presidential Commission on the Establishment of a Democratic One-Party State was holding hearings prior to making its report, it received a brief from the Tanganyika Law Society urging the inclusion of a Bill of Rights in the new constitution. This brief noted, *inter alia*, 'It is by incorporating a guarantee of these rights (i.e. "fundamental rights of man") in the Constitution that we can ensure it of universal respect.' Among the fundamental rights which were enumerated was 'the right of property'. *The Annual Survey of Commonwealth Law* (Butterworth, London) always includes a chapter entitled 'Fundamental Rights and Civil Liberties', and in this chapter there is always a section on 'Freedom of Property', which is, presumably, a fundamental right. Does the emphasis on the right to property say anything about the purpose of Bills of Rights ? In this connection, s.75 of the Constitution of Kenya is interesting. This section guarantees property rights, limits the state's power of compulsory acquisition, and provides that anyone whose property is compulsorily acquired shall be paid 'full' compensation and shall have direct access to the High Court on any question regarding compensation. The undoubted aim of this section was to guarantee the property rights of white settlers against the independent government of

Kenya. (See Odinga, *Not Yet Uhuru*, Heinemann, London, 1968, pp. 257-69.) On African property rights during the colonial period in Kenya see *Ol le Njogo* v. *A.G.* (1914) 5 E.A.L.R. 70.

NOTE In connection with the Presidential Commission's remark about the cynicism engendered by empty Bills of Rights, it might be noted that the 1965 Constitution of Rhodesia contained an elaborate Bill of Rights running to fifteen sections (ss. 66-81). It declared that '. . . every person in Rhodesia enjoys the fundamental rights and freedoms of the individual'. These rights were then enumerated as: life, liberty, security of the person, the enjoyment of property, the protection of the law, freedom of conscience, freedom of expression, freedom of assembly, freedom of association, and respect for private and family life. All persons were guaranteed the enjoyment of these rights regardless of '. . . race, tribe, place of origin, political opinions, colour, or creed'. Another example of an empty Bill of Rights could certainly be found in the United States: that country's Bill of Rights was adopted in 1791; slavery was abolished in the United States in 1865.

A class analysis may help us put Bills of Rights in their correct light. If the state exists for the purpose of suppressing a particular class, then clearly a Bill of Rights is unlikely to be of assistance to any member of that class in his struggles with the state. On the other hand, those members of the ruling class who are directly wielding state power will not wish to antagonize other members of their own class. A Bill of Rights may provide a useful instrument for protecting members of the ruling class against the over-zealousness of the servants of the state.[9]

A state trying to make radical alterations in its class structure might find itself hamstrung by a Bill of Rights which demanded impartial, non-discriminatory treatment of all subjects. To return to the example used at the beginning of this section, a Bill of Rights which absolutely prohibited racial discrimination of any kind would pose a serious obstacle to a government which wished to do away with the institutionalized racism of the colonial period. (As an example of discriminatory legislation, see the Civil Service Act, Cap. 509, s.20. It could be argued that fair employment practices legislation affecting at least the private sector of the economy would be desirable. Of special importance would be provisions that persons performing similar work receive similar pay, regardless of race or sex.)

In any case, the recommendations of the Presidential Commission were accepted and Tanzania does not have a Bill of Rights. However, the Interim Constitution does contain a preamble which refers to some of the basic elements of personal freedom. It must be noted, however, that preambles to statutes have no legislative force and are merely ancillary to the particular

[9] This was, in fact, the function of such constitutional safeguards as existed in colonial times. See Ghai and McAuslan, *Public Law and Political Change in Kenya*, pp. 506-9.

piece of legislation. Thus the statements contained in the preamble to Tanzania's constitution are of a moral rather than a legal effect.[10]

INTERIM CONSTITUTION OF TANZANIA[11]

● Whereas freedom, justice, fraternity and concord are founded upon the recognition of the equality of all men and of their inherent dignity, and upon the recognition of the rights of all men to protection of life, liberty and property, to freedom of conscience, freedom of expression and freedom of association, to participate in their own government, and to receive a just return of their labours:

And when men are united together in a community it is their duty to respect the rights and dignity of their fellow men, to uphold the laws of the State, and to conduct the affairs of the State so that its resources are preserved, developed and enjoyed for the benefit of its citizens as a whole and so as to prevent the exploitation of one man by another:

And whereas such rights are best maintained and protected and such duties are most equitably disposed in a democratic society where the government is responsible to a freely elected Parliament representative of the People and where the courts of law are free and impartial:

Now therefore this Constitution, which makes provision for the Government of Tanzania as such a democratic society is hereby enacted

● by the Parliament of the United Republic of Tanzania.

QUESTION Why was the preamble written into the constitution if it has no legal effect? For a very interesting Canadian case in which a court, operating under a parliamentary constitution, used a legislative declaration of basic rights to invalidate a portion of a conflicting Act of Parliament, see *R. v. Drybones* [1970] S.C.R. 282.

NOTE The present Constitution is the fourth the nation has possessed. Neither the Independence Constitution (Tanganyika Constitution) Order in Council, 1961, nor the Republican Constitution (Constitution of Tanganyika) C.A. Act No. I, Cap. 499 contained a Bill of Rights, but both were prefaced by preambles which, except for the last sentence of each, were identical. The preamble to the Republican Constitution reads as follows:

Whereas recognition of the inherent dignity and of the equal and inalienable rights of all members of the human family is the foundation of freedom, justice and peace:

And whereas the said rights include the right of the individual, whatever his race, tribe, place of origin, political opinions, colour, creed or sex, but subject to respect for the rights and freedoms of others and for the public interest,

[10] On Bills of Rights generally, see de Smith, *The New Commonwealth and its Constitutions*, Stevens and Sons, London, 1964, ch. V.
[11] Act No. 43 of 1965, Preamble.

to life, liberty, security of the person, the enjoyment of property, the protection of the law, freedom of conscience, freedom of expression, freedom of assembly and association, and respect for his private and family life:

And whereas the said rights are best maintained and protected in a democratic society where the government is responsible to a freely-elected Parliament representative of the people and where the courts of law are independent and impartial:

Now therefore, this Constitution, which makes provision for the government of Tanganyika as such a democratic society, is hereby enacted by the Constituent Assembly of Tanganyika.

Are there any changes in emphasis between the preamble to the Republican Constitution and the preamble to the present Constitution? Why might these changes have come about?

NOTE Reference should also be made to the TANU Constitution and especially to its preamble, the TANU Creed.

The Preamble to the Constitution states that a freely elected representative parliament and free and impartial courts are the institutions best suited to guaranteeing personal freedom. Let us then look in more detail at these two institutions.

B · PARLIAMENT AND THE PARTY

INTERIM CONSTITUTION OF TANZANIA[12]

● 3.—(1) There shall be one political Party in Tanzania.

(2) Until the union of the Tanganyika African National Union with the Afro-Shirazi Party (which United Party shall constitute the one political Party), the Party shall, in and for Tanganyika, be the Tanganyika African National Union and, in and for Zanzibar, be the Afro-Shirazi Party.

(3) All political activity in Tanzania, other than that of the organs of state of the United Republic, the organs of the Executive and Legislature for Zanzibar, or such local government authorities as may be established by or under a law of the appropriate legislative authority, shall be
● conducted by or under the auspices of the Party.

In the following extract from a speech given to the TANU National Conference in early 1963, the President outlines the reasons underlying the decision to establish a *de jure* one-party state.

[12] Act No. 43 of 1965.

J. K. Nyerere
DEMOCRACY AND THE PARTY SYSTEM[13]

● Now my argument is that a two-party system can be justified only when the parties are divided over some fundamental issue; otherwise it merely encourages the growth of factionalism. Or, to put it another way, the only time when a political group can represent the interests of a section of the community, without being a faction, is when that group fights to remove a grievous wrong from society. But then the differences, between this group and those responsible for the wrong it fights, are fundamental; and there can therefore be no question of national unity until the differences have been removed by change. And 'change' in that context is a euphemism, because any change in fundamentals is properly termed 'revolution'. What is more, the reason why the word 'revolution' is generally associated with armed insurrection is that the existence of really fundamental differences within any society poses a 'civil war' situation, and has often led to bloody revolution.

. . . In any country which is divided over fundamental issues you have the 'civil war' situation we have been talking about. If, on the other hand, you have a two-party system where the differences between the parties are not fundamental, then you immediately reduce politics to the level of a football match. A football match may, of course, attract some very able players; it may also be entertaining; but it is still only a game, and only the most ardent fans (who are not usually the most intelligent) take the game very seriously. This, in fact, is not unlike what has happened in many of the so-called democratic countries today, where some of the most intelligent members of society have become disgusted by the hypocrisy of the party games called politics, and take no interest in them. They can see no party whose 'line' they could support without reservation and are therefore left with no way of serving their country in the political field, even should they wish to; except, perhaps, by writing a book! For the politics of a country governed by the two-party system are not, and cannot be, national politics; they are the politics of groups, whose differences, more often than not, are of small concern to the majority of the people . . .

Let us take the case of two major parties which differ only on minor issues. Both have the interests of the people at heart, or so they claim. Both believe that education is a good thing, and that it should be made available to everybody; both believe that a fair living wage should be paid to all workers; both believe that medical care should be within the reach of all, and so on. All these things are fundamental, and it is not

13 *Freedom and Unity*, pp. 196-7.

likely that any political party today would dare tell the electorate it did not believe in them. So it is a fairly reasonable assumption that which-ever party may win the elections, its aim will be to provide the people with as many of those benefits as it can. Is it not a little absurd, then, that every few years the country should be asked to choose which of the 'opposing' parties should do the job which both agree should be done ? Surely, given that fundamental agreement, it would be far more sensible if both sides were to disband their football teams and let the electorate choose the best individuals from among them all; and if those individuals were then to meet in the parliament to discuss the details
● of the job and co-operate in getting it done!

QUESTION According to Lenin, what is the only 'fundamental issue' which can divide parties ?

On 8 June 1965, when presenting to Parliament the proposed con-stitutional changes establishing the one-party state, the President advanced an additional reason for making these changes:

> I do not believe there is anything wrong in making these changes in our funda-mental law—in our constitution. In July 1961, I said that in relation to the form of our future society, and in relation to our political institutions, we must 'grope our way forward'. This means that we must learn by thinking about our own experience, and about that of other people. We refuse to adopt the institutions of other countries even where they have served those countries well—because it is our conditions that have to be served by our institutions. We refuse to put ourselves in a strait-jacket of constitutional devices—even of our own making. The constitution of Tanzania must serve the people of Tanzania. We do not intend that the people of Tanzania should serve the constitution.

The role of Parliament within the one-party state was discussed in great detail by the Presidential Commission on the Establishment of a Democratic One-Party State. The Commission was aware of the National Assembly's shortcomings, but recommended against a fusion of it with the National Executive Committee of TANU. It hoped that the establishment of a *de jure* one-party state would lead to an increase in Parliament's effectiveness, and suggested further specific changes designed to achieve this purpose.[14] These proposals, and the operation of Parliament since the adoption of the Interim Constitution in 1965, have been analysed by Cliffe[15] and by Tordoff,[16] who have concluded, along with other commentators, that Parliament can control and criticize government and, occasionally, come forward with

[14] *Report*, pp. 16-22.
[15] Lionel Cliffe, *One-Party Democracy: The 1965 Tanzania General Elections*, East African Publishing House, Nairobi, 1967; and 'Democracy in a One-Party State: The Tanzanian Experience', *The Parliamentarian*, vol. XLIX, 1968, p. 206.
[16] William Tordoff, *Government and Politics in Tanzania*, East African Publishing House, Nairobi, 1967, ch. 1.

initiatives of its own. In support of his argument, Tordoff notes that Parliament has on occasion forced the government to withdraw proposed legislation and has passed several private members' motions and one private member's Bill. Cliffe suggests that since 1965 Parliament has become a more vocal instrument '[which] scrutinizes executive actions more fully than was formerly the case'. He further suggests that Parliament has been more actively involved in the planning process and has become less of a rubber stamp.[17] It is submitted that the general thesis advanced by these commentators needs some revision.

There are two important aspects of Parliament's traditional role which we shall look at: its position as the supreme law-making authority, and its ability to criticize the actions of the executive.

However, before analysing Parliament's effectiveness in performing these functions, certain limitations inherent in its constitution and operation must be noted. First, the composition of the National Assembly is important, for although a hundred and twenty of its members are directly elected from mainland constituencies, a further ninety-seven members hold their seats *ex officio*, through executive appointment, or through indirect election.[18] Secondly, although legislative power is formally vested in Parliament (Interim Constitution, s. 49) this power is neither absolute nor exclusive. By s. 52 of the Constitution, the National Assembly may not proceed with money bills without the permission of the President, and by s. 51, the provisions of the Constitution itself and of certain other specified Acts are entrenched. The President may veto any legislation enacted by the Assembly, but his veto can be overridden according to s. 50. In addition, the Act of Union with Zanzibar gives the President the power to legislate by decree on matters involved in the implementation of the Union (Cap. 557, s. 8 (2)). Thirdly, as a limit on Parliament's control over the executive, Ministers are appointed by and responsible to the President, not to the National Assembly (Interim Constitution, ss. 13-17). Fourthly, certain practices tend to circumscribe Parliament's role. Among these are: the Assembly sits on an average of only about seventy to eighty days per year; legislation is consistently enacted which delegates wide legislative powers to the executive; and, largely because of severe demands on the Parliamentary Draftsmen, Bills are regularly sent for enactment with Certificates of Urgency. Finally there is an almost total lack of office, secretarial, and research facilities available to MPs.

While it is true that since Independence, and especially in the late 1960s, Parliament has enacted an extraordinary amount of legislation, the members of the National Assembly have not played a particularly active role in this

---

[17] *The Parliamentarian*, op. cit., p. 211.
[18] Interim Constitution, ss. 24, 30, 31, 33; Act No. 56 of 1968; for the electoral system, see Cliffe, *One-Party Democracy*, ch. II.

process. Consider Parliament's role in the legislative implementation of the Arusha Declaration: the Declaration was discussed and adopted at a meeting of the National Executive Committee of TANU; Parliament was simply expected to give legislative effect to policies already decided upon. Thus, in a matter of two days the National Assembly passed legislation nationalizing the banks and establishing the National Bank of Commerce, establishing the State Trading Corporation and nationalizing major commercial enterprises, nationalizing certain sectors of agricultural production and expanding the National Agricultural Products Board, nationalizing the insurance business and placing it under the National Insurance Corporation, and nationalizing most of Tanzania's industry (Acts Nos. 1 to 5 of 1967).

Although it is not suggested that Parliament should have been permitted to reject the Arusha Declaration, it can hardly be said that Parliament had any more than a purely formal role in enacting such important legislation. In such a short period, members certainly could not have considered, let alone debated, the details of the Acts involved. This situation illustrates some of the contradictions in the position of a legislature in a country trying to achieve economic independence. Had Parliament debated these Acts for a longer period, the advance warning might have enabled the capitalists whose property was being nationalized to take steps which would have lessened the effect of the Party's decisions. The question arises whether in a country like Tanzania, Parliament must inevitably play a reactionary role, hamstrung as it is by '. . . the inherent inability of bourgeois democracy to achieve the social revolution'.[19]

The procedure whereby the Second Five-Year Plan was adopted may further clarify Parliament's position, and the decision-making process generally. The Plan was drafted, largely *in camera*, by officials of the Ministry of Economic Affairs and Development Planning. In the early months of 1969 the draft Plan was subjected to intensive scrutiny by the Cabinet, although few changes were made. The Plan was submitted to the N.E.C. in mid-May for its approval, and then it was sent to the National Conference of TANU, at which time it was made public. Not until two weeks later was the Plan laid before Parliament.[20] A five-year plan is, of course, not specifically legislation, and is likely of no legal effect, but the method by which Tanzania's present plan was adopted indicates a great deal about policy-making priorities and procedures. In fact, the procedure to be used was laid down by the N.E.C. itself which decided that the Plan would '. . . first be submitted to the TANU N.E.C., *the supreme organ of the nation*, before it is submitted to the National Assembly'.[21] This closed planning process has been criticized by an economist

---

[19] Peter Worsley, *The Third World*, p. 218, and see generally, pp. 176-230.
[20] *The Nationalist*, 20 May 1969, 31 May 1969, and 14 June 1969.
[21] *Ibid.*, 21 October 1968, emphasis added.

very much involved in development planning in Tanzania, who has suggested that successful planning requires 'a large degree of broad participation' and open discussion of policies.[22]

In early 1970, it was announced that the government planned to bring retail trade under state control, and the Minister of Commerce and Industries was called before the N.E.C. to outline the action he was contemplating and the legislation he would introduce before Parliament to effect the takeover.[23] It is possible then that in addition to discussing and establishing policies, the N.E.C. will also undertake the task of reviewing specific pieces of legislation before they are sent to Parliament for enactment.

What conclusions can be drawn about Parliament's legislative role ? First, it is clear that broader issues of policy are to be decided by the N.E.C. and are not to be the subject of debate in the National Assembly.[24] Secondly, specific legislative proposals may be reviewed by the N.E.C. and simply sent to Parliament for ratification. Thirdly, constitutional and operational factors severely limit Parliament's possible effectiveness. In sum, the legislative role of the National Assembly is that of legitimator. Policies and the specific means through which they will be effected are decided elsewhere, and the National Assembly is summoned as required to legitimate these decisions.

It should be noted that even when MPs have taken a legislative initiative they have not shown themselves to be particularly progressive. For example, two victories by the legislature over the executive have been its refusal to extend the provisions of the Affiliation Ordinance (Cap. 278) to Africans in 1963, and the rejection of a Bill which would have done away with most corporal punishment.[25]

In Parliament's other role as a critic of the executive and a watchdog on government activity, the Assembly's performance has been considerably better. In his address to the new National Assembly after the 1965 election, President Nyerere stressed the importance of this role and reminded members of their right to question ministers. The President added that the Assembly, through its careful observation of government activity, would make a significant contribution to national development.[26] Even though members continued to permit legislation 'of the most complex and far-reaching kind' to be passed without 'careful examination of detailed principles',[27] they used their power to question ministers not only for purposes of clarification,

---

[22] K. E. Svendsen, 'The Present Stage of Economic Planning in Tanzania' in A. H. Rweyemamu (ed.), *Nation-Building in Tanzania*, East African Publishing House, Nairobi, 1970, pp. 84-5.
[23] *The Standard*, 17 March 1970.
[24] Nyerere, 'Democracy and the Party System'; One-Party State Commission, *Report*.
[25] *The Standard*, 23 October 1969.
[26] J. K. Nyerere, *Freedom and Socialism*, p. 94; see also J. K. Nyerere, *Arusha Declaration Parliament*, Government Printer, Dar es Salaam, 1970.
[27] One-Party State Commission, *Report*, p. 20.

but also to point out and criticize shortcomings. During the seventy-eight sitting days held between 13 June 1967 and 26 July 1968, MPs asked a total of 1,345 questions. As opportunity for formal debate on national issues decreased in the National Assembly, an expanded method of questioning, employing a number of supplementaries, became the major means whereby members could publicly take the Government to task.[28]

The sittings of Parliament which took place in July and October 1968 were extremely important because they resulted in a clear definition of the degree to which members might be permitted to criticize the Government. They were extremely lively sittings, undoubtedly the liveliest in the history of the National Assembly, as members voiced critical opinions on a wide range of subjects. Certain of these criticisms are particularly relevant to this discussion. On 9 July, Mr Mwakitange asked the Government to deny that it was planning to award a gratuity amounting to twenty-five per cent of their annual salaries to all ministers, junior ministers, regional commissioners, and area commissioners. This gratuity would presumably be awarded to soften the financial blow of the leadership provisions of the Arusha Declaration. When a government spokesman was unable to explain away the whole matter, a private member's motion was passed criticizing the Government and calling on it to drop its plans to pay the gratuities. No more was heard concerning the scheme, and the MPs appeared to have won an important victory.

Another area of criticism involved the political relationship between regional commissioners and MPs from their regions. A major power struggle in West Lake Region was transferred to the floor of the Assembly, with two MPs from the region accusing the Regional Commissioner in very bitter terms of using autocratic methods to carry out an ujamaa village programme. A committee was appointed to travel to West Lake Region and investigate the matter, but, significantly, this committee was set up by the Central Committee of TANU, not by Parliament.

On a more general level, many members criticized the dominant position of the Party in national life, called for the creation of other political parties, and asserted that Parliament, not the Party, was the supreme organ in Tanzania. In reply to several of these criticisms, the Second Vice-President stated that TANU and the A.S.P. were supreme and that MPs opposed to their policies should quit Parliament. He also reminded them that the N.E.C. had the power to expel people from the Party.[29]

[28] See R. F. Hopkins, 'The Role of the MP in Tanzania' (mimeo), African Studies Association, New York City, 1968. This article also appears in *American Political Science Review*, vol. LXIV, no. 3, 1970, p. 754 and as chapter V of Hopkins, *Political Roles in a New State: Tanzania's First Decade*, Yale, New Haven, 1971. This last work is a supremely unintelligible example of contemporary methodology in U.S. 'political science'.
[29] *The Standard*, 10, 11, 12, 19, 23 and 27 July 1968.

At its October meeting, the N.E.C. reacted to these parliamentary challenges to the authority of the Party. Upon receiving the report from the West Lake investigation committee exonerating the Regional Commissioner, the N.E.C. expelled from the Party the two MPs involved in this dispute. Five other MPs who had led the critical attacks in Parliament were also expelled. (At the same time, the N.E.C. expelled Mr Kambona and Mr Anangisye, but clearly for different reasons.) The general reason given for all the expulsions was that the MPs concerned had 'grossly violated the Party Creed' and opposed the Party and its policies.[30]

Sections 27, 30, 32, and 33 of the Interim Constitution when read together require that a person be, *inter alia*, a Party member in order to be qualified to become a Member of Parliament. By s. 35 (1), if a sitting MP loses any one of the qualifications necessary for becoming an MP, his seat is automatically vacated. Thus the effect of the N.E.C.'s action in expelling these people from the Party was, at the same time, to remove them from Parliament. (It is interesting to note that under the 1965 TANU Constitution, the power to expel people from the Party rested with the more representative National Conference, while under the 1967 TANU Constitution (s. 32 (4) (j) this power was given to the N.E.C. It should also be noted that in 1965 subscription to Party 'beliefs, aims, and objects' became a condition of Party membership. (Interim Constitution, s.5.))

From these incidents we may draw certain conclusions about the boundaries within which MPs are required to exercise their power to criticize. In general, MPs may *criticize*, but they may not *oppose*. This is not a very precise distinction, but certain statements of Party leaders have helped to clarify it. The following list, based on such statements, indicates areas of conduct specifically prohibited to MPs:

—they may not criticize a government policy on principle, only on practical grounds.

—they may not criticize a policy decision of the N.E.C.

—they may not be contemptuous of Party principles and Party ideology.

—they may not speak with cynicism of Tanzania's socialist goals.

—they may not question whether TANU should have authority over them.[31]

In a more positive vein, the President, when dissolving Parliament in July 1970, stated that its purpose as critic of the government was to ensure that '... policies are implemented properly, fairly and with decent humanity'. (*Arusha Declaration Parliament*, p. 8.)

---

[30] *The Nationalist*, 19 October 1968. For a sound analysis of this incident, see J. S. Saul, 'The Nature of Tanzania's Political System: part II', *Journal of Commonwealth Political Studies*, vol. X, no. 3, 1972, p. 198.

[31] See *The Nationalist*, 12 June 1966 and 21 October 1968; Hopkins, op. cit., pp. 32-4; H. U. E. Thoden van Velzen and J. J. Sterkenburg, 'The Party Supreme', *Kroniek von Afrika*, 1969, pp. 65-74.

It is clear that a socialist ideology requires the subordination of state power to the authority of the party. Sekou Touré speaks of the 'dictatorship of the whole people' and asserts that any institutions interposed between the party and the exercise of state power serve merely to frustrate the expression of the people's will.[32] The Constitution of the Communist Party of China provides that 'The organs of the dictatorship of the proletariat . . . must all accept the leadership of the party' (Art. 5). Current practice in Tanzania appears to reflect a similar view, at least in so far as Parliament is concerned. Maintenance of Party discipline, control of Party membership, development of ideology, and the determination of policy in strategic and tactical terms—these are the functions of the Party, and particularly of the N.E.C. Parliament may not oppose either broad or specific policies, and it may not delay the implementation of the Party's will. In other words, it must not get in the Party's way. (As Sekou Touré stated: 'We are not interested in parliamentarianism. We are running a revolution.'[33])

In spite of these limitations, it is submitted that Parliament in Tanzania still has a role. It must not attempt to prevent the government from performing its basic function as executor of Party policy, but it should ensure that the methods of executing those policies are fair and just. Thus, while the National Assembly is not the cornerstone of political life doubtless envisaged by the drafters of Tanganyika's Independence Constitution, it remains, along with the Party, the courts, and the Permanent Commission of Enquiry, one of the institutions through which the people exercise their basic rights (*Arusha Declaration Parliament*, p. 3). One cannot, however, be too optimistic about the future of Parliament. With the removal of Parliament's dominance in the legislative field, the role reserved for it is the essentially negative one of a check on government activity. This role would seem to guarantee further clashes with the party hierarchy, clashes which can only lead to a greater weakening of Parliament. Certainly MPs do have a role in mobilizing their constituents and explaining party and government policy, but their basic function seems bound to restrict their initiative and creativity. However, in assessing the vitality of such institutions, it is appropriate to remember that Tanzania is unusual among African states in that it has held two open and democratic general elections since independence.

NOTE An assessment of the democratic nature of the party is beyond the scope of this chapter, but it is clearly an important question in relation to such a ubiquitous institution as TANU. The following passage, which refers to the C.P.P. in pre-Coup Ghana, outlines the dimensions of such an analysis:

[32] A. S. Touré, *The Doctrine and Methods of the Democratic Party of Guinea*, Part I (no date), pp. 26-36.
[33] op. cit., Part I, p. 148.

The most important condition of the success of the socialist experiment in a newly-independent state is the ability of the party-state apparatus actively to engage the broad mass of the working people in the country's construction . . . [The problem here is] to democratize the party's structures, procedures and leadership at all levels . . . [This can only be done] through active and continuous association of the people with political and economic decisions involved in reconstruction and development, especially at the grass-roots level, rather than through administering 'ideology' and sermons from above. (Mohan, 'Nkrumah and Nkrumahism', op. cit., p. 219.)

Crucial to such an analysis would be an investigation of the decision-making process within the party—whether policy matters are the subject of wide debate and criticism at all levels of the party, or whether the higher strata of the party tend merely to ratify decisions already taken by the bureaucrats. (On TANU generally, see Henry Bienen, *Tanzania: Party Transformation and Economic Development*, 2nd ed., Princeton University Press, Princeton, New Jersey, 1970.)

NOTE A brief comparison between the N.E.C. and the National Assembly may be useful. The N.E.C. consists of about eighty members. This number is made up of *ex officio* members, nominated members, and members elected from various levels of the party organization. In a limited, constitutionalist sense, the N.E.C. is not representative, although such an analysis avoids the real point that an institution's representative character is determined not by the way it is constituted, but by the degree to which it objectively embodies the will of the people. Meetings of the N.E.C., which are held in private, take place four or five times a year. The N.E.C. has the power to call witnesses and order the production of documents. The One-Party State Commission noted that in the N.E.C., '. . . every aspect of Government policy has been the subject of rigorous scrutiny and the exchange of views has been frank, fearless and on the basis of complete equality'. The Commission attributed these features of N.E.C. meetings primarily to the fact that they were held in private. (*Report*, pp. 20-21.)

C · THE COURTS

In the next chapter we examine specific devices through which the courts are able to exercise some control over the executive. In this chapter, we are concerned with the degree to which they are able to play this role. We consider the extent to which the courts are independent of the executive, precisely what is meant by an 'independent judiciary' in Tanzania, and to what extent this is a useful and appropriate concept.

An independent judiciary does not mean that those people employed by the state to resolve specific contradictions between individuals, or between the state and an individual, can do so entirely as they please. There are both implicit and explicit limits on the way they perform their role. Among the implicit limits are values acquired as a result of the particular person's class, cultural and educational background. The important explicit limits are the substantive rules of law which are to be applied, and the procedural rules which govern their application. Therefore, when we speak of the independence of the judiciary we really mean the judges' freedom of operation within these limits.

We must also ask whether the whole concept of an independent judiciary is illusory. Judges are members of the ruling class by birth or assimilation (regardless of what class that may be) and hired employees of the State who depend ultimately on the coercive power of the executive for the enforcement of their decisions. To disregard these conditions in an attempt to be totally independent would only make the judges' function meaningless.[34] To many interpreters of the liberal-democratic theory of government, the independence of the judiciary simply means that when a government formed by members of Party 'X' is in power, it should not meddle with judges who were appointed by Party 'Y' at some earlier time. When both Party 'X' and Party 'Y' represent the interests of essentially the same class, serious problems are unlikely to rise. Difficulties are encountered, as in the famous Roosevelt-Supreme Court dispute in the United States, when the judges represent the interests of one class and the executive represents, or appears to represent, those of another. Looking at the independence of the judiciary in this light, it is not difficult to see why judicial systems inherited from colonialism have come into conflict with progressive post-colonial régimes.[35]

Under colonial rule, there was no formal separation of the executive and the judiciary at the lower levels. It was held by the High Court of Tanganyika, however, that this fact alone would not prevent anyone from getting a fair trial. (*Re Hermann Milde* (1937) I T.L.R. (R) 129.) The Court of Appeal for Eastern Africa appeared to accept a similar principle, but on one occasion indicated that the fact that a magistrate was also a district officer might, in the circumstances of the case, be a factor to be considered in deciding whether an accused person had received a fair trial. (*Andreas s/o Mathias* v. *R.* (1954) 21 E.A.C.A. 285.) A major trend in the administration of justice

---

34 Most judges appear to accept this point of view. See Sir Charles Newbold, 'The Role of a Judge as a Policy Maker', *Eastern Africa Law Review*, vol. II, no. 2, 1969, p. 127; and *Uganda* v. *Commissioner of Prisons; ex parte Matovu* [1966] E.A. 514. For differing comments on the preceding case, see *Eastern Africa Law Review*, vol. I, no. 1, 1968, p. 61; and *University of Western Ontario Law Review*, vol. VII, 1968, p. 93.
35 Compare Touré, op. cit., Part II, p. 31, and the sentiments expressed in J. W. Katende, 'The Sayings of Mr. Justice Lewis', *Transition*, no. 37, 1968, p. 40. The career of Lewis, J. represents one way in which an individual judge dealt with problems of class struggle. After an eight-year stay on the Ugandan High Court, during which he took many opportunities to register his disapproval of things African, he found the prospect of Independence too disturbing and moved to the bench of Southern Rhodesia. His finest hour came when he wrote the judgement which gave the Smith government of 'Rhodesia' internal legality: *Madzimbamuto and others* v. *Lardner-Burke*, GD/CIV/23/66; overruled [1969] I A.C. 645 (PC).

since the 1950s has been the separation of the executive and the judiciary at all levels, and we will now attempt to analyse the results of this process.[36]

J. P. W. B. McAuslan and Y. P. Ghai
CONSTITUTIONAL INNOVATION
AND POLITICAL STABILITY IN TANZANIA[37]

● Two propositions about the courts may be advanced. First, since independence, a determined effort has been made to modernize and judicialize the system of courts so that they can provide a better service for the consumer. The magistracy has been separated from the administration, all magistrates must now have some rudimentary training before starting on their duties, an increased number of magistrates have been appointed, and so far as possible sufficient court-houses established to ensure easy access for everyone. Salaries have also been raised, and a system of promotion based on examinations and competence has been introduced so as to attract good-quality persons to the magistracy. Initial appointments all the way through are in the hands of boards composed of judicial and administrative-cum political persons. All courts in their judicial work are subject to the ultimate control of the High Court, with, in certain cases, an appeal to the Court of Appeal for Eastern Africa.

Secondly, it would be idle to pretend that the courts are, or in the foreseeable future will be, the bastions of control, which is the role that colonial constitution-makers invariably try to cast them in. This is not because the courts have been shackled by an authoritarian régime; the reasons are more complex than that. Among the most important is that courts in colonial times were by and large deliberate allies of the régime, and this long-standing attitude is not one that can be forgotten overnight by the courts, by the administrators, or by the people. Another reason for the restricted role of the courts is that to approach them for a remedy against the state is quite easy for an educated person, particularly a member of the small middle class, brought up to accept as axiomatic most of the values which the courts consider they exist to uphold; but these people are still an extremely small minority.

The courts have continued to perform their traditional functions of controlling administrative action as provided by law. In this respect

---

[36] For accounts of the process itself, see the Judiciary *Annual Reports* for 1962, 1963, 1964, and 1965, and the African Conference on Local Courts and Customary Law, *Report*, Dar es Salaam, 1963, pp. 101-8. For a discussion of the colonial position, see J. S. Read, 'The Search for Justice' in H. F. Morris and J. S. Read, *Indirect Rule and the Search for Justice*, Oxford University Press, London, 1972, p. 287.
[37] *Journal of Modern African Studies*, vol. IV, no. 4, 1966, pp. 487-8.

their jurisdiction and rules are similar to the law in England. It is, however, unclear what role the courts will play, or be allowed to play, when the action in question is not so much administrative as political, for example those of the Regional Commissioners, who in Morogoro closed the local club, dismissed the committee, and appointed another in its place, and in Mwanza confiscated the property of two local Asian residents and handed that of one to the TANU Youth League. With the strengthening of the executive and the party, there have inevitably arisen some doubts as to the efficiency of court remedies. Legal control presupposes a large body of law generally adhered to; and recently the Government has shown impatience with the restrictions imposed by the law. Adverse judgements, were the courts to deliver such, could be overruled by legislative action, as happened with the decision awarding damages to Chief Marealle for wrongful dismissal from office by the Kilimanjaro District Council. This points to the need for alternative methods of control more acceptable alike to the
● Government and the public.

NOTE The Marealle case referred to above is of sufficient interest to warrant a more detailed examination. In 1951, the Chagga Council, then the Native Authority in what is now Kilimanjaro District, decided that a paramount chief should be appointed for all the Chagga. After a popular election Thomas Marealle was installed in January 1952 as Mangi Mkuu, apparently for life. He remained in office until 1959 when certain difficulties arose with the Council. A referendum was held and, as a result, Marealle was removed from office in December 1959. In 1961 he sued the Kilimanjaro District Council, as successors to the Chagga Council, for breach of contract, claiming as damages the salary and other benefits he would have received had he remained in office for life. The case was held up until it was decided whether the High Court had jurisdiction in such a matter. (*Marealle* v. *Chagga Council* [1963] E.A. 131 (CA).) By the time the main issue came up for trial, the Government of Tanganyika had abolished all hereditary chieftainships as part of a series of moves designed to democratize local administration. (African Chiefs (Ordinance Repeal) Act, 1963, Cap. 517; for a detailed description of post-independence changes in local administration, see Dryden, *Local Administration in Tanzania*, East African Publishing House, Nairobi, 1968, pp. 98-109.) In the High Court, Murphy, J. discounted the possible effects of this change on the action, and awarded the plaintiff the sum of Sh. 919,900.00 as compensation for the loss of his office. (*Marealle* v. *Kilimanjaro District Council*, High Court of Tanganyika at Arusha, Civil Case No. 44 of 1961.) This sum would have been sufficient to bankrupt the Kilimanjaro District Council. More seriously, Marealle's success in the High Court could well have encouraged other dispossessed chiefs to attempt similar actions. Judgement was given on 17 October 1963; on 29 November 1963 the Government introduced a Bill in the National Assembly to overrule the Court's decision. The statement of objects and reasons appended to the Bill read in part, 'It is not considered that the new District Councils should be liable for any legal consequences which followed on the termination of the appointments, or abolition of the offices, of Chiefs or the disestablishment of native authorities . . . It is known that in one case a district council has been held liable for damages to a former Chief on account of the abolition of his office.' Mr Kawawa, who introduced the Bill, made its purpose clear. 'Government must have the power to stop a few people who want to suck the blood of many others.' (*The Standard,* 5 December 1963.) The Bill passed through the three readings, '. . . in the space of a few minutes', and became law as the Chiefs (Abolition of Office: Consequential Provisions) Act, 1963 (ibid., Cap. 535). The Act provided that no suit could be instituted '. . . by or on behalf of a former Chief against a local authority making or in respect of any claim for damages, for breach of contract, or for inducing or conspiracy to induce a breach of contract, or for compensation, arising out of the termination of such former Chief's appointment or tenure of office as Chief or native authority, or out of the abolition of any office of Chief or native authority.' Any proceedings which were under way were to be stayed. While not directly referring to the Marealle case, the Act provided that no decree in respect of any such suit was to be enforced without the consent of the President, and subject to such conditions as he might wish to impose (ss. 3, 4 and 5).

J. K. Nyerere
EDUCATION AND THE LAW[38]

● It is essential in a democratic society which believes in the equality of all of its citizens that every individual should be subject to the law. Further, it is of paramount importance that the execution of the law should be without fear or favour. Our Judiciary at every level must be independent of the executive arm of the state. Real freedom requires that any citizen feels confident that his case will be impartially judged,
● even if it is a case against the Prime Minister himself.

The conviction expressed in this speech was tested two years later when the special court which tried the ringleaders of the January 1964 Army Mutiny, passed what were generally considered to be extremely lenient sentences.

J. K. Nyerere
COMMENT ON THE MUTINEERS' SENTENCES[39]

● There has been some considerable criticism of the very lenient sentences passed on the fourteen soldiers convicted of conspiracy and taking part in the mutiny of the Tanganyika Rifles in January of this year. The Government wishes to make clear that it shares the feeling that the penalties imposed by decision of the High Court Judge and the two

[38] *Freedom and Unity,* p. 131.
[39] ibid., pp. 298-9.

Army Officers bore no relation to the seriousness of the offences and the damage which was done to our country.

Despite this criticism, the Government does not intend to vary the sentences imposed in these cases. To interfere with the Court's decision would be to do exactly that thing for which the nation condemns the soldiers—it would be to abrogate the rule of law. The soldiers knew that there were laws about the way they should behave and that there was machinery to deal with any grievances they had. By leading a mutiny the convicted soldiers invited people to break the peace and to abandon law. We saw something of the results of the absence of law in the succeeding hours.

The rule of law is the basis on which rests the freedom and equality of our citizens. It must remain the foundation of our state. We must not allow even our disgust with the mutineers to overcome our
● principles.

REPORT OF THE PRESIDENTIAL COMMISSION ON
THE ESTABLISHMENT OF
A DEMOCRATIC ONE-PARTY STATE[40]

● *The Rule of Law and the Independence of the Judiciary*
The independence of the Judiciary is the foundation of the rule of law. The Commission believes that this is true as much in a One-Party State as it is where the law of the Constitution recognizes an opposition. We have, however, formed a strong impression that there is a good deal of misunderstanding about what this important concept really means. What is essential for the maintenance of the rule of law is that judges and magistrates should decide the cases that come before them in accordance with the evidence. They should not be influenced by extraneous factors. In criminal cases they should not convict or acquit because they believe that a particular verdict will please the Government. In civil cases they should not consider the relative importance of the parties or the political consequences of their decision. Their job is to find the facts and apply the relevant principles of law.

It is in this sense that judges must be independent. Their independence does not mean that they should regard themselves, or be regarded by others, as a caste apart. Respect for the law and concern for the proper administration of justice must spring from the people themselves; it cannot be imposed from above. If the judges are seen to share the hopes and fears of the ordinary citizen, if their work is seen as part of a collective effort by the community as a whole, the people

[40] p. 33.

will respond by identifying themselves with the law and with the problems facing judges and magistrates in administering justice impartially.

The Commission therefore attaches great importance to finding ways of associating the people with the judicial process. For practical reasons, we are unable to recommend the introduction of trial by jury. However, we note that the law already provides that Assessors should sit with the Primary Court Magistrates in both civil and criminal cases and with the High Court in criminal cases at the first instance. We approve of these provisions and recommend that the Government should now give consideration to the extension of the Assessor system
● to the District Courts.

The principle of the independence of the judiciary has been incorporated into the Constitution.

INTERIM CONSTITUTION OF TANZANIA[41]

● 56.—(1) There shall be a High Court of the United Republic which shall have such jurisdiction and powers as may be conferred on it by this Constitution or any other law.

(2) The judges of the High Court of the United Republic shall be the Chief Justice of Tanzania and such number of other judges, not being less than eight (hereinafter referred to as 'the puisne judges') as may be prescribed by Parliament:
Provided that the office of a puisne judge shall not be abolished while there is a substantive holder thereof.

(3) The High Court shall be a superior court of record and, save as otherwise provided by Act of Parliament, shall have all the powers of such a court.

57.—(1) The Chief Justice of Tanzania shall be appointed by the President.

(2) The puisne judges of the High Court of the United Republic shall be appointed by the President after consultation with the Chief Justice.

    (3) (a) Subject to the provisions of subsection (4), a person shall not be qualified for appointment as a judge of the High Court unless—

        (i) he is, or has been, a judge of a court having unlimited jurisdiction in civil and criminal matters in some part of the Commonwealth, or in any country outside

41 Act No. 43 of 1965.

the Commonwealth that may be prescribed by Act
of Parliament, or a court having jurisdiction in appeals
from any such court; or,

(ii) he holds one of the specified qualifications and has
held one or other of those qualifications for a total
period of not less than five years.

(b) In this subsection and in subsections (4) and (6) 'the
specified qualifications' means the professional qualifications specified by the Advocates Ordinance (or by or under
any law amending or replacing that Ordinance) one of which
must be held by any person before he may apply under
that Ordinance (or under any such law) to be admitted as
an advocate in Tanganyika.

(4) Where the President is satisfied that by reason of special
circumstances a person who holds one of the specified qualifications
is worthy, capable and suitable to be appointed a judge of the High
Court notwithstanding that he has not held some one or other of
those qualifications for a total period of not less than five years, the
President may dispense with the requirement that such a person
shall have held some one or other of the specified qualifications for a
total period of not less than five years and may, after such consultation
aforesaid, appoint him a judge of the High Court.

(5) If the office of the Chief Justice is vacant or if the Chief Justice
is for any reason unable to perform the functions of his office, then,
until a person has been appointed to and has assumed the functions of
that office or until the person holding that office has resumed those
functions, as the case may be, those functions shall be performed by
such one of the puisne judges as may be designated in that behalf by the
President.

(6) If the office of any puisne judge is vacant or if any such judge is
appointed to act as Chief Justice or is for any reason unable to perform
the functions of his office, or if the Chief Justice advises the President
that the state of business in the High Court so requires, the President
may appoint a person qualified for appointment as a judge of the High
Court to act as a puisne judge of that Court:

Provided that—

(a) notwithstanding the provisions of subsection (1) of section
58 of this Constitution, no person shall be disqualified for
appointment under this subsection by reason only of his
age;

(b) the President may dispense with the requirement that a
person shall not be qualified for an appointment as a judge

of the High Court unless he has held some one or other of the specified qualifications for a total period of not less than five years in the case of an appointment of a person who has one of the specified qualifications to act as a puisne judge of the High Court for the like reason as he may dispense with that requirement under the provisions of subsection (4).

(7) Any person appointed under subsection (6) of this section to act as a puisne judge shall continue to act for the period of his appointment or, if no such period is specified, until his appointment is revoked by the President:

Provided that, notwithstanding the expiration of the period of his appointment or the revocation of his appointment, he may thereafter continue to act as a puisne judge for so long as may be necessary to enable him to deliver judgement or to do any other thing in relation to proceedings that were commenced before him previously thereto.

58.—(1) Subject to the provisions of this section, a person holding the office of a judge of the High Court shall vacate that office on attaining the age of sixty-two years: Provided that the President may permit such a person to continue in office until he has attained the age of sixty-five years.

(2) Notwithstanding that he has attained the age at which he is required by the provisions of this section to vacate his office, a person holding the office of a judge of the High Court may continue in office for so long after attaining that age as may be necessary to enable him to deliver judgement or to do any other thing in relation to proceedings that were commenced before him before he attained that age.

(3) A judge of the High Court may be removed from office only for inability to perform the functions of his office (whether arising from infirmity of body or mind or from any other cause) or for misbehaviour, and shall not be so removed except in accordance with the provisions of subsection (5) of this section.

(4) If the President considers that the question of removing a judge under this section ought to be investigated, then—

(a) he shall appoint a tribunal which shall consist of a chairman and not less than two other members, the chairman and at least one half of the other members being persons who hold or have held office as judges of a court having unlimited jurisdiction in civil and criminal matters in some part of the Commonwealth, or in any country outside the Commonwealth that may be prescribed by Parliament, or a court having jurisdiction in appeals from any such court;

(b) the tribunal shall enquire into the matter and report on the facts thereof to the President and advise the President whether the judge ought to be removed from office under this section for inability as aforesaid or for misbehaviour.

(5) Where a tribunal appointed under subsection (4) advises the President that a judge ought to be removed from office for inability as aforesaid or misbehaviour, the President shall remove such judge from office.

(6) If the question of removing a judge from office has been referred to a tribunal under subsection (4) of this section, the President may suspend the judge from performing the functions of his office, and any such suspension may at any time be revoked by the President and shall in any case cease to have effect if the tribunal advises the President that the judge ought not to be removed from office.

(7) The provisions of this section shall be without prejudice to the provisions of subsection (7) of section 57 of this Constitution.

59. A Judge of the High Court shall not enter upon the duties of his office unless he has taken and subscribed the oath of allegiance and such oath for the due execution of his office as may be prescribed by Act of Parliament.

60.—(1) There shall be a Judicial Service Commission in and for the United Republic in Tanganyika which shall consist of—

(a) the Chief Justice of Tanzania, who shall be Chairman;

(b) such puisne judge of the High Court of the United Republic as may be for the time being designated in that bchalf by the President after consultation with the Chief Justice;

(c) a member appointed by the President.

(2) A person shall not be qualified to be appointed under the provisions of paragraph (c) of subsection (1) of this section if he is a member of the National Assembly or the holder of an office prescribed by Parliament for the purpose of this section.

61.—(1) Subject to the provisions of any Act of Parliament, the power—

(a) to appoint persons to hold offices to which this section applies (including the power of confirming appointments and promotions) is vested in the President;

(b) to exercise disciplinary control over persons holding or acting in such offices, to terminate appointments and to remove such persons from office, is vested in the Judicial Service Commission.

(2) The offices to which this section applies are the offices of Registrar and Deputy Registrar of the High Court of the United Republic, Resident Magistrate and any other magistrate, and such other offices connected with any court (other than a court-martial) as, subject to the provisions of this Constitution, may be prescribed by Act of Parliament:

Provided that this section shall not apply to any such office or magistrate of a court in Zanzibar.

(3) The power of the President to abolish offices in the service of the United Republic shall not be exercised in respect of any office to which this section applies while there is a substantive holder of that office, unless the Judicial Service Commission concurs in such abolition.

77.—(1) There shall be paid to the holders of the offices to which this section applies such salary and such allowances as may be prescribed by Act of Parliament.

(2) The salaries and any allowances payable to the holders of the offices to which this section applies, and where any such holder is appointed on terms by which he is entitled to a pension or gratuity, such pension or gratuity shall be a charge on the Consolidated Fund of the United Republic.

(3) The salary payable to the holder of any office to which this section applies and his terms of office, other than allowances, shall not be altered to his disadvantage after his appointment.

(4) Where a person's salary or terms of office depend upon his option, the salary or terms for which he opts shall, for the purpose of subsection (3) of this section, be deemed to be more advantageous to him than any others for which he might have opted.

(5) This section applies to the offices of judge of the High Court of the United Republic, of chairman and member of the Permanent Commission, and of Controller and Auditor-General of the United
● Republic.

NOTE Detailed provisions concerning the functioning of the Judicial Service Commission are contained in the Judicial Service Act, Cap. 508. The Commission may remove a judicial officer if it considers his removal to be in the public interest, but before it does so, a disciplinary charge must be made, and an enquiry held at which the officer is given an opportunity to answer the charge (s. 19). A Special Commission is established under the Act to deal with matters concerning Primary Court Magistrates. The members of the Special Commission are the Chief Justice, the puisne judge who is for the time being serving on the Judicial Service Commission, and two members appointed by the Minister responsible for legal affairs (presently the Second Vice-President). The Minister may also delegate the functions of the Special Commission to Regional Boards set up for this purpose and chaired by Regional Commissioners (s. 21B). Regional Boards receive recommendations for the appointment of persons as Primary Court Magistrates from District Boards. The Chairman of the District Board is the District Chairman of TANU. The other members of the Board are two nominees of the Party's District Executive Committee, the Area Secretary, and one District Magistrate. District Boards are given also the power to investigate complaints against Primary Court Magistrates (ibid., as amended by s. 21 of the Administration of Justice (Miscellaneous Amendments) Act, 1971, Act No. 26 of 1971). In addition, the Act attempts to guarantee the independence of the Judiciary by providing that the administration of the judicial service is vested in the Chief Justice (s. 25). Under the Independence Constitution, the Chief Justice was to be appointed by the Governor-General on the advice of the Prime Minister. Power to appoint the other judges of the High Court was vested in the Judicial Service Commission. With the adoption of republic status, the appointment of all judges was placed in the hands of the President. This change can be seen as a part of the process of redressing the imbalance created at Independence whereby the control of significant areas of state administration was denied to the executive. See *Government Paper No. 1 of 1962*, op. cit.

NOTE The provisions of the Constitution quoted above do not in fact apply to all the present judges of the High Court. Non-citizen judges serve on a contract basis, while several of the Tanzanian citizens raised to the bench in recent years were appointed as Acting Judges.

NOTE The provisions in the Republican Constitution concerning appointment and removal of judges were almost identical to those in the present constitution. One exception is found in s. 58(4) of the present constitution. This section requires that the chairman and at least half of the members of the tribunal set up to consider the removal of a judge should be present or former judges. The corresponding provisions of the Republican Constitution required that *all* members of the tribunal be present or former judges (see s. 48 (4)). Why might this change have been made?

NOTE One aspect of the judicial service not dealt with constitutionally, and which could lead to abuse, is the question of the transfer of magistrates from one post to another. For example, a Regional Commissioner might desire the removal of a particular magistrate, and attempt to use his influence to cause the magistrate to be transferred to another region. No constitutional or statutory provisions would have been violated in such a case, but the independence of the judiciary would, in one region at any rate, have been prejudiced. Given that magistrates are constantly retiring, dying, being appointed, promoted, and transferred, would it be possible or desirable to design regulations which could avoid this sort of abuse? How much reliance should be put on legislation itself as a guarantor of 'freedom' or 'democracy'?

NOTE The provisions relating to security of tenure of judges of the Court of Appeal for East Africa are to be found in the Court of Appeal for Eastern

Africa Act, 1962 (EACSO No. 13 of 1962), as amended by the Court of Appeal for Eastern Africa (Amendment) Act, 1964 (EACSO No. 5 of 1964), ss. 3, 4, 6, and 8. The power of appointment rests with the Authority of the East African Community, that is, the three Presidents, while the provisions for removal and disciplining of judges are essentially similar to those noted above. For the constitutional position of the Court of Appeal, see *Opoloto* v. *A.G.* (*Uganda*) (*No. 1*) [1969] E.A. 496 (CA).

The question of what an 'independent judiciary' means in a socialist state which is attempting rapid economic development must still be answered.

J. K. Nyerere

THE JUDICIARY AND THE PEOPLE[42]

● Justice demands many things. It demands that the innocent be assured of personal security; and also that the guilty should be punished. It demands impartiality between individual citizens—that the law should be the same for all. And it demands an understanding by the judiciary of the people, and by the people of the judiciary; for without this mutual understanding the people's basic sense of justice in their relations with each other may be outraged by the very instrument which they have created to implement justice.

And we do in practice assist the judges by making them 'independent' of power politics. There is a separate hierarchy and system of command for the judiciary, and once a man is appointed it is extremely difficult to displace him. These things are intended to help secure impartiality.

But they must not do more. They must not lead to the belief that a judge can be, or should be, 'neutral' on the basic issues of our society. The fact that judges interpret the law makes it vital that they should be part of the society which is governed by the law. Their interpretation must be made in the light of the assumptions and aspirations of the society in which they live. Otherwise their interpretations may appear ridiculous to that society, and may lead to the whole concept of law
● being held in contempt by the people.

QUESTION What is the 'whole concept of law' ?

R. M. Kawawa

SPEECH TO THE JUDGES' AND MAGISTRATES' CONFERENCE[43]

● It is the wish of the people of Tanzania that their Judiciary should be independent. I appreciate the fact that this principle is very much

---

[42] *Freedom and Socialism*, Oxford University Press, Dar es Salaam, 1968, pp. 110 and 112.
[43] Dar es Salaam, 11 November 1968.

liked by all members of the Judiciary and is acceptable to them. However, this popular and sacred principle needs careful guidance. It is the Judicial officers who are mainly responsible for giving this principle its correct interpretation. It is mainly through their behaviour and actions which will demonstrate to the public that our Political Party and our Parliament were not wrong in adopting this principle. I know that their work is sometimes interfered with by some ill-informed leaders but this should not detract them from their correct stand. If our Judicial officers are right the public will always be with them.

Judicial officers like other people serving in different institutions of our country, are servants of the people, and as such they must identify themselves with the people they are serving; by this I mean our Judicial officers should know the people as much as or even more than they know the Laws of this country. For the Laws are meant to serve the people and not the people to serve the Laws.

Again as I have said before, trouble is nearly always at the primary court level. It is at this level that we come across instances of the abuse or misconception of the principle. Even at this level I must say the position has improved steadily. There are fewer and fewer cases

● of this nature.

R. M. Kawawa
SPEECH TO THE JUDGES' AND MAGISTRATES' CONFERENCE[44]

● This country is now fully committed to a policy of socialism and self-reliance. Steps have been taken on various fronts towards the implementation of this policy. For example, a sizeable number of institutions have been nationalized or have at least been placed under public control. Of course that is not enough for an equally important task is to ensure that these institutions are now put to even better use.

However, as the Arusha Declaration makes it quite clear, nationaliza-tion is not the most important thing; rather the Declaration states clearly that self-reliance is really the hub of the matter. The message is simple. It is that Tanzania must rely principally on herself for her own development. And that Tanzania, being an agricultural country, emphasis must be on the development of the agricultural sector and up-lifting of the standards of the rural communities.

It may be asked what relevance all this has to a conference of judges and magistrates ? And this is the central point of my speech today.

[44] Dar es Salaam, 27 November 1967.

In my view, the Judiciary is as much involved in these things as any other organ of state. The Judiciary is entrusted with the very important responsibility of administering justice in accordance with the laws and accepted norms of the country. It is involved in the day-to-day examination and interpretation of these laws and norms. In many ways therefore it is the most ideal organ for detecting their effectiveness or otherwise and their justice or injustice. Given, therefore, the broad basis of the country's policies, the Judiciary should at once be able to discover to what extent the laws of the country and practices of the courts conform to those policies.

Take for example the country's clearly stated policy of laying greater emphasis on rural communities. The question could be asked: to what extent do the facilities of the judicial system reflect this policy? Is the machinery of justice in rural areas as satisfactory as it should be? How swiftly is justice available in rural areas or do people have to travel long distances and wait many months before they can get justice? This indeed is a problem that for some time now has been exercising the mind of the Government.

There are rather a large number of complaints about the inadequacy of the courts in the country, inadequacy which in turn leads to long delays before injustices are redressed. Of course this is partly due to lack of resources with which the Government can provide a more adequate system of courts. But isn't there anything we can do to redress or reduce this inadequacy instead of sitting down and waiting for the day when the Government will have sufficient funds with which to build more court houses and employ more staff? Are we
● making the maximum use of the system we have at present?

NOTE In these speeches, Mr Kawawa is giving expression to very widespread feelings of dissatisfaction with the courts. At the 1969-70 Judges' and Magistrates' Conference, one speaker stated that 'dangerous complaints' and 'persistent dissatisfaction' concerning the work of the Judiciary had been heard in Parliament and Party meetings, and noted in the press. For verification of the existence of this dissatisfaction, he referred to the inordinate number of complaints about the Judiciary in the annual reports of the Permanent Commission of Enquiry. (*The Standard*, 7 January 1970.) The main source of the trouble seems to be in the Primary Courts, the bottom rung of Tanzania's court structure. The great bulk of the nation's judicial business is carried out by the approximately 500 Primary Court Magistrates. In criminal matters they can send people to prison for a year, order the payment of a fine of Sh. 1,000.00, and impose 12 strokes of corporal punishment. (These limits may be exceeded where the Primary Court has jurisdiction in respect of an offence falling under the Minimum Sentences Act.) The basic civil jurisdiction of the Primary Courts is over matters involving customary law or Islamic law, but there is no monetary limit on their jurisdiction in such matters. Debts not exceeding Sh. 2,000.00 owing to public authorities and small non-customary contracts may also be litigated in Primary Courts. (See the Magistrates Courts Act, 1963, Cap. 537 and the Third and Fourth Schedules thereto. For an analysis of the Act, see Eugene Cotran, 'Integration of Courts and Application of Customary Law in Tanganyika', *East African Law Journal*, vol. I, no. 2, 1965, p. 108.) The minimum qualifications for appointment as a Primary Court Magistrate are good character, integrity, education to Standard X, and an age of at least 28 years. The normal pre-service training consists of a six-months' course at the Institute of Development Management, Mzumbe, Morogoro, after which a successful candidate is appointed to the bench. (See T. M. Jackson, *Guide to the Legal Profession in East Africa*, Sweet and Maxwell, London, 1970, pp. 45-6.) In the 1965 *Annual Report* of the Judiciary, it was noted that the quality of some Primary Court Magistrates was 'exceedingly low'. (Government Printer, Dar es Salaam, 1968, p. 5.)

It is not possible to gauge the accuracy of criticism levelled against the Primary Courts or to determine the proportion of Primary Court Magistrates who are subject to such criticism. The major areas of criticism are delay, inefficiency, arrogance, isolation from the people, and dishonesty. The seriousness of the situation is indicated by the increasing frequency of complaints and the fact that even the Second Vice-President, Regional Commissioners (*The Standard*, 3 February 1970), MPs (ibid., 15 July 1970), and the Government's newspaper (ibid., 7 January 1970) have indulged in such criticism. An implicit recognition of this situation can be seen in speeches given by members of the senior judiciary, and especially by the Chief Justice, to Primary Court Magistrates. Speaking in August 1970, the Chief Justice reminded Primary Court Magistrates of the necessity of being honest and explained that the independence of the judiciary did not mean isolation from the public. He also said that the judiciary should take an active part in building a socialist Tanzania. (See *The Standard*, 24 August 1970; see also ibid., 22 June 1970.)

While one can speculate on the causes of this situation, the more obvious ones—inexperience, too much power, lack of training—may not reveal the whole picture. In his article, 'The Codification of Customary Law in Tanzania' (*East African Law Journal*, vol. II, no. 2, 1966, p. 105), R.E.S. Tanner argues that the establishment of adversary procedures in the Primary Courts and the enforcement of written declarations of customary law is so contrary to established systems of dispute-solving that confidence in these courts is bound to be drastically diminished. He further argues that the usual position of the Primary Court Magistrate as a non-resident of the District where he is posted, saddled with the task of enforcing an alien system of justice can only be maintained through the exercise of the most skilful diplomacy.

Whatever the causes of this situation, it has become necessary for the Government, which maintains the courts and pays the magistrates, to take some sort of action, if only to defend its own interests. Thus, the purpose of recent government action has not been specifically to interfere with the courts, but rather, to deal with a situation of potential political danger which the judiciary itself has been unable to rectify. The basic trend in government action has been an attempt at 'dejudicialization' of the work of Primary Courts. Viewed from another direction, this process could also be seen as a movement towards a system of People's Courts.

In this connection, let us look first at the role of assessors in the Primary Courts. As originally conceived, assessors were to be persons learned in customary law who would advise the magistrate and assist him to interpret the law in the light of the customs and way of life of the local people. As a secondary purpose, they were also to act as representatives of the general public in the judicial process. Under the Magistrates' Courts Act, 1963 as originally enacted, assessors were only to sit in cases where customary or Islamic law governed the issues (s. 8), their opinions were not binding on the court (s. 8), and they were required to have a knowledge of customary law or local laws (s. 63). By Act No. 67 of 1964, assessors were required to sit in all cases in Primary Courts, and while they were still required to be residents of the area in which the court was situated, it was no longer necessary that they be knowledgeable in customary law. The most important changes were made by Act No. 18 of 1969. As a result of this legislation at least two assessors must sit with the magistrate in all cases, and the decision of the majority of the assessors and the magistrate together shall be the decision of the court. Thus, there will be in most cases in Primary Courts a three-man bench. One member of this bench will be a full-time judicial officer while the other two will be part-time representatives of the community. The magistrate is still to some extent *primus inter pares* because in the case of an equality of votes, he is allowed a casting vote in addition to his deliberative vote. Under s. 63 of Cap. 537, assessors are to be empanelled through the local authority of the particular district. In practice, assessors are usually chosen through the TANU district organisation. (See R. W. Moisey, 'The Role of Assessors in the Courts of Tanzania', *East African Law Journal*, vol III, no. 4, 1967, p. 348; J. S. Warioba, 'The Role of Assessors in Criminal Trials in Tanganyika', *Journal of the Denning Law Society*, vol. I, no. 3, 1965, p. 65. Moisey notes a tendency in most Primary Courts towards 'permanent' assessors. Presumably this practice would have to be scrapped in order to allow the new system to function with maximum efficiency.)

Act No. 18 of 1969 also takes what would seem to be an important step in the direction of people's courts through attempting to regularize informal arbitration and conciliation proceedings. It is provided that a Primary Court may, with the consent of all the parties to a civil proceeding, refer that dispute to an Arbitration Tribunal. There is to be at least one Arbitration Tribunal in each ward which shall consist of five members to be nominated by the TANU Branch Committee having jurisdiction over the particular ward. The proceedings of the tribunal are to be public and any settlement it reaches must have the consent of all parties to the dispute. Once a settlement is reached, however, it may be enforced as if it were an order of a Primary Court. In addition to disputes referred to it via a Primary Court, the Arbitration Tribunal may hear disputes referred to it by any party to a dispute provided that the other parties consent. The Tribunal has no power to fine or punish any party to a dispute, or any other person. Finally, it should be noted that there is no appeal from a settlement reached at an Arbitration Tribunal. A party who claims that he was coerced into accepting the settlement, or that he did not consent to the settlement as recorded, may attempt to impeach the settlement in a Primary Court. If he is successful, the Primary Court will then determine the dispute *de novo*. (The Arbitration Tribunals Regulations, 1969, G.N. No. 219 of 1969.)

A third important measure is the establishment of Ward Development Committees with quasi-judicial powers. (Ward Development Committees Act, 1969, Act No. 6 of 1969.) This legislation is significant in that it gives a non-judicial body the power, albeit indirectly, to levy fines. The Ward Development Committees Act will be dealt with more fully in Chapter IV.

As noted above, the changes which took place in the judicial structure after independence were designed to create a unified, multi-tier system of courts, staffed at all levels by full-time, independent, judicial officers. While recent legislative changes may or may not indicate a movement in the direction of people's courts, they do indicate that no constitutional institution is to be considered inviolable. The validity of any institution will depend on the degree to which it is able to contribute to national development. If an institution is either interfering with or obstructing national development, it may be altered. No established institution is guaranteed by the mere fact of its existence. As President Nyerere has said, 'We refuse to put ourselves in a strait-jacket of constitutional devices—even of our own making.' For a discussion of, *inter alia*, the development of people's courts in a rural, revolutionary setting, see William Hinton, *Fanshen: A Documentary of Revolution in a Chinese Village*, op. cit.; for an account of people's courts in Cuba, see José Yglesias, *In the Fist of the Revolution*, Penguin Books, London, 1970, pp. 190-200. See also Mohammed Bedjaoui, *Law and the Algerian Revolution*, International Association of Democratic Lawyers, Brussels, 1961, pp. 42-52.

One can also regard the changes enumerated above as an attempt by the Party to control the administration of justice at the lowest level, both through the established courts and through the traditional methods of resolving disputes. The establishment in 1971 of District Boards, dominated by Party members, with wide powers in relation to Primary Court Magistrates, is an example of such a trend. This may not necessarily be the same thing as establishing a system of people's courts.

The reaction of the judiciary to these changes is interesting. When the government proposed them in 1968, the then Chief Justice commented favourably on the three-man bench in Primary Courts, but he expressed reservations about institutionalization of arbitration proceedings. In supporting the proposed new role of assessors in Primary Courts, the Chief Justice further suggested that the practice of having more or less permanent assessors should be changed. He was opposed to institutionalization of arbitration for two reasons. First, he felt that this would simply create another layer of courts. Villagers would still begin dispute settlement through informal arbitration—failing settlement, they would move to formal arbitration and ultimately, as before, to the Primary Court. The result would be simply to delay the settlement of disputes. Secondly, he feared that formal arbitration tribunals would appear as rivals to the Primary Court structure. (P. T. Georges, 'Report on Judges' and Magistrates' Conferences, November 1967–March 1968', *Eastern Africa Law Review*, vol I, no. 2, 1968, pp. 168-70, and 172.) On other occasions, Chief Justice Georges gave his enthusiastic support to the changes taking place, stating that the courts were undergoing a 'revolution without violence', that they were 'the people's courts'. (*The Standard*, 24 February and 24 August 1970.)

Certain steps have been taken and others are contemplated which will increase disciplinary control over magistrates. Section 16 of the Penal Code formerly provided that a judicial officer was generally protected from all criminal liability in the exercise of his judicial functions, even if he acted in excess of his authority or omitted to perform a required function. The new s. 16 limits this protection to bona fide acts or omissions. (Act No. 2 of 1970.) The Attorney-General explained that although it was necessary to safeguard magistrates in the performance of their duties, it was also necessary to take steps against those magistrates who wilfully mistreated the people. (*The Standard*, 20 March 1970.) Plans have been announced to appoint Supervisory Magistrates, who would supervise, discipline, and encourage Primary Court and District Magistrates. (*The Standard*, 16 July 1970.) During the 1970 debate on his department's estimates, the Second Vice-President stated that he would have no mercy with Primary Court Magistrates who gave a bad name to the Judiciary, and called upon the people to report any incidents to local TANU offices. (*The Standard*, 18 July 1970.)

Part of the problem of the Primary Courts stems from the insufficient number of both magistrates and courthouses. In the debate referred to above, Mr Kawawa announced plans to appoint a further one hundred and twenty Primary Court Magistrates. The bulk of the Judiciary's projects in the Second Five-Year Plan involve courthouse construction in the rural areas.

NOTE In July 1969, a major confrontation occurred in Zambia between the executive and the judiciary. On 16 June 1969, two uniformed Portuguese soldiers crossed, inadvertently they claimed, into Zambia from Angola and were arrested by Zambian border authorities. A magistrate convicted the two on a charge of illegal entry into Zambia and sentenced them to a fine of K. 2,000 (Sh. 20,000) each or two years' imprisonment in default of payment. The Portuguese appealed to the High Court where Evans, J. set aside the Magistrate's sentence on the grounds that the offence was '. . . trivial, merely a technical breach of the regulations'. He added that '. . . the situation did not redound to the credit of the Zambian authorities'. On 14 July, President Kaunda called a press conference during which he attacked the Judge and his finding. 'It [the judiciary] is part and parcel of this society. . . . Who does not know that we in Zambia live in a state of emergency, partly caused by the hostile, warlike actions of the Portuguese . . . literally Zambia is at war with the minority regimes around us.' The two Portuguese were detained. Chief Justice Skinner then issued a statement supporting the decision of Mr Justice Evans. Skinner, though Irish-born, was a Zambian citizen and had been associated with Kaunda and UNIP during the independence struggle. On 16 July, members of the Zambia Youth Service demonstrated outside the High Court in Lusaka and then invaded the building itself, forcing Skinner and Evans to barricade themselves in their offices. Following this action, and statements by the President that he intended to take steps to Zambianize the Judiciary, the Chief Justice left Zambia on 18 July for a holiday in the United Kingdom. On 23 September, despite an apology from President Kaunda, he announced his resignation as Chief Justice of Zambia. (*The Standard*, 15 July 1969; 18 July 1969; 19 July 1969; and 24 September 1969). As an interesting footnote to this dispute, about one year later Mr Justice Skinner returned to Africa as Chief Justice of Malawi. All other expatriate judges in Malawi had resigned over changes in the legal system. (*The Guardian*, London, 7 October 1970.)

NOTE The incident described above should lead us to question whether the Judiciary can function independently so long as it contains within its ranks large numbers of non-nationals. At the time of independence in Tanzania, the only African judicial officers were local court holders, two district commissioners, and a handful of district officers. At the present time, all primary court magistrates and district magistrates are Tanzanians. As of 1 September 1970, of the 44 resident magistrates, three were Nigerians, five were Malawians, and the rest were Tanzanians. Tanzania was the first country in East Africa to appoint a woman resident magistrate. (*Sunday News*, 7 June 1970.) The first appointments of Tanzanians as puisne judges of the High Court were made in August 1964. (The Judiciary, *Annual Report, 1964*, Government Printer, Dar es Salaam, 1966, p. 1.) By the end of 1970, over half the judges in the High Court were Tanzanian citizens, and the first Tanzanian Chief Justice, Mr Justice Saidi, was appointed in 1971. The first Tanzanian citizen to be a Justice of Appeal on the Court of Appeal for East Africa was appointed in May 1970. (*The Standard*, 6 May 1970.)

Tanzania has clearly made significant steps in the nationalization of its judiciary, but the fact that the higher judiciary has been one of the last major institutions to be Africanized must affect its freedom of action. Although there have been undeniable changes, Colin Leys summed the problem up several years ago, 'The judiciary is all too often expatriate or at least not representative of the indigenous majority, who have often learned to look to politicians and politics to protect them from the courts, rather than the other way around.' (*Journal of the Parliaments of the Commonwealth*, vol. XLIV, no. 2, 1963, p. 135.)

NOTE On the question of ideological commitment of the judiciary in East Africa, see *Transition*, nos. 36 and 37 (1968). This lively discussion led, unfortunately, to the demise of *Transition*.

P. T. Georges
THE COURT IN THE TANZANIA ONE-PARTY STATE[45]

● Before the granting of independence, the position of the courts in this *de facto* one-party state was not a matter of much concern. The judges, resident magistrates and district officers who did magisterial work were all appointees of the Colonial Office, and as such distinctly outside the direct influence of the party and its politics. With indepen-

[45] *East African Law and Social Change*, G. F. A. Sawyerr (ed.), East African Publishing House, Nairobi, 1967, pp. 26-46 (abbreviated).

dence all this has changed and it is both useful and necessary to examine the extent to which the courts have been able to play their traditional role as upholders of the rule of law in the context of the one-party state.

It was not until independence that the complete separation of the judiciary and the executive was achieved at the lower levels of the judiciary with which most people came into contact.

The difficulties created by this fusion of the judicial and executive functions were, of course, clearly perceived, and in Local Government Memorandum No. 2, which was published shortly after the enactment of the Local Courts Ordinance, it was stated that the policy of the separation of the judiciary and the executive should be implemented and that every opportunity should in future be taken to relieve chiefs of as much court work as possible and to encourage them to appoint judicial deputies for this purpose; similarly, Liwalis should wherever possible be relieved of executive responsibilities so that they may become Kadhis and in the true sense of that word, i.e. judges learned in the Mohammedan law.

Of particular significance is a statement at page 17 of the Memorandum:

The dispensation of justice without regard to administrative convenience is another long-term aim which will not be easy of achievement but which nevertheless must not be lost sight of. It will not be easy to achieve because of the combination of judicial and executive functions in both court holders and supervising officers. Yet the tendency to use the Courts as machinery for the enforcement of policy which may be unwelcome must be curbed. Circumstances sometimes arise in which the Courts may be used, justification being the overriding necessity for the preservation of good government, but such occasions will be rare.

This brings into sharp focus the inheritance of the colonial era: the admission that courts may be used for the enforcement of policy, unwelcome though it may be, and that use of the courts may be justified by the overriding necessity to preserve order and good government. It would be a signal achievement indeed if a young society bred in an atmosphere where such use of the courts was permissible and openly admitted could, in a reasonable period, solve the problem which is the legacy of that attitude. But the attempt has been made; the judiciary and the legislature are now separated. The executive officer is now confined to his administration, and the Primary Court magistrate and the district magistrate deal with the problems of the courts.

The physical separation of powers has not, however, been without difficulties. The administrative officers who have succeeded their

English counterparts have not failed to notice that their powers are not so wide. The judicial officers whose exclusive domain has been carved out of what was once administrative territory are nervous of any encroachment and tend to see a threat in every move, which is a healthy reaction, though often provocative of difficulties.

Even more troublesome has been the fact that at the Primary Court level, the Primary Court magistrate and district executive officer, who between them share the powers of the old native chiefs, must continue to occupy the single building which in the past served as court and administrative centre for a single functionary. The buildings are, of course, quite small, and in this narrow space difficulties of personal adjustment can be exaggerated into national problems. It is in that context that the problem may be exacerbated by the fact of the one-party state. Normally, the relationship between the executive and the party would be closer than that between the judiciary and the party, and if the weight of the party is brought to bear in such a dispute on the side of the executive, the position of the Primary Court magistrate may well become intolerable.

Happily, such conflicts have been few. It is hoped that when each of the departments is housed in separate quarters these problems will become rarer yet. The long term aim that justice should be administered without reference to administrative convenience has already been achieved. It is likely that problems of personal adjustment will persist. The tension between judges and the most senior administrative officers, resident magistrates and the administrative officers at their level in the provincial administration was always present. It will only subside when there is a complete understanding among the members of each group of the role they play in the development of society. With time there is no doubt that understanding will be developed.

In another direction also, the independence of the judiciary has been strengthened. The extent of direct executive influence on the choice of judicial officers has been lessened.

Under the Local Courts Ordinance, 1951, the provincial commissioner in each province appointed the members of the court; he determined by his warrant the terms of their appointment and the order of precedence among them. He could also dismiss members of the court. The district commissioner had the power to suspend. There would appear to have been no rules determining how he was to act in these matters. The Magistrates' Courts Act, 1963, placed the power to appoint Primary Court magistrates in the hands of the minister for the time being responsible for legal affairs, but he does not act on his own.

He acts on the recommendations of a Judicial Service Special Commission which is presided over by the Chief Justice and has as its other members the judge who is for the time being serving on the Judicial Service Commission and two other members appointed by the President—one of whom is usually a senior attorney in the Ministry of Justice. This Commission also has the power to promote Primary Court magistrates. The Judicial Service Special Commission itself acts through regional boards constituted by the minister. These boards are usually presided over by the regional commissioner—a political figure, but the district magistrate and resident magistrate are also members. They interview applicants and make recommendations to the Judicial Service Special Commission. The Commission considers their recommendations and then submits the names to the minister responsible for legal affairs, who makes the appointment. It has not yet happened that the minister has objected to an appointment. In practice his final right to make the appointment operates in the nature of a veto on the recommendations of the Judicial Service Special Commission and does not amount to a direct right of selection.

The power to appoint resident magistrates and district magistrates is vested in the President, but he has delegated that power to the Judicial Service Commission, and that body actually makes the appointment. The Judicial Service Commission is presided over by the Chief Justice and with him serve a judge of the High Court, nominated by the President after consultation with the Chief Justice, and any other person, usually a senior attorney in the Attorney-General's Chamber.

Judges are appointed by the President after consultation with the Chief Justice, and the Chief Justice is himself appointed by the President. At this level it is clear that political consideration may very well play a part. Barring a method of promotion based on competitive examination among members of the subordinate judiciary it appears to be difficult to avoid the possibility of political influence in the appointment of judges. The ideal method would be that of placing the appointment of judges themselves in the hands of the Judicial Service Commission and leaving to the executive authority the choice only of the Chief Justice. Here the Constitution places the power in the hands of the President after consultation with the Chief Justice. A great deal will depend on the amount of weight which is given to that consultation. Granted that there is mutual confidence between the President and the Chief Justice as ought normally to exist, the mechanism of consultation could be as effective as that of appointment by a Judicial Service Commission presided over by the Chief Justice.

Before any lawyer reaches the bench, he should have had a variety of experience from which he would have formed views which will affect his opinions as propounded in the form of judgements from the bench. I would go further and say that anyone so detached from the society as not to hold some view on the important issues which agitate it at any time is not in every sense fitted to be a judge. Law does not operate in a vacuum, but in a society, and it is right that a judge should recognize that his pronouncements must affect that society. Such discretion as he has to exercise should be exercised towards helping rather than hindering the solutions of social problems. To fail to realize this can lead only to unhappy conflict between the judiciary and the executive, which too often leads only to the defeat of the judiciary and a lowering of its prestige. What can destroy the bench and weaken the role of the courts in the maintenance of the rule of law is the appointment of officers who lack professional competence, professional discipline and personal integrity. It is in that sense that a purely politically motivated appointment is dangerous. Consultation with the Chief Justice should be a safeguard against that possibility.

If it is important to insulate the appointment of judicial officers from political pressures, it is even more important to insulate them from those pressures during their tenure of office so that they can act fearlessly without thought of reprisals.

As has been noted above, Local Court holders could be dismissed by the provincial commissioner or suspended by the district commissioner at will. The tenure of the Primary Court magistrate is secure.

The power to exercise disciplinary control over Primary Court magistrates and to terminate appointments and to remove them from office is vested in the Judicial Service Special Commission. Dismissal, however, must have the President's consent. The President has delegated that right to the minister for the time being in charge of legal affairs.

Regulations have been drawn up to regulate the procedure for disciplining and dismissing Primary Court magistrates. Complaints against Primary Court magistrates in respect of their judicial conduct are to be made to the registrar, and in respect of extra-judicial conduct to the regional board. The board is empowered to investigate the complaint and forward their recommendations to the Registrar. If the registrar thinks that disciplinary proceedings are necessary and that the complaint if proved would justify dismissal, he shall after such investigations as he considers necessary forward a statement of charges to the magistrate concerned with a brief statement of the allegations being made against him where these are not clear from the charges themselves. He will at the same time call upon the magistrate to exculpate himsel ˙ by a given date.

If the magistrate does not reply, or if his reply in the opinion of the registrar is not exculpatory, an investigating officer or committee is appointed to enquire into the charges. The chairman of the committee or the single investigatory officer must be a judge, judicial officer or civil servant with legal qualifications.

A proper enquiry must then be held at which the magistrate must be allowed to appear and ask questions of witnesses brought to establish the charges. He may, with the permission of the investigator, be represented by an advocate or by a public officer. At the close of the enquiry, the investigating officer reports to the Commission stating whether the charges or any of them have been established, setting out circumstances of aggravation or mitigation, if any, and generally expressing his views on the matter. On this the Commission acts.

Where the registrar thinks that the complaint is such as not to justify dismissal, the mechanism of an investigation may be eliminated if the Commission thinks it unnecessary, and it may act on the statement of charges and the magistrate's reply thereto. It may, of course, also order an enquiry, but not as formal in character as that required where dismissal is contemplated.

There is additional power in the Commission to remove a Primary Court magistrate from office where it is in the public interest that he should be removed. The Commission must notify the magistrate of the grounds on which his removal is contemplated and allow him an opportunity to show cause why he should not be removed.

It will be seen from the above that the tenure of office of this most junior member of the judicial hierarchy is amply safeguarded. His position has improved tremendously since independence.

One point deserves mention with regard to judges. Although overseas judges theoretically hold office during good behaviour, the factual situation is that they fall within the terms of the Tanganyika (Compensation and Retiring Benefits) Order in Council, 1961. With the introduction of the Republican Constitution, the Africanization provisions of the Order in Council were preserved by section 17 of the Republic of Tanganyika (Consequential, Transitional and Tempo-rary Provisions) Act, 1962. All overseas judges in fact now serve on an arrangement which enables either side to terminate the appoint-ment by giving six months' notice. To date the Government has not exercised its rights under the section to terminate the services of any judge. Several have exercised their right to end their appointments—often because a stage is reached where retirement at a comparatively early age can be achieved with the maximum of benefits. There is nothing to indicate that overseas judges in any way feel that the possibility of their appointments being terminated is in any way a threat. It is likely on their side that the freedom of action the position allows would be thought desirable.

It should be noted that unlike many of the newly independent countries, the Constitution of Tanzania does not set out a declaration of human rights. Where that is done, the courts would normally have the jurisdiction to pronounce on legislation and to declare it invalid where it infringed any of the enumerated rights. It may well be that the High Court of Tanzania has no such power. Of course, this situation is not new. The courts before independence had no such power. It seems unlikely that the courts would seek such a role today though it could be urged that they could legitimately pronounce against any law which patently cut across any of the aims for which the Constitution has been established, e.g. the existence of free and impartial courts. The argument would be fascinating.[46]

No doubt, however, there are dangers—dangers which do not necessarily arise from the nature of the one-party state, but which may pose a greater threat because this is a one-party state. The challenge is to fit the ideals of an independent judiciary into a pattern which is basically different from that with which it is traditionally associated.

The inheritance of colonialism increases the problems. It was only natural in colonial days to think of the courts as one of the mechanisms through which the metropolitan power exercised its domination. In the struggle for independence deliberate challenges to the law were the order of the day for the important leaders and their more dedicated followers. A prison sentence or at the very least a conviction was the hallmark of devotion to the cause. The courts were certainly not viewed in the light of stalwart champions of individual liberty.

Now the position has changed. A new image must be created. The courts must be seen as being no longer a mechanism for repression in the interests of the preservation of 'order and good government'. The transition is not easy, particularly as lawyers, magistrates and judges tend to conservatism rather than radicalism. In Tanzania there is the additional difficulty that at independence there was no really indigenous bar and very few local men on the bench. There would, therefore, be an impression of a gap between the people and those

---

[46] For a decision on precisely this point which supports the Chief Justice's view, see *Liyanage* v. *The Queen* [1967] A.C. 259 (PC)

connected with the administration of justice, a gap which would cause misunderstanding and foster suspicion.

The result was a growing concern over what the term 'independence of the judiciary' meant and what the result of such independence would be in a society where the party was so powerful. In that regard some rethinking is necessary. The concept of the judge as the neutral, belonging to no party in the multi-party democracy, can have no meaning here where there is one party. If he stands aloof seeming to play the apolitical role which is supposed to be his, his motives will doubtlessly be suspected. A new way must be found.

It is too much to expect the politicians to do that job for the judiciary. Largely we will have to do it ourselves so that a public opinion will gradually be created, permeating throughout the Party that the courts must be preserved because of the indispensable role which they play. The leaders at the top realize it and often stress it. But the task demands more than the occasional pronouncement. For these reasons, I see no harm and much good in party membership by members of the judiciary and use of the opportunities which membership offers to show a positive interest in helping the process of rapid national development and to stress the importance of the courts in the achievement of that goal.

This, of course, demands a substantial degree of professional skill on the part of the judiciary. Largely one wins respect through the competence one shows in action. The difficulties here are serious, more so at the level of the Primary Courts where there is the greatest amount of contact between the people and the magistrate, and also between the lower level politician and the magistrate. Many of the magistrates were recruited from among those who held office as Local Court-holders before the integration of the systems. In many cases their basic education was sadly lacking. The Government has realized the problem and has tackled it with energy. Training courses were commenced at the Local Government Training Centre at Mzumbe to instruct the magistrates in the new law they would have to administer and to try to equip them with the new skills in legal analysis they would need. Those who show particular promise are given further refresher courses to increase their skills further. Gradually, as the least suitable of the earlier recruits are weeded out, younger men with more formal education are being appointed, and the prospects of building a competent junior judiciary in a comparatively short time are brightening.

At the higher levels the problems, though present, are not as acute. The Law School at University College, Dar es Salaam, has begun

to release an increasing number of academically well trained law graduates. With experience in the field they should in a reasonably short time be competent to serve in a manner which will command
● respect.

NOTE For a general discussion of the suitability of English constitutional structures and procedures in Africa, see Seidman, 'Administrative Law and Legitimacy in Anglo-Phonic Africa', University of East Africa Social Sciences Council Conference, *Proceedings*, Kampala, 1968. For the colonial courts, see J. S. R. Cole and W. N. Denison, *Tanganyika: The Development of its Laws and Constitution*, op. cit., pp. 90-109.

NOTE According to Claire Palley, ' . . . a judiciary is prone to reflect the values of the mass of the people and to appeal to the same values'. ('Rethinking the Judicial Role', *Zambia Law Journal*, vol. I, no. 1, 1969, p. 32.) This statement describes what is obviously an ideal situation and one desirable of achievement, but is it an accurate description of the role of the judiciary in colonial Africa, or, for that matter, in any bourgeois state? One might comment that only when the courts and the law have been changed from tools of the bourgeoisie into instruments of the masses, can such a situation be realized.

CHAPTER THREE

EXECUTIVE AND ADMINISTRATIVE POWERS

In Chapter I we noted the class content of state power, and in Chapter II we discussed the legislative and judicial branches of government. In this chapter the exercise of power (that is, certain aspects of the executive function) is examined. First, we look at the specific powers that the state is capable of exercising, the types and range of these powers, and secondly the controls that are possible over their exercise.[1]

Since all the powers to be investigated are statutory, we will be concerned centrally with questions of statutory interpretation. Although parliamentary legislative supremacy allows the law to be changed at any time and for any purpose, a basic requirement of the Rule of Law that the state and its servants exercise only those powers granted to them by law remains part of the Tanzanian Constitution.

In analysing powers granted by statute, it is desirable to follow some fairly consistent approach, first, to determine as precisely as possible the nature and scope of the power and secondly, to analyse the circumstances under which the power may be exercised. The latter includes the person or class by whom the power is exercised, the procedure followed in deciding to exercise the power, and the persons in respect of whom the power may be exercised. Finally, one should take note of the provisions, if any, which permit the exercise of the power to be reviewed.

We will begin by looking at certain powers exercised by the President, then at the powers exercised by Regional Commissioners, and finally investigate in a general way the role the courts play in controlling the exercise of statutory powers. Although we will examine only legal or formal control mechanisms and procedures, it should be remembered that a large number of informal controls based on political, financial, personal, ethnic, and class relationships undoubtedly exist.

A · THE PRESIDENT

The President of Tanzania is given tremendous power under the Constitution. For example, executive power in Tanzania is vested in the President, he is not generally required to follow the advice of any other person or body,

[1] For examples of the broad range of powers exercised by state officials plus some of the ways in which these powers can be abused, see the extracts from the annual reports of the Permanent Commission of Enquiry in Chapter V.

and he is given executive control over the public service.[2] For purposes of this section, however, we are concerned with those powers which permit the President directly to affect the individual. We will deal first with powers granted to the Governor prior to Independence and still exercised by the President today. (Between Independence and the establishment of the Republic, these powers were exercised by the Governor-General, on the advice of either the Prime Minister or the Cabinet.) These powers have been preserved despite the many constitutional changes which have taken place since 1961, and have devolved upon the President under the provisions of the Republic of Tanganyika (Consequential, Transitional and Temporary Provisions) Act, 1962 (Cap. 500) and the Interim Constitution (Consequential, Transitional and Temporary Provisions) Act, 1965 (Act No. 45 of 1965).

DEPORTATION ORDINANCE: CAP 38

● 1. This Ordinance may be cited as the Deportation Ordinance.

2. Where it is shown by evidence on oath, to the satisfaction of the President, that any person is conducting himself so as to be dangerous to peace and good order in any part of Tanganyika, or is endeavouring to excite enmity between the people of Tanganyika and the Republic, or is intriguing against the Republic's power and authority in Tanganyika, the President may, if he thinks fit, by order under his hand and official seal, order that person to be deported from any part of Tanganyika to any other part of Tanganyika.

3. An appeal shall not lie from any order of deportation under this Ordinance.

5. Where, under this Ordinance, a person is to be deported, he shall by warrant of the President under his hand and seal, be detained, if necessary, in custody or in prison, until a fit opportunity for his deportation occurs.

6. The warrant of the President shall be sufficient authority to the person to whom it is directed or delivered for execution to receive and detain the person therein prescribed, and to carry him to the place named according to the warrant.

7. The expenses of deportation, including expenses of maintenance, shall be defrayed in such manner as the President directs.

8. The President may by order under his hand and official seal, vary or rescind any order of deportation made under this Ordinance, or, without varying or rescinding the order of deportation, may grant permission in writing to the person deported to leave for a temporary purpose the part of Tanganyika to which he has been deported for

[2] Interim Constitution, ss. 6 (2), 12, 21.

some other part named in such permission. Such permission may be granted subject to such conditions as to the President may seem proper, and any person who shall fail to comply with the conditions attached to any permission granted to him as aforesaid, shall be liable to the penalties provided in the next section.

9. If any person deported under this Ordinance leaves the part of Tanganyika to which he has been deported, or returns to the part of Tanganyika from which he has been deported without the permission in writing of the President, he shall be liable to imprisonment for any period not exceeding three months, with or without a fine not exceeding one thousand shillings; and he shall also be liable to be forthwith

● again deported.

NOTE The powers granted under the Deportation Ordinance are complemented by those found in the Expulsion of Undesirables Ordinance, Cap. 39. Under this second ordinance the President may, if he believes such action to be conducive to public good or advisable in the interests of public morals, order any person who is not a 'native' of Tanzania to leave the country (s. 2). Such an order may also be made in respect of a person who is not a native of Tanzania who has been convicted of a felony by a court other than a Primary Court, and the court has so recommended (s. 2). An order made under the Ordinance may be reviewed by an ad hoc board, but the President is not obliged to follow the recommendations of the board and no court of law has any jurisdiction to review, quash, reverse, or interfere with any proceeding, act or order made under the Ordinance (ss. 9-12; 20). It appears to have been the colonial practice for the Government to use Cap. 38 to deal with 'natives' and Cap. 39 to deal with 'non-natives'. Since Independence, the distinction appears to be based on citizenship. Thus, citizens who are not 'natives' of Tanzania have received deportation orders under Cap. 38. The powers under Cap. 39 were used immediately after Independence to expel a number of Europeans who were not willing to adjust to the change. (See *The Standard* for December 1961 and January 1962.) Two other points should be made about Cap. 38. First, there is no term fixed for the operation of a deportation order and no review machinery or procedures are established. Second, the person deported is not incarcerated. Within the area to which he has been deported, he is a free man. Thus an advocate who was deported to Sumbawanga District in December 1963, was permitted to continue with the practice of law, provided of course, that he did not leave Sumbawanga.

EMERGENCY POWERS ORDER IN COUNCIL, 1939

● 3.—(1) If the President is satisfied that a public emergency exists, he may by Proclamation declare that the provisions of Part II of this Order shall come into operation in Tanganyika, and thereupon those provisions shall come into operation accordingly; and they shall continue in operation until the President by a further Proclamation directs that they shall cease to have effect, where upon they shall cease to have effect except as respects things previously done or omitted to be done.

(2) A Proclamation under subsection (1) of this section may, if the President thinks fit, be made so as to apply only to such part of Tanganyika as may be specified in the Proclamation (in this subsection called 'the emergency area') in which case Regulations made under the said Part II shall, except as otherwise expressly provided in such Regulations, have effect only in the emergency area:

Provided that, for the avoidance of doubts, it is hereby declared that the expression 'Tanganyika' in the said Part II shall not be construed as referring only to the emergency area.

PART II—REGULATIONS

6.—(1) The President may make such Regulations as appear to him to be necessary or expedient for securing the public safety, the defence of Tanganyika, the maintenance of public order and the suppression of mutiny, rebellion and riot, and for maintaining supplies and services essential to the life of the community.

(2) Without prejudice to the generality of the powers conferred by the preceding subsection, the Regulations may, so far as appears to the President to be necessary or expedient for any of the purposes mentioned in that subsection:

(a) make provision for the detention of persons and the deportation and exclusion of persons from Tanganyika;

(b) authorize:
   (i) the taking possession or control, on behalf of the Republic, of any property or undertaking;
   (ii) the acquisition on behalf of the Republic of any property other than land;

(c) authorize the entering and search of any premises;

(d) provide for amending any law, for suspending the operation of any law, and for applying any law with or without modification;

(e) provide for charging, in respect of the grant or issue of any license, permit, certificate or other document for the purposes of the Regulations, such fee as may be prescribed by or under the Regulations;

(f) provide for payment of compensation and remuneration to

(g) persons affected by the Regulations;
provide for the apprehension, trial and punishment of persons offending against the Regulations;

Provided that nothing in this section shall authorize the making of provision for the trial of persons by Military Courts.

7.   The Regulations may provide for empowering such authorities or persons as may be specified in the Regulations to make orders and rules for any of the purposes for which such Regulations are authorized by this Order to be made, and may contain such incidental and supplementary provisions as appear to the President to be necessary or expedient for the purposes of the Regulations.

8.   A Regulation or any order or rule made in pursuance of such a Regulation shall have effect notwithstanding any thing inconsistent therewith contained in any law; and any provision of a law which may be inconsistent with any Regulation or any such order or rule shall, whether that provision shall or shall not have been amended, modified, or suspended in its operation under section 6 of this Order, to the extent of such inconsistency have no effect so long as such Regulation, order or rule shall remain in force.

9. Every document purporting to be an instrument made or issued by the President or other authority or person in pursuance of this Order, or of any Regulation, and to be signed by or on behalf of the President or such other authority or person, shall be received in evidence, and shall, until the contrary is proved, be deemed to be an instrument
● made or issued by the President or that authority or person.

NOTE   The above powers which were granted to all colonial Governors by the English Crown were specifically preserved for the President of Tanganyika by s. 28 of Cap. 500. While Kenya and Uganda have not preserved these same colonial emergency powers, legislation exists which gives the respective President roughly similar powers.

COLLECTIVE PUNISHMENT ORDINANCE: CAP. 74

● 1. This Ordinance may be cited as the Collective Punishment Ordinance.

2. The President may impose fines on all or any inhabitants of any village, area or district, or members of any tribe, sub-tribe, or community if, after inquiry, he is satisfied:

(a)   That they or any of them have colluded with or harboured or failed to take all reasonable means to prevent the escape of any criminal;

(b)   that they or any of them have suppressed or combined to suppress evidence in any criminal case;

(c)   that stolen property having been traced to within the limits of any village, area or district, they have failed or neglected to restore the property or to trace it beyond the limits of such village, area or district;

and may order the whole or any part of the fines recovered to be applied in compensation for the injury caused by the offence of which the criminal is accused or to which the criminal case relates, or in compensation to the owner of the stolen property; except within a Township, the occurrence of any theft or of any unlawful removal or damage with respect to any telegraph line, railway material, bridges or other property of a public nature shall be prima facie evidence that an offence under this section has been committed by the inhabitants of the village, area or district in which such theft or unlawful removal or damage has occurred.

3. When within any village, area or district a person is dangerously or fatally wounded by unlawful attack, or the body is found of a person believed to have been unlawfully killed, the inhabitants of such village, area or district or the members of any tribe, sub-tribe, or community resident therein, shall be deemed to have committed an offence under the last foregoing section and may in like manner be fined by the President, unless they can show that they:

(a) had not an opportunity of preventing the offence or arresting the offender; or

(b) have used all reasonable means to bring the offender to justice.

4. The President may, in making any order under this Ordinance, determine the limits of any village, area or district or define a tribe, sub-tribe, or community for the purpose of such order.

5. A fine imposed under this Ordinance may be recovered by distress.

6. An inquiry under this Ordinance shall be conducted by a magistrate, or other judicial officer, in the same manner, as far as may be, as an inquiry under the laws relating to Criminal Procedure.

7. An appeal shall not lie from any order made under this Ordinance, which shall be final and shall not be liable to be contested by suit or otherwise.[3]

The following are post-Independence enactments which have conferred certain powers on the President.

PREVENTIVE DETENTION ACT, 1962: CAP. 490

1. This Act may be cited as the Preventive Detention Act, 1962.

2.—(1) Where:

(a) it is shown to the satisfaction of the President that any person is conducting himself so as to be dangerous to peace and good

---

[3] It appears that the power to fine under this Ordinance has not been used in recent years.

order in any part of Tanganyika, or is acting in a manner prejudicial to the defence of Tanganyika or the security of the State; or

(b) The President is satisfied that an order under this section is necessary to prevent any person acting in a manner prejudicial to peace and good order in any part of Tanganyika, or to the defence of Tanganyika or the security of the State,

the President may, by order under his hand and the Public Seal, direct the detention of that person.

(2) Unless the President is satisfied that it is not feasible or practicable to require that any particular item of information shall be given on oath, he shall require that any information on which he satisfies himself that a person is conducting himself or acting in any such manner aforesaid or that it is necessary that an order be made, as the case may be, shall be given on oath.

3. No order made under this Act shall be questioned in any court.

4.—(1) An order under this Act shall constitute an authority to any police officer to arrest the person in respect of whom it is made and for any police officer or prison officer to detain such person as a civil prisoner in custody or in prison and such person shall, while detained in pursuance of the order, be in lawful custody.

(2) The President may make regulations:

(a) Applying to persons detained under orders made under this Act, any of the provisions of the Prisons Act or of any rules made thereunder relating to convicted criminal prisoners and disapplying in relation to such persons any of such provisions relating to civil prisoners; and

(b) prohibiting, regulating and controlling visits to, and correspondence to or from, such persons,

and where the President makes any such regulations, the Prisons Act and any rules made thereunder shall have effect in relation to such persons subject to the provisions of such regulations.

5. The President may:

(a) rescind any order made under this Act;

(b) direct that the operation of an order made under this Act be suspended subject to such conditions, if any, as may be specified in such direction:

  (i) requiring the person in respect of whom the order is made to notify his movements in such manner, at such times and to such authority or person as may be specified; and

  (ii) requiring him to enter into a bond with or without

securities for the observance of any such conditions aforesaid,

and if that person fails to comply with a condition attached to such a direction, he shall, whether or not the direction is revoked, be detained under the original order.

6. A person detained under this Act shall, not later than fifteen days from the beginning of his detention, be informed of the grounds on which he is being detained and shall be afforded an opportunity of making representations in writing to the President with respect to the order under which he is detained.

7.—(1) There shall be an Advisory Committee which shall consist of:

(a) a chairman and two members appointed by the President; and

(b) two members appointed by the Chief Justice.

(2) A member of the Advisory Committee may resign his membership by writing under his hand addressed to the person by whom he was appointed.

(3) The quorum of the Advisory Committee shall be three, of whom one shall be the chairman, one shall be another member appointed by the President, and one shall be a member appointed by the Chief Justice.

(4) The President shall refer to the Advisory Committee every order made under this Act:

(a) where representations have been made in pursuance of section 6, as soon as may be after the making of such representations;

(b) where no such representations have been made, within a year of the order being made, and thereafter at intervals not exceeding a year (unless such order has previously been rescinded), and shall inform the Committee of the grounds on which the order was made and such other matters relating to the person detained as are relevant to this continued detention, and shall provide the Committee with a copy of all representations made by the person detained.

(5) The Committee shall be afforded an opportunity of interviewing any person detained under an order referred to them under this section, at the place where such person is detained.

(6) The Committee shall advise the President whether, in their opinion, an order made under this Act should be continued or rescinded or suspended, but the President shall not be required to act in accordance with the advice of the Committee.

QUESTION Would the validity of a particular Preventive Detention Order be affected by a failure to observe the procedural requirements of ss. 6 and 7 ? See *Re Mandavia* (1952) 26 K.L.R. 52; brief remarks by Professor Ghai in *Eastern Africa Law Review*, vol. I, no. 1, 1968, pp. 74-75; and M. C. J. Kagzi, 'Judicial Control of Executive Discretion under Preventive Detention Law: An Indian Experience', *Public Law*, 1965, p. 30. The High Court of Zambia has held that where procedural requirements are not complied with a detention order is invalid. *Chipango* v. *R.* unreported, 1970 HP Const/Ref/2.

J. K. Nyerere
OPENING OF THE UNIVERSITY COLLEGE CAMPUS[4]

● Take the question of detention without trial. This is a desperately serious matter. It means that you are imprisoning a man when he has not broken any written law, or when you cannot be sure of proving beyond reasonable doubt that he has done so. You are restricting his liberty, and making him suffer materially and spiritually, for what you believe he intends to do, or is trying to do, or for what you believe he has done. Few things are more dangerous to the freedom of a society than that. For freedom is indivisible, and with such an opportunity open to the Government of the day, the freedom of every citizen is reduced. To suspend the Rule of Law under any circumstances is to leave open the possibility of the grossest injustices being perpetrated.

Yet, knowing these things, I have still supported the introduction of a law which gives the Government power to detain people without trial. I have myself signed Detention Orders. I have done these things as an inevitable part of my responsibilities as President of the Republic. For even on so important and fundamental an issue as this, other principles conflict. Our Union has neither the long tradition of nationhood, nor the strong physical means of national security, which older countries take for granted. While the vast mass of the people give full and active support to their country and its government, a handful of individuals can still put our nation into jeopardy, and reduce to ashes the effort of millions.

It becomes a question of emphasis and priorities. There is never a single 'correct' answer when a conflict of principles is concerned. For it is comparatively easy to build a nation of well-fed robots who have no ideas of their own, or to have a society where everyone can talk while they are starving. But we are aiming at achieving ALL the freedoms, and that means thinking at every stage of the progress ● both about the principle and about the techniques of advance.

NOTE In their book, *Tanganyika: The Development of its Laws and Constitution*, op. cit., Cole and Denison assert that the Tanganyika Preventive

---

[4] *Freedom and Unity*, pp. 312-13.

Detention Act, 'closely resembles' that which used to exist in Ghana (p. 262). There are, in fact, several major differences, in that the Ghanaian Act applied only to citizens, there was no privative clause excluding the jurisdiction of the courts, a detention order was valid only up to five years, and no review machinery was established. (See the Ghana Preventive Detention Act, 1958, Act No. 17 of 1958, and amending and consolidating legislation, Acts 132, 199, and 240.) The Bill for Tanzania's Preventive Detention Act was introduced in the National Assembly on 26 September 1962, and passed through all three readings in just over an hour. At a press conference held after the Act had been passed, Julius Nyerere (then a private MP) stated that the Government was prepared to take the risk of locking up innocent people in order to prevent harm to the state. He said that the Act was not intended as a political weapon but was designed to safeguard the security of the state. Kasanga Tumbo, leader of the Peoples' Democratic Party in the National Assembly, who was himself detained from January 1964 until July 1966, was very critical of the Act and called it '. . . a declaration of a state of emergency on the peaceful people of Tanganyika'. (*The Standard*, 28 September 1962.) Nyerere replied that preventive detention was aimed solely at traitors. (*The Standard*, 4 October 1962.) The power to detain was not used to any significant degree until 1964. (See Tordoff, *Government and Politics in Tanzania*, p. 163.) With the revolution in Zanzibar, the Army Mutiny on the mainland, and the beginning of armed struggle in Mozambique, Tanzania became extremely security conscious. (See Bienen, 'National Security in Tanganyika After the Mutiny', *Transition*, no. 21, 1965, p. 39.) After the Zanzibar revolution, approximately twelve members of its independence Cabinet were detained. It has been estimated that immediately following the Mutiny, more than five hundred people were put in preventive detention. (Tordoff, loc. cit.) These were mainly soldiers of the Tanganyika Rifles who had taken part in the Mutiny, and trade unionists, including the President of the Tanganyika Federation of Labour. The trade unionists were the only organized group within Tanganyika which had responded favourably to the mutineers. (Bienen, p. 43.) As early as 13 February, large numbers of trade unionists were released. (*The Standard*, 14 February 1964.) Gradually, over the next two years all those detained as a result of the Mutiny were released. By April 1965, only 14 Tanzanian civilians (apart from the members of the former Zanzibar Cabinet) and approximately 20 members of the Tanganyika Rifles were in detention. (*The Standard*, 9 April 1965.) On 25 July 1966, it was announced that all the Tanzanians detained as a result of the Mutiny had been freed. (*The Standard*, 26 July 1966.) According to Mr Job Lusinde, then Minister for Home Affairs, the general policy followed in this regard was, that detainees would be released ' . . . as and when it was established [that] their freedom no longer constituted a danger to national security'. (*The Standard*, 14 September 1965.) The members of the former Zanzibar Cabinet have not fared so well and it appears that approximately seven of them are still in detention. It has been reported that in mid-1969 three members of the Sultan's Cabinet who had been in preventive detention on the mainland since 1964 were released. They asked permission to go abroad, but as the Zanzibar authorities demanded their return and gave an understanding that they would remain at liberty in Zanzibar, they were sent back, and were apparently imprisoned. (*The Times*, London, 30 October 1969.)

In August 1967, Mr Hanga (then Vice-President of Zanzibar), his body-guard, Mr Anangisye (a mainland MP), two brothers of Oscar Kambona, and three officials of the Ministry of Foreign Affairs alleged to be sympathetic to Kambona, were detained for being involved in a planned coup. (See an article by Colin Legum in *The Observer*, London, 20 August 1967.) In October 1969, another Kambona-inspired coup attempt resulted in the detention of its alleged leaders and a considerable number of their supporters, friends, and relatives. However, it was later announced that the alleged leaders of the plot would be placed on trial for treason. (*The Nationalist*, 27 October, 1969.)

Since late 1964, the ranks of those in detention have been swelled by a general category of 'spies'. At any given time there have been twenty-five to thirty-five of such people in preventive detention, most of them Malawians or South Africans. (See, for example, *The Standard*, 13 and 14 February 1970.)

It appears that since the beginning of 1969, the President has given more personal attention to the use of preventive detention, having previously delegated the power to the Minister for Home Affairs who was given a relatively free hand in its use. This change may have resulted from pressure exerted by Ministers who are opposed in principle to preventive detention, and could explain why the seven people involved in the October 1969 coup attempt were brought to trial rather than kept in detention. In passing sentence on the six people found guilty in the treason trial, Chief Justice Georges expressed the hope that this approach of bringing people to trial rather than placing them in detention would be followed in other cases. (*The Times*, London, 10 February 1971.)

On the basis of the admittedly sketchy evidence available, it seems fair to conclude that preventive detention has been used essentially to fulfil its stated aim of dealing with serious threats to the security of the state. Still, there have been cases where questionable use of the power has been made. Fourteen peasants in Ukerewe District were informed that the land they were farming was to be set aside as the site for an ujamaa village. Some time before the development of this village began, the peasants were ordered to move off the land. When they refused to do so, they were placed in preventive detention and held there for over a year until their release in mid-1969. It is doubtful if these peasants constituted a serious threat to the security of the state. Also open to some doubt is the case of the four Patel brothers of Dar es Salaam who were detained because they were allegedly involved in a range of undisclosed corrupt activities. After being held in detention for almost a year they were released in June 1970, and immediately declared prohibited immigrants. (*The Standard*, 13 June 1970.)

In November 1969, police arrested thirty-nine people, including civil servants, as part of a crackdown on various alleged rackets and corrupt practices involving immigration and passport matters. (*The Standard*, 28 November 1969.) On 14 December, the President publicly defended his action of having detained these people under the Preventive Detention Act, by pointing out the difficulties that would have been encountered had normal criminal procedure been followed. First, police investigations would have been seriously hampered if the suspects had been released on bail, and, second, it would be very difficult to prove charges of this kind. (*The Standard*, 15 December 1969.) In an editorial on 16 December, *The Standard* supported the President and added, 'Here, surely, is a case where guilty men should not be allowed to escape through some legal technicality.' In early February, 1970, ten of the people detained were released. (*The Standard*, 5 February 1970.) On 21 April 1970, all the non-Tanzanians involved were released, all their property was confiscated, and they were expelled from the country. Naturalized citizens involved were released, had their property confiscated, their citizenship revoked, and they were then expelled from the country. The twelve remaining people, who were all citizens by birth, remained in detention. (*The Standard*, 22 April 1970.) A Government statement released the same day acknowledged the seriousness of these steps, but stressed that any action necessary to fight bribery and corruption would be taken. (For a somewhat dated comment on the use of the Preventive Detention Act and Caps. 38 and 39, see McAuslan, 'The Republican Constitution of Tanganyika', *International and Comparative Law Quarterly*, vol. XIII, 1964, pp. 564-6.)

NEWSPAPER ORDINANCE: CAP. 229

● 21A.—(1) Where the President is of the opinion that it is in the public interest or in the interest of peace and good order to do so, he may, by order in the Gazette, direct that the newspaper named in the order shall cease publication as from the date (hereinafter referred to as the effective date) specified in the order.

(2) Every order made under subsection (1) shall specify:

(*a*) the title or name of the newspaper in respect of which it is made; and

(*b*) the names of the proprietor, printer and publisher of such newspaper:

Provided that no order made under subsection (1) shall be invalid by reason of non-description or misdescription of the proprietor, printer or publisher or any of them.

(3) Where an order under subsection (1) is made in respect of any newspaper:

(*a*) any person who, on or after the effective date, prints or publishes or causes to be printed or published the newspaper named in the order shall be guilty of an offence and shall be liable on conviction to a fine not exceeding twenty thousand shillings or to imprisonment for a term not exceeding five years or to both such fine and imprisonment;

(*b*) any person who, on or after the effective date, sells, offers to sell, exposes for sale, distributes or exhibits, or causes to be exhibited, in any public place any copy or part of a copy of the newspaper named in the order, whether or not such copy or part was printed or published prior to the effective date, shall be guilty of an offence and shall be liable on conviction to a fine not exceeding ten thousand shillings or to imprisonment not exceeding two years or to both such fine and imprisonment.

(4) Where any person is convicted of an offence under this section the court by which such person is convicted may, notwithstanding the provisions of section 7 of the Criminal Procedure Code, impose the maximum fine prescribed by this section for such offence.

(5) For the purposes of this section 'public place' shall have the ● meaning ascribed thereto in the Penal Code.

NOTE The section quoted above was passed in May 1968 to give the Government power to suppress a political publication put out by individuals loyal to Oscar Kambona. The President has a complementary power, under s. 51 of the Penal Code, which is to be exercised 'in his absolute discretion', to prohibit any publication, periodical or otherwise, the importation of which would in his opinion be contrary to the 'public interest'. This power was exercised in October 1968 to prohibit the importation of any papers published in Kenya by the foreign-owned Nation chain. (This ban was lifted when *The Standard* was nationalized in February 1970.) The President may also prohibit for the same reasons, the importation of any or all the works of a specified author or publisher. Section 52 lays down penalties for the importation, possession or sale of any prohibited publication.

Although this chapter is concerned with executive powers, it should be noted in passing that other sections of the Penal Code place limitations on communication. Section 56 creates a number of seditious offences, s. 63 makes it an offence to publish false news 'likely to cause fear and alarm to the public', and s. 175 prohibits traffic in obscene publications. The administration of these provisions is left to the courts as part of the criminal law. See *Wallace-Johnson* v. *R.* [1940] A.C. 231 (PC), and *D.P.P.* v. *Obi* [1961] All N.L.R. 186.

Freedom of expression in colonial times was as restricted as one would expect. For example, the powers granted under s. 51 of the Penal Code were then exercised by the Governor-in-Council, and were used to protect the people of Tanganyika from, *inter alia*, Marxist-Leninist publications, Jehovah's Witness publications and, apparently, anything by or about George Padmore. (Cap. 16—Subsidiary Legislation—Supp. 59.) In this regard, one can find an entertaining description of colonialist mentality in James Hooker's biography of Padmore, *Black Revolutionary: George Padmore's Path from Communism to Pan-Africanism*, Pall Mall, London, 1967.

The Kenya Government in 1951 attempted to ban the importation of 'any publication dealing with sex or the psychological or the medical aspects of sex or birth control.' As J. S. Read points out ('Censored: Notes on Banned Books in Africa', *Transition*, no. 32, 1967, p. 37), this ban would have excluded, 'most modern fiction and a majority of the classics including much of Shakespeare'.

In independent Africa the problems surrounding freedom of the press have been exacerbated by the fact that a significant proportion of the press is foreign-owned and either unsympathetic to or uninterested in national development. The late Tom Mboya pointed out in 1962 that the nationalist struggle in Africa faced general press opposition and that what was needed after independence was 'a national press that is in every sense rooted in the country of its publication, instead of being an organ or an echo of interests overseas'. ('Relations Between the Press and Governments in Africa', *Transition*, no. 4, 1962, p. 11.) In a speech given in 1963, Nkrumah suggested that the major responsibility of the journalist lies in mobilizing and educating the people to continue with the African revolution. (*The African Journalist*, Tanzania Publishers, Dar es Salaam, 1965.) The issue was expressed succinctly in 1967 by the Ugandan Foreign Minister, Mr Odaka, when he said that the first problem that needed solving was press *ownership*, the second was press *freedom*. (Quoted in Daniel Nelson, 'Newspapers in Uganda', *Transition*, no. 35, 1968, p. 29.) This problem of foreign ownership of the press and other information media is one that is faced by all ex-colonial states. (See, for example, C. L. R. James, *The Black Jacobins*, Random House, New York City, 1963, p. 406.) It has, however, been heightened in Africa by a tendency of the post-independence courts to give far greater protection to the freedom of foreign-owned newspapers to criticize African governments, than pre-independence courts gave to African-owned newspapers in their criticism of colonial governments. (J. F. Scotton, 'Judicial Independence and Political Expression in East Africa', *East African Law Journal*, vol. VI, no. 1, 1970, p. 1.) For a descriptive discussion of the press in Tanzania, see John C. Condon, 'Nation-Building and Image-Building in the Tanzanian Press', *Journal of Modern African Studies*, vol. V, no. 3, 1967, p. 335.

On 4 February 1970, the Government nationalized *The Standard*, the largest English language daily in Tanzania. The fact that the major newspaper in a socialist African state was owned by the Lonrho Corporation, a British company with extensive interests in South Africa, was a source of considerable tension and embarrassment. The party-owned newspaper, *The Nationalist*, consistently referred to *The Standard* as 'the local imperialist-owned daily'. In a statement released at the time of the nationalization, President Nyerere described the Government's action as 'both nationalistic and socialistic'. He then laid down new editorial standards within which the paper was to function. Generally, *The Standard* was to be a socialist newspaper and would support the socialist ideology of Tanzania as defined in the Arusha Declaration. It was free to express opinions on any 'particular proposal' put forward by the Government or TANU, to initiate discussion on any subject relevant to the development of a socialist and democratic society in Tanzania, to criticize particular acts of individual TANU or government leaders, and to criticize the implementation of agreed policies. (Compare these ground rules with the limits set out in Chapter II on the National Assembly's power to criticize.) The editor was to be appointed by the President, but would have full autonomy in the day to day administration of the paper. Finally, the paper was to be '. . . guided by the principle that free debate is an essential element of true socialism'. (*The Standard*, 5 February 1970.) Despite some pious hand-wringing in the western press about freedom of the press in Tanzania (see, for example, *Africa Report*, vol. XV, no. 5, 1970, p. 8; *The Globe and Mail*, Toronto, 7 February 1970), *The Standard* became a much more critical, exciting, and intelligent newspaper after the takeover.

Paradoxically, the *fact* of nationalization expanded freedom of expression by removing the *fear* of nationalization which had formerly emasculated the newspaper. As examples of the paper's new critical stance, *The Standard* broke a scandal about illegal detentions (13 February 1970 and following), loudly disagreed with a Regional Commissioner (2 April, 3 April, and 4 April 1970), took the National Development Corporation to task for its allegedly non-socialist ways (27 April 1970), and expressed serious doubts about the Government's tourism policy (25 May 1970 and following). On the other hand, *The Standard* avoided certain delicate issues. For example, when in January 1970, violence broke out near Mbeya involving Americans working on the Great North Road and Chinese working on the Tan-Zam Railway, *The Standard* ignored the incident. And, in July 1970, the paper acceded to an official request that it should not give any coverage to the testimony of a particular witness in the treason trial then being held in Dar es Salaam. The formation of the *Daily News* in 1972 through the amalgamation of *The Nationalist* and *The Standard* can be seen as an attempt to bring the press under greater party, as opposed to government, control.

'Freedom of the press' is a concept which, like 'freedom' itself, has suffered in clarity through cold war ideological conflict. There seems little value in debating whether censorship by business interests is preferable to censorship by bureaucrats, for this is the level at which much of the discussion on the subject is carried out. In his essay, 'The Prevention of Literature', George Orwell may have been nearer to the heart of the matter when he said, 'The controversy over freedom of speech and the Press is at bottom a controversy over the desirability, or otherwise, of telling lies. What is really at issue is the right to report contemporary events truthfully, or as truthfully as is consistent with the ignorance, bias, and self-deception from which every observer necessarily suffers.' (*Inside the Whale and Other Essays*, Penguin Books, London, 1962, p. 161.)

NOTE An important aspect of the problem of freedom of expression after the colonial experience, is that of protecting and developing the national culture. Fanon points out in his vitally important essay, 'Racism and Culture' (*Toward the African Revolution*, Grove Press, New York City, 1967, p. 29), that if African culture is to redevelop itself, it must become liberated from the restraints and prejudices and, ultimately, the *definitions* of colonialism. Yet how may a culture free itself from the psychological shackles of colonialism and avoid turning inward to an incestuous sterility? Undoubtedly the first step towards cultural liberation will be the determination of the objective content of the new culture. In the early stages of the Vietnamese Revolution the following approach was suggested: 'In dealing with traditional culture and foreign culture, we should refrain from systematic denigration or blind imitation. We should instead cultivate a critical spirit, assimilating what is good in other cultures, and rejecting what is bad.' (Tru'o'ng-Chinh, *The Resistance Will Win*, 3rd ed., Foreign Languages Publishing House, Hanoi, 1966, p. 64.) More important than the objective content of the new culture is the process by which it attains its freedom from the culture of colonialism. Commenting on his trip to Cuba in 1970, Richard Gott stated, '. . . what strikes one most forcibly is the failure of the revolution to overcome the legacy of the past. Today's Cuba is the product of its history rather than its

Revolution. It needs a cultural revolution if it is to break away from this heritage.' (*The Guardian*, London, 15 October 1970.)

Tanzania has committed itself to revitalizing and redeveloping its culture so that it will produce a national culture that is both African and socialist. During the process of this development it must protect its culture from the crude imperialism of foreign films, radio, and publications, without, at the same time, stifling the initiative and creativity essential for cultural growth. Some of the steps which have been taken seem to be prudent and beyond criticism. For example, authorities have banned certain western publications and films which reflect the shallow material values of capitalism. On the other hand, it is questionable whether the banning of 'soul music' in Dar es Salaam can be defended on the same basis. (*The Standard*, 13 November 1969; *The Nationalist*, 15 November 1969.) Of particular interest in this context is 'Operation Vijana'. At a meeting held on 2 October 1968, the TANU Youth League (T.Y.L.) General Council called on the Government to prohibit miniskirts, wigs, skin bleaches, and other foreign cultural intrusions. They also announced 'Operation Vijana' which was to begin on 1 January 1969. The aim of Operation Vijana was '. . . to wipe out all renegade practices, foster national culture and carry forward the Tanzanian revolution'. In practice, the whole exercise became an attempt to stamp out certain western habits of dress among Tanzanian youth. Specially trained T.Y.L. cadres were to patrol the streets and point out to people wearing the forbidden clothing (minis, tight jeans, and so on) that such practices were no longer acceptable in Tanzania. These cadres were provided with identity cards, wore uniforms, and were the only persons authorized to police the implementation of Operation Vijana. They were not, either formally or informally, given any powers of arrest and were directed to act politely towards transgressors. The operation was launched to the accompaniment of great publicity and enthusiasm. Cadres patrolled the streets for about one month, but then Operation Vijana appeared to run out of steam, largely due to the fact that the T.Y.L. cadres involved had to return to secondary school.

At the time of Operation Vijana, there was considerable talk that this represented the beginning of a cultural revolution in Tanzania. This talk subsided as Operation Vijana revealed the organizational weaknesses of the T.Y.L.

Some extremely contradictory pressures are involved in cultural development. For example, while Operation Vijana was attempting to eradicate certain forms of western dress, the Regional Commissioner for Arusha Region continued his campaign to persuade the Maasai to reject their traditional dress and adopt western clothing. (For 'Operation Vijana' see *The Nationalist*, 3 October 1968 and 30 December 1968 to 3 January 1969; for a comment on the banning of soul music in Dar es Salaam, see J. K. Obatala, 'U.S. Soul Music in Africa', *The African Communist*, no. 41, 1970, p. 80.) It should be noted that cultural imperialism is not the private preserve of the western states. In July 1969, officials of the Chinese Embassy in Dar es Salaam tried unsuccessfully to force the banning of the American film, 'Shoes of the Fisherman', because it contained scenes which were critical of the Chinese leadership.

What should be the role of the artist in the process of cultural renewal and, more important for the purposes of this study, what should be the state's reaction to the artist? Wole Soyinka, who spent almost two years in detention in Nigeria, is not very optimistic about the role which African states will allow to the artist. He sees the task of the writer, for example, as being the critical conscience of his society, but he sees great difficulties in performing this task. 'Where he [the writer] is purged from the long deception and has begun to express new wisdoms, the gates of the preventive detention fortress opened up and closed on him.' ('The Writer in an African State', *Transition*, no. 31, 1967, p. 11.)

As TANU has not yet formulated a programme of cultural development, it may be useful to quote the sections of the PAIGC Programme which refer to this subject:

Art. VII. b. 3.   Total elimination of the complexes created by colonialism, and of the consequences of colonialist culture and exploitation.

4.   . . . Protection and development of national literature and arts.

5.   Utilization of all values and advances of human and universal culture in the service of the progress of the peoples of Guinea and Cabo Verde. Contribution by the culture of these peoples to the progress of humanity in general.
(Amilcar Cabral, *Revolution in Guinea*, op. cit., pp. 139-40.)

For an excellent portrayal of the crippling effect of colonialism on cultural development, see V. S. Naipaul, *The Middle Passage*, Penguin Books, London, 1969. For accounts by two writers of their personal struggles against the cultural effects of colonialism, see Aimé Césaire, *Return to My Native Land*, Penguin, London, 1969; and Eldridge Cleaver, *Soul on Ice*, Cape, 1969.

To end our investigation of the powers of the President, let us look at an example of a situation where only swift executive action was adequate to deal with a serious crisis.

G. H. Boehringer

DEVELOPMENTS IN CRIMINOLOGY IN TANZANIA[5]

● In late December 1966, President Nyerere went to Mwanza for a rest prior to an extended tour of northwestern Tanganyika, an area in which cattle theft has been a particularly difficult problem to deal with. On 28 December 1966, *The Standard* reported that ten tribesmen had been killed in a cattle raid by the Wamang'ati, a tribe noted for this kind of activity. Two days later, *The Standard* reported seven more dead were found, the battle having been fought with spears, clubs and bows and arrows. On 5 January 1967, *The Standard* reported that President Nyerere had called for the arrest of all cattle thieves

---

[5] University of East Africa Social Sciences Council Conference, *Proceedings*, Kampala, 1968, fn. 17.

in North Mara where he was speaking, and an area where the offence is prevalent. On 31 January 1967, the Mara Regional Development Committee congratulated President Nyerere for helping it to solve the cattle theft problem. *The Standard* of that date announced that over 1,300 suspects had been arrested. (It is interesting to note that three subsequent reports in *The Standard*, 7 January, 11 January, 26 January state that President Nyerere had called for the arrest of 'suspected' cattle thieves.) On 22 April 1967, *The Standard* reported the Minister for Home Affairs, Mr Sijaona, as stating that 4,200 people had been rounded up; that the cattle thieves among them would be deported from their home areas and resettled permanently elsewhere, to act as a deterrent. It was also announced they would not be taken to court, but screened by teams set up within the Regions; he announced that 1,061 had already been released. At a Press Conference in March 1967, the President stated that he believed in the criminal law and procedure adopted from the British, but that in this particular case, especially due to police shortage, it would not have solved the problem; therefore, he had used the traditional 'chieftain's law' and given the people permission to round up the thieves. He noted that 4,000 people had been rounded up and cattle theft had stopped. See the *Sunday News*, 5 March 1967. All but 62 had been released according to the Minister for Home Affairs, Mr. Maswanya; report in *The Standard*, 8 May 1968. It was announced in 1968 that 10,000 of the Wamang'ati (cattle theft is a common activity with economic and cultural implications amongst this tribe) might be re-settled in new villages to break their traditional pattern of raiding and killing.
● *The Standard*, 10 June 1968.

NOTE In connection with the above incident, reference should also be made to the Stock Theft Ordinance, Cap. 422.

NOTE An extremely important feature of the role of the President is that he need not exercise personally any of the powers granted to him. He may delegate any of his powers or duties to any other person unless he is specifically prohibited from doing so by the Constitution or any other law. He may not, however, delegate powers given to him under legislation of the East African Community. Notwithstanding the delegation of a particular power, the President may still continue to exercise it himself. The President may also transfer to himself or to any other person, the powers or duties of anyone holding an office in the service of the United Republic. (Transfer and Delegation of Powers Act, Cap. 511, ss. 2, 3, 4.)

NOTE Julius Nyerere is also President of TANU. For the powers and duties of the holder of that office, see the TANU Constitution.

B · REGIONAL COMMISSIONERS AND AREA COMMISSIONERS

In this section we investigate powers granted prior to independence to Provincial Commissioners or District Commissioners which are presently exercised by Regional Commissioners or Area Commissioners.

TOWNSHIPS (REMOVAL OF UNDESIRABLE PERSONS) ORDINANCE: CAP. 104

● 1. This Ordinance may be cited as the Townships (Removal of Undesirable Persons) Ordinance.

2. In this Ordinance, unless the context otherwise requires:
'Area Commissioner' means the administrative officer for the time being in charge of a district;
'district court' means a subordinate court established under the Magistrate Courts Act presided over by a Resident Magistrate.

3.—(1) Where the Area Commissioner has reasonable cause to believe that a person belongs to one of the categories specified in subsection (3) of this section and that the presence of such person within any township or other area within his district to which this Ordinance extends is, by reason of any of the matters mentioned in subsection (2) of this section, undesirable in the public interest, he may make an order (in this Ordinance referred to as a Removal Order) requiring such person:

(a)   to leave the said township or other area not later than a date to be specified in the order;

(b)   to proceed to such place as may be designated in the order, either under the escort of a person to be specified in the order or independently; and

(c)   thereafter to remain outside the said township or other area either during a period to be specified in the order or until further order.

(2) A Removal Order may be made on any of the following grounds, that is to say:

(a)   that the person has been sentenced to a term of imprisonment (other than in default of payment of fine or compensation) for an offence against the person or in relation to property, or for an offence against the Native Liquor Ordinance or the Intoxicating Liquors Ordinance; or

(b)   that the person has no regular employment or other reputable means of livelihood.

(3) A Removal Order may be made in respect of a person belonging to one or other of the following categories, that is to say:

(a) persons of any age which according to law or custom should render them subject to control, where the person whose duty it is to exercise such control is resident within Tanganyika but outside the township or other area; and

(b) persons having no settled home within the township or other area whose district of origin or last place of ordinary residence is within Tanganyika but outside the township or other area.

(4) For the purposes of paragraph (b) of subsection (3) a person shall be deemed to have a settled home within a township or other area if he satisfies the Area Commissioner:

(a) that one or other of his parents is ordinarily resident in such township or other area; or

(b) that he is, and has been for a period or periods amounting in the aggregate to not less than three years during the four years immediately preceding the month then current, ordinarily resident in such township or other area:

Provided that a person shall not be deemed to have a settled home in such township or other area under the provisions of paragraph (b) of this subsection if the Area Commissioner is satisfied from the mode of life of such person or otherwise that notwithstanding his period of residence within such township or other area he has no settled home in such township or other area and is not likely in the near future to acquire a settled home in such township or other area.

(5) This Ordinance extends to such townships and other areas as the President may, by order published in the Gazette, direct that it shall extend.

4. Every person in relation to whom a Removal Order has been made shall be provided with such subsistence allowance, in cash or in kind, as the Area Commissioner thinks sufficient to enable him to reach the place designated in the Order.

5.—(1) A person in respect of whom a Removal Order has been made may appeal against such Order to a district court.

(2) The district court on receiving notice of appeal against a Removal Order within the prescribed time may by order suspend the operation of such Removal Order on such terms (including detention in custody or the provision of sureties or the entering into recognizances or reporting to the police) as may appear expedient, pending the determination of the appeal:

Provided that any such suspension shall cease to have effect if no appeal against such Removal Order is lodged in the manner and within the time prescribed.

(3) The district court at the hearing of such appeal may receive evidence and may affirm or, on cause shown, cancel or vary the Removal Order.

(4) Either party may appeal to the High Court from the decision of the district court in such appeal on a matter of law only and the decision of the High Court shall be final and conclusive on all parties.

(5) The appellant and the Area Commissioner shall have the right to appear or be represented before the district court or the High Court at the hearing of any appeal.

(6) The High Court may make rules prescribing the manner in which and the time within which notice of appeal may be given and an appeal lodged and generally the procedure to be followed in any appeal to a district court or the High Court under this section.

6.—(1) Any person in relation to whom a Removal Order is made who wilfully fails to comply with any of the terms of such Order shall be guilty of an offence against this Ordinance:

Provided that the Area Commissioner may in writing suspend the operation of a Removal Order for such period and on such terms as he thinks fit.

(2) Any person found guilty of an offence against this Ordinance shall be liable to a fine not exceeding two hundred shillings or to imprisonment for a term not exceeding three months or to both such fine and imprisonment.

(3) A second or subsequent Removal Order may be made in relation to any person who is convicted of any offence against this Ordinance.

7.—(1) Any person in relation to whom it is proposed to make a Removal Order may be arrested by any police officer without warrant and may be detained in custody for a period not exceeding one month for the purpose of enabling the Area Commissioner to make such inquiries as may be necessary.

(2) During any period of detention under subsection (1) of this section such person shall be treated as a person awaiting trial and not as a convicted prisoner.

8. Any police officer may arrest without warrant any person who he has reason to believe is guilty of an offence against this Ordinance.

9. In any prosecution for any offence against this Ordinance any document purporting to be a Removal Order made in pursuance of the provisions of this Ordinance may be admitted in evidence without proof of its authenticity.

NOTE To determine whether the provisions of this Ordinance apply to a particular urban area, consult the subsidiary legislation made pursuant to Cap. 104.

NOTE This Ordinance was obviously intended to give the executive the power to deal with what is one of Africa's most serious social problems—the continual influx of large numbers of uneducated, untrained, and, therefore, unemployable people into urban areas. In this context, we should read Cap. 104 in connection with the Destitute Persons Ordinance, Cap. 41. Section 3 (1) of this Ordinance reads as follows:

> Where it is shown to the satisfaction of a Magistrate that any person is a destitute person, the magistrate may in his discretion order that person:
> (a) to find work and to report to the magistrate before a named date;
> (b) to be detained in custody for a period not exceeding one month with a view to work being found for him; or
> (c) if he is a native who is not dwelling in his usual place of residence, to return before a named date to his usual place of residence in Tanganyika.

By s. 2, 'destitute person' means 'any person without employment and unable to show that he has visible and sufficient means of subsistence'. These two statutes, then, give to the Government the necessary legal power to remove the destitute and unemployed from the cities and towns. In Dar es Salaam the usual way of exercising these powers has been by means of 'roundups'. At irregular intervals during the year the police round up beggars, prostitutes, idlers, and petty criminals. These unfortunates are then sent back to their villages. (See, for example, *The Nationalist*, 24 February 1969, and 25 February 1969; and *The Standard*, 24 February 1969.) In some cases the distinction between those who fall under the terms of either Cap. 41 or Cap. 104, and those who do not, becomes somewhat unclear. The following is an extract from an interview with a welfare officer concerning a major roundup which was then underway:

> Q. If women are really found practising prostitution, then why is it that they are not charged and taken to court?
> A. There must be proof that the woman was really enticing a man with intent to commit prostitution before such steps can be taken. It is difficult to find such evidence, so the best way is to repatriate them.
> (*The Nationalist*, 21 August 1968.)

On 1 July 1969, the responsibility for the Maintenance and Repatriation of Destitutes was transferred from the Ministry of Home Affairs, where it had come under the Police, to the Social Welfare and Probation Division of the Ministry of Health and Social Welfare. Under the new system, the Police continue to round people up, and keep them under supervision, but they are interviewed by officers of the Social Welfare Division who make recommendations as to the action that should be taken. If a removal order under Cap. 104 is deemed desirable, the person concerned is sent home under police escort and the local Area Commissioner and TANU leaders are requested to keep him under observation. The costs of repatriations made under Cap. 41 or Cap. 104 come out of Social Welfare Division votes, though in Cap. 41 cases some attempt is made to get a contribution from the

individual's family. If the officer of the Social Welfare Division who is
handling the case discovers that someone who has been rounded up is
lawfully employed, he will recommend that the person be released and remain
in the urban area. This whole procedure takes time and, as the Social Welfare
Division is understaffed, people must often wait in destitute camps for
lengthy periods. The police do not appear to be entirely happy with this
situation. They argue that as unemployment is the basic cause of crime in the
urban areas, the basic function of the authorities in respect of unemployed
people, once they have been rounded up, should be to repatriate them.
The feeling is that this task is not being performed as expeditiously as might
be wished. (*Sunday News*, 5 April 1970.)

During a typical month, August 1969, twenty-eight people were removed
from Dar es Salaam under Cap. 104, and two children, twenty-three adults,
and forty-seven elderly persons were repatriated from Dar es Salaam under
Cap. 41. Efforts such as these have not yet solved the problem, and as of
mid-1970, police 'roundups' continued. For example, on 30 April 1970,
'hundreds' of 'habitual criminals' and unemployed were rounded up by
police in Dar es Salaam. People who looked suspicious were stopped and
questioned about their residences and places of work, and 'many' of those
who failed to satisfy the police on these points were arrested. (*The Standard*,
1 May 1970.) Roundups have also taken place in Tanga. (*The Standard*,
9 July 1970.)

There seems to be a growing awareness that other methods of dealing
with the problem may be more appropriate and effective. Speaking on 19
December 1969, Mr T. E. J. Mwangosi, the Commissioner for Social Welfare,
stated that it was not morally right to treat ordinary citizens, who happened
to be destitute through no fault of their own, in a humiliating way by rounding
them up and forcing them to return to their homes. He added that he was
interested in more investigation of the problem and its causes and that he
wished to adopt a more humane approach to the problem. (*The Standard*,
20 December 1969.) In an article in *The Standard* of 11 June 1970, entitled,
'The Scapegoats of Society', Naijuka Kasiwaki was extremely critical of
what he called 'colonialist and unsocialist' ways of handling destitutes in
urban areas. In later statements officials of the Ministry of Health and
Social Welfare have acknowledged that it is incorrect to treat destitutes as
second-class citizens, and that the solution lies in cutting off the flow of
people to the towns. (In this context, consider a request from officials of
this Ministry to the railway authorities, that destitutes should not be
permitted to travel on buses or trains without an authorizing letter from
their Area Commissioner or a Medical Officer. It might be noted that under
the common law, a common carrier, such as the East African Railways
Corporation, is obliged to carry any person who can pay the fare.) On leaving
his post as Secretary-General of the T.Y.L., Joseph Nyerere stated that the
solution to movement from the rural areas would depend largely on the kind
of leadership exercised at the village level. He stressed that the main problem
facing the T.Y.L. was to control the flow of young people to the towns
by making the rural areas more relevant to their youthful aspirations. (*The
Standard*, 28 April 1970.) The Social Welfare Division has recognized for
some time that preventive measures are the best solution to the problem.
Since early 1969, the Division, in cooperation with TANU, has been running

educational programmes in the rural areas designed to dissuade people from moving to urban centres, particularly to Dar es Salaam.

Kenya has attempted to deal with the same general problem by means of very stringent legislation (Vagrancy Act, 1968, No. 61), which one commentator has likened in its administration to the colonial pass laws. (P. LePelley, 'Vagrancy and the Law in Kenya', *East African Law Journal*, vol. V, no. 3, 1969, p. 195.) If one analyses the operation of such laws, it becomes apparent that their essential purpose is the control and suppression of the urban proletariat. Why should it be necessary to maintain laws of this kind, and even to expand their application? (See Romano Ledda, 'Social Classes and Political Struggle in Africa', *International Socialist Journal*, August 1967, p. 560.) Very little has been written about urban life in Tanzania. Probably the book which best captures the flavour of Dar es Salaam, although it is now extremely dated, is Leslie, *A Survey of Dar es Salaam*, Oxford University Press, London, 1963. See also, 'Dar es Salaam: City, Port and Region', *Tanzania Notes and Records*, no. 71, 1970.

POLICE FORCE ORDINANCE:
CAP. 322

● 40.—(1) Subject to the provisions of any order made under subsection (8), no assembly or procession in any public place shall be convened, collected, formed or organized by any person except in accordance with a valid permit issued under the provisions of subsection (2).

(2) Any person who is desirous of convening, collecting, forming or organizing any assembly or procession in any public place shall first make application for a permit in that behalf to the Area Commissioner for the district in which such place is situated or, if there is no Area Commissioner for such district, to the Regional Commissioner for the Region of which that district is a part, and, if the Area Commissioner or the Regional Commissioner, as the case may be, is satisfied, having regard to all the circumstances, including (without prejudice to the generality of the foregoing) the availability of a sufficient number of police officers to direct the conduct of the proposed assembly or procession, that the assembly or procession is not likely to cause a breach of the peace, or to prejudice the public safety or the maintenance of public order or to be used for any unlawful purpose, he shall, subject to the provisions of subsection (3), issue a permit in such form as the Commissioner may approve, authorizing such person to convene, collect, form or organize such assembly or procession, as the case may be, and defining the conditions subject to which such assembly or procession is authorized.

(3) The Area Commissioner or the Regional Commissioner, as the case may be, may refuse to grant a permit:

(a) if the applicant, or any person or organization or body of

persons associated directly or indirectly with the application
or intended or likely, in the opinion of the Area Commissioner
or Regional Commissioner, as the case may be, to be associated
with or concerned in the holding of the assembly or procession,
has, in the course of or in relation to any assembly or procession
within the preceding twelve months contravened the provisions
of this Ordinance or of any other law or any condition of a
permit issued under this section or any section replaced by
this section; or

(b)   if the assembly or procession has been advertised or otherwise
publicised in contravention of the provisions of subsection (7).

(3A) Where a permit has been refused under subsection (3), the
applicant therefor may appeal against such refusal to the Minister
whose decision shall be final.

(4) The Area Commissioner or Regional Commissioner, as the
case may be, who has issued a permit under this section in respect
of such assembly or procession may at any time:

(a)   cancel such permit if he is satisfied that the assembly or procession is likely to cause a breach of the peace, or to prejudice
the public safety or the maintenance of public order, or to be
used for any unlawful purpose, or if any condition of such
permit is being or has been contravened; or

(b)   vary the conditions of such permit.

(5) No cancellation of a permit and no variation of any condition
of a permit under the provisions of subsection (4) shall have effect
until notice in writing thereof has been:

(a)   communicated to the person to whom the permit was issued
or left at the usual abode or place of business of such
person; and

(b)   posted up in such place or places or otherwise publicised in
such manner as, in the opinion of the person cancelling such
permit or varying such condition, will give effective publicity
to such notice.

(6) The officer in charge of police, any police officer above the
rank of inspector or any magistrate, may stop or prevent the holding
of any assembly or procession in a public place which has been convened, collected, formed or organized otherwise than in accordance
with a permit issued under subsection (2), or in regard to which
any condition of a permit has been or is being contravened, and may,
for any of the purposes aforesaid, give or issue such orders as he may
consider necessary or expedient, including orders for the dispersal
of any such assembly or procession as aforesaid.

(7) No assembly or procession in respect of which a permit under this section is required shall be advertised or otherwise publicised until such permit has been issued.

(8) The President may by order declare that the provisions of this section shall not apply to any assembly or procession convened, collected, formed, or organized exclusively for one or more, or for a combination of one or more of such purposes as may be specified

● in such order.

QUESTION Is an *ngoma* an 'assembly' within the meaning of s. 40 (1)?

NOTE Prior to independence the power granted under s. 40 of Cap. 322 was exercised by the police commander in the district. Why was this situation changed?

WITCHCRAFT ORDINANCE: CAP. 18

● 8.—(1) If it shall be reported to an Area Commissioner that a person is suspected of practising witchcraft, and the Area Commissioner, after due inquiry, shall be satisfied that the person so suspected causes or is likely to cause fear, annoyance or injury in mind, person or property to any other person by means of pretended witchcraft or is practising witchcraft for gain or reward, he may, for reasons to be recorded, order the person so suspected to reside in any specified locality within his district until such order may be varied or revoked, and further or in the alternative may order such person to report to the Area Commissioner or to a District Council at such intervals not being less than seven days as he shall direct until such order

● shall be varied or revoked.

NOTE Other sections of this Act create offences in respect of which a charge must be laid and a trial held. Any order made by an Area Commissioner under s. 8 (1), must be forwarded to the Regional Commissioner along with the reasons for making the order. The Regional Commissioner may then vary or quash such order, or he may direct the individual concerned to reside in a specified locality within the region. The President may also vary or quash orders, and may likewise direct the person against whom an order has been made to reside in any specified locality within the country. Two further things should be noted about this Ordinance. First, there is no section in the Ordinance which attempts to exclude the jurisdiction of the courts, as does, for example, s. 3 of the Preventive Detention Act. Second, note that s.8(1) lays down fairly precise conditions as to when the Area Commissioner may exercise this particular power. Compare the language used in 2.8(1) to that used in s.2 of the Deportation Ordinance; s.2(1) of the Preventive Detention Act; s.21 A of the Newspaper Ordinance; and s.7(1) of the Regions and Regional Commissioners Act. Do the two factors noted indicate anything about the possibility of controlling the exercise of this power?

NOTE The power created by s.8(1) has been used as recently as July 1970. See *The Standard*, 2 July 1970.

Since Independence, Regional Commissioners and Area Commissioners have also been given the following powers.

REGIONS AND REGIONAL COMMISSIONERS ACT, 1962: CAP. 461

● 7.—(1) When the Regional Commissioner has reason to believe that any person is likely to commit a breach of the peace or disturb the public tranquillity, or to do any act that may probably occasion a breach of the peace or disturb the public tranquillity, and that such breach cannot be prevented otherwise than by detaining such person in custody, the Commissioner may arrest or order a police officer verbally or in writing to arrest such person.

(2) A person arrested under the powers conferred by this section shall be taken as soon as is practicable before a magistrate empowered under section 41 of the Criminal Procedure Code to deal with the case and, if such person is not brought before such a magistrate within forty-eight hours after he was taken into custody, he shall be released and shall not be again arrested for the same cause in pursuance of the powers conferred by this section.

(3) Where a Regional Commissioner arrests or orders the arrest of any person under the powers conferred by this section, he shall, at the time of making or ordering the arrest or forthwith thereafter, record his reasons therefor in writing. The Commissioner shall deliver a copy of his recorded reasons, or cause a copy thereof to be delivered, to the magistrate or, if such person has been released before he is brought before the magistrate, as soon as is practicable after such release: Provided that the production of a copy of recorded reasons under this section shall not authorize the magistrate to dispense with any provision requiring information to be given on oath.

(4) A magistrate before whom a person is brought under this section may, in his discretion, detain such person in custody until the completion of the inquiry prescribed by section 51 of the Criminal Procedure
● Code.

NOTE Section 7 of the Area Commissioners Act (Cap. 466) has, *mutatis mutandis*, exactly the same wording as the above.

NOTE Regional Commissioners, Area Commissioners and the Minister responsible for refugee matters (presently the Second Vice-President) are given wide powers under the Refugees (Control) Act, 1965 (Act No. 2 of

1966). This Act covers all aspects of the life of refugees in Tanzania. A wide discretion is granted to deport refugees from Tanzania (s.9), or to order them to live in refugee settlements (s.12). Once in a settlement the refugee must obey all rules made by the Minister or a Regional Commissioner or an Area Commissioner. He may be arrested without warrant by an Administrative Officer, a settlement commandant, a police officer, a prisons officer, or a member of the T.P.D.F. for any offence or for a refugee 'disciplinary offence'. Once a refugee is arrested, he may be held in custody, apparently indefinitely, pending the institution of proceedings for the offence or disciplinary offence (s.16). Disciplinary offences include leaving a settlement, breaking the rules of a settlement, and acting 'in a manner prejudicial to good order and discipline' in a settlement (s.13). Under s.10 of the Act, the Minister, a Regional Commissioner, or an Area Commissioner, may detain a refugee if he is satisfied that the refugee is acting in a manner prejudicial to peace and good order in Tanzania, or is prejudicing the relations of Tanzania and any foreign government. Further, if it appears to the Minister, a Regional Commissioner or Area Commissioner, that a refugee has committed any offence outside Tanzania, such refugee may be detained. Detention is for an indefinite period, but the Minister is required to review all refugee detention orders once every three months. These powers have been used at the request of the recognized liberation movements to put away any of their fellow countrymen whom they suspect of spying on them or with whom they have other quarrels. In some cases these people have been kept in detention for as long as four years. This practice has been justified on the grounds that as spying on a liberation movement or attempting to sabotage its activities was not an offence in Tanzania (and does not come within the ambit of the Preventive Detention Act), some kind of measures were needed to provide security for these movements. With the passage of the National Security Act, 1970 (Act No. 3 of 1970) under which espionage or sabotage directed against a liberation movement is made an offence (s.9), it might be argued that some of this justification has disappeared. Under international law some doubt exists as to whether it is proper to classify freedom fighters temporarily in Tanzania as refugees. If such people are not refugees in a legal sense then presumably the provisions of the Refugees (Control) Act could not be made applicable to them. This problem has been solved by the simple device of declaring that, for example, all nationals of Namibia or Rhodesia entering Tanzania without proper exit papers from their country of origin are 'refugees' for the purposes of the Act. (G.N. No. 198 of 1969.)

Before concluding this section it should be noted that while Regional Commissioners and Area Commissioners hold wide powers, they are somewhat less omnipotent than their colonial predecessors, the Provincial Commissioners and District Commissioners. The fact that Regional Commissioners are *ex officio* Members of Parliament, and normally are appointed as Regional Secretaries of TANU, means that forums exist in which these officials can be criticized and called to account. In this respect it is important to note that Regional and Area Commissioners perform a dual role, which is part administrative and part political. Thus, while a Regional Commissioner is the administrative head of a Region, he is also Regional Secretary of the Party and a member of the N.E.C. and the National Conference. Likewise, in addition to his administrative responsibilities, an Area Commissioner will normally be District Secretary of the Party and a member of the National Conference. It is also significant that neither Regional Commissioners nor Area Commissioners possess any judicial powers. As noted, prior to 1962, Provincial Commissioners and District Commissioners performed important judicial and administrative functions in relation to both the subordinate courts and the local courts. These powers devolved on full-time magistrates as part of the general post-Independence impetus towards separating judicial and executive functions at all levels.[6]

NOTE During the colonial period, considerable power—executive, administrative, and judicial—was exercised by Chiefs. This system was established in pursuance of the theory of 'indirect rule' introduced into Tanganyika by Governor Cameron. After independence, it was decided to establish a more democratic system of local government. The chiefs were stripped of their executive powers by the simple expedient of repealing the statute which had established chieftainship. (African Chiefs Ordinance (Repeal) Act, 1963, Cap. 517.) It was assumed that the chiefs were divested of their judicial functions by giving jurisdiction in customary law matters to the Primary Courts under the Magistrates Courts Act. It was, however, found necessary in 1969 to make the situation absolutely clear. Thus the African Chiefs Act (Act No. 53 of 1969) was enacted to provide that Chiefs were not to exercise any function under customary law or otherwise. While the process of removing the Chiefs from positions of authority has, in certain cases, given rise to considerable conflict (see, e.g., Andrew Maguire, *Towards Uhuru in Tanzania*, Cambridge University Press, London, 1969), nothing approaching the struggles of Nkrumah and Obote against traditional authorities has been experienced. In fact, many former Tanzanian chiefs have been given positions of considerable importance and influence.

NOTE   See also the Public Order Ordinance, Cap. 304.

NOTE   This chapter has included no discussion of the powers of party officials. The basic reason for this is that while party officials have considerable authority, they do not, in their capacity as party officials, have any legal powers. Examples of party officials misusing their authority may be found in the extracts from the Annual Reports of the Permanent Commission of Enquiry in Chapter V. For a discussion of this problem, see Norman Miller, 'The Rural African Party: Political Participation in Tanzania' in *American Political Science Review*, vol. LXIV, no. 2, 1970, p. 548.

C · JUDICIAL CONTROLS

In this section we investigate certain rules which permit the courts to exercise a degree of control over the powers wielded by the executive.

[6] This was in fact declared to be the policy of the colonial government as long ago as

First, however, we shall review certain points raised in Chapters I and II concerning the nature and purpose of colonial administration, the role of the courts in the processes of that administration, and the somewhat ambivalent position in which the courts find themselves today. The subordinate courts before independence were wholehearted instruments of the imperial system, and it would have been absurd for either administrator or 'native' to regard these courts as defenders of the people's rights. In any case, the legal remedies available to curb the administration could be sought only in the High Court which, for geographical, cultural, and financial reasons, was beyond the reach of most people. This is not to say that the High Court was totally blind to the authoritarian nature of the régime. Its members were professionally trained lawyers who frequently offered searing criticisms of administrative officers' bland disregard for the most basic principles of justice. Yet in addition to the chasm which separated it from the people, the High Court had to contend also with an extremely jealous government, and the legislature which it controlled. Thus, any significant function that the courts might have had in checking administrative action was severely limited in advance by the type of legislation enacted. Consequently one finds relatively few cases in colonial East Africa dealing with judicial review of the actions of public authorities, and virtually none of these involves an African plaintiff. This situation might be regarded as an application of the principle that in a class-oriented society, legal rights and guarantees are designed to protect members of the ruling class, but are not intended to apply to relations between the state and the oppressed class.

Because the courts had long been identified as upholders of colonial rule, it is not surprising that the post-independence government viewed them with some suspicion. In the years immediately following independence, this atmosphere of mistrust was heightened by the tendency of the courts to show a greater concern for the rights of the subject *vis-à-vis* an African government than they did *vis-à-vis* the colonial government. When we add to these factors the present tendency of TANU to bring all aspects of the national life under its control, we can easily see why the courts have been unable to assume a major role in curbing possible abuses on the part of the state.

We now investigate certain specific rules of law governing the circumstances under which the courts may attempt to control executive action.

The rules concerning judicial control of administrative action are largely

---

1949, though it did not make much significant progress in this direction. See the African Conference on Local Courts and Customary Law, *Report*, op. cit., p. 102. For a discussion of the roles and duties of Regional Commissioners and Area Commissioners, see S. Dryden, *Local Administration in Tanzania*, ch. II; and Tordoff, *Government and Politics in Tanzania*, ch. IV.

intelligible only in the context of the particular power the exercise of which it is sought to control. In the first two sections of this chapter, we looked at those powers which allow restrictions to be placed on the freedom of the individual. While it is impossible to detail the many other powers possessed by the government, it is important to remember that these are extremely wide, particularly those concerning the regulation of economic activity. For example, the ability of the Tanzanian Government to control agriculture and land use is extremely broad. Agricultural officers are empowered to enter land or premises for purposes of inspection, to eradicate pests or diseases, to control certain crops, to grade and to license, and to seize and detain certain prohibited articles. Likewise the Minister for Lands, Housing and Urban Development may revoke rights of occupancy, order the forfeiture of government leases, alter customary leaseholds, and acquire land for public purposes.[7]

Because Tanzanian Law recognizes the supremacy of Parliament and because the Interim Constitution does not contain any limits on the power of the legislature to interfere with individual rights, the scope of review by the courts is confined essentially to statutory interpretation. In other words, because Parliament has unlimited ability to enact legislation, it thereby also has unlimited ability to confer powers on the government and its officials; therefore any limitation on the scope of a particular power must be found in the words of the statute which created that power. We can also approach the problem from another direction and say that officials at all levels possess certain powers because those powers were conferred upon them by particular legislative acts. Thus, a given official may exercise only those powers granted to him by law, and in order to determine precisely what those powers are, we must look to the wording of the relevant statute.[8]

In interpreting statutes, the courts do not attempt to give comprehensive opinions which will apply to all situations. The courts are called upon in specific situations when an individual or group believes that a particular official or governmental body has acted unlawfully, or, in less common cases, the government itself will ask the courts to determine whether a contemplated action is permissible.

[7] See the Plant Protection Ordinance, Cap. 133; the Produce Export Ordinance, Cap. 137; the Sugar (Control) Ordinance, Cap. 141; the Tea Ordinance, Cap. 291; the Cotton Ordinance, Cap. 362; the Pyrethrum Ordinance, Cap. 421; the Coffee Industry Ordinance, Cap. 422; the Agricultural Products (Control and Marketing) Act, 1962, Cap. 486; the Land Ordinance, Cap. 113; the Land Acquisition Act, 1967, Act No. 47 of 1967; the Urban Leasehold (Acquisition and Regrant) Act, 1968, Act No. 22 of 1968; the Customary Leaseholds (Enfranchisement) Act, 1968, Act No. 47 of 1968 as amended by No. 43 of 1969; and the Graves (Removal) Act, 1969, Act No. 9 of 1969.
[8] A noted Belgian Marxist has argued that one means of preventing the growth of bureaucratic power in a socialist state is to require that officials always obey the law. Ernest Mandel, *The Marxist Theory of the State*, Merit Publishers, New York City, 1969, p. 29.

In one important sense the courts are not confined solely to the words of statutes when a question of interpretation arises. We shall see that there are rules used by the courts in statutory interpretation which, in spite of the principle of parliamentary supremacy, do constitute a kind of residual bill of rights. These rules recognize that while the legislature has the ability to interfere with any 'rights', it may only succeed in doing so if it expresses this intention in unequivocal language, and, in certain cases, such interference will only be upheld if it is carried out according to certain procedures. Thus, while the courts always insist that their only purpose in interpreting statutes is to discover the intention of the legislature in enacting a particular statute, and then to give effect to that intention, the methods they use for discovering that intention often allow them to inject their own ideas of justice into the process of government.

Two important legislative practices severely limit the ability of the courts to control the exercise of statutory powers. First, the legislature may insert words into an act which are designed to prevent the courts reviewing the exercise of the power established by the act. This can be done in two ways. On the one hand, specific words may be used to exclude the jurisdiction of the courts. Thus, we have s. 3 of the Preventive Detention Act: 'No order made under this Act shall be questioned in any court.' If '... there are express words clearly defining the intention of the legislature' to deprive the citizen of access to the courts, then the courts themselves are bound to give effect to such words. (*Re Marle's Application* [1958] E.A. 153 (K).) However, it has been held that an exclusionary clause of this kind is only sufficient to protect from review acts which are prima facie within the scope of the power granted. Where the limits of the statutory power are exceeded, its purported exercise will be in law a complete nullity and there will therefore be nothing to which the protection of the exclusionary clause can attach. In such a case, the way will then be opened for judicial review. (*Anisminic* v. *Foreign Compensation Commission* [1969] 1 All E.R. 208 (HL).) For example, ss. 2(1) (a) and 2(1) (b) of the Preventive Detention Act lay down the circumstances under which the power to detain is to be exercised. In a case where a person has been detained for a reason not apparently subsumed within either of these sections, it could be argued that the Act does not give the power to make such an order. If this were so, the order in question would be a nullity, the protection of s. 3 would not attach, and a court could intervene, presumably by way of habeas corpus proceedings. (In favour of this view, see *Re Desai* (1954) 2 T.L.R. (R) 192; opposed, see *Chite* v. *East African Community* [1970] E.A. 487 (K)). On the other hand, a clause may be inserted which says that a power is to be exercised 'if the Minister is satisfied' that a particular state of affairs exists. (For example, s.2 of the Preventive Detention Act.) Thus the question of whether a power has been exercised lawfully remains a subjective matter for the discretion of the person to whom the power has been entrusted. The English courts have recently held that even in such cases the discretion created is not without limits and that a judge may enquire whether any objective basis existed for the exercise of the Minister's discretion. (*Padfield* v. *Minister of Agriculture, Fisheries, and Food* [1968] 1 All E.R. 694.) East African cases indicate, however, that the courts will be extremely loath to review the exercise by a Minister of such a discretion. (For example, *Uganda* v. *Commissioner of Prisons* [1966] E.A. 514 (U); *Re Ibrahim* [1970] E.A. 162 (U).)

The second common device is for the legislature to grant powers, which according to the words used, are limitless. The courts can only limit the exercise of a particular power within the boundaries set by the statute granting the power. When that statute does not indicate any limits on the power, the courts are rendered incapable of controlling its exercise. For example, s. 5(1) (f) of the Price Control Ordinance (Cap. 309), reads as follows:

> The Price Controller may from time to time by order published in the Gazette or displayed in a prominent position in the district headquarters of the district or districts to which such order applies prescribe the type of packing, weight, size, quality and the processing and ingredients of any goods manufactured in Tanganyika.

Since the courts are required to find the meaning of a piece of legislation from the words used in the legislation itself, it is difficult to see how they would be able to place limits on the exercise of a power which is plainly limitless.[9]

Finally, it must be remembered that the courts do not go out looking for unjust acts, they must wait until individuals bring specific matters before them. Regardless of all the financial, historical, geographical and cultural barriers which prevent the people of Tanzania from making full use of the courts, can the remedies which exist be referred to as 'rights' when the mass of the people are unaware of their existence? To put it another way, is there any point in talking about controls on executive power when most people are unaware that there are legal limits on the power of government

[9] For an expansion of the ideas expressed above, see a paper by Professor Seidman, 'Administrative Law and Legitimacy in Anglo-Phonic Africa', op. cit.; and for an analysis, which, after thirty years is still the *locus classicus* on statutory interpretation, see Professor Willis's, 'Statute Interpretation in a Nutshell', *Canadian Bar Review*, vol. XVI, 1938, p. 1. For statutory interpretation in Tanzania, see S. K. Huber, 'Statutory Interpretation and Judicial Discretion', *Journal of the Denning Law Society*, vol. II, no. 1, 1967, p. 99; 'Bail Under the Official and Other Secrets Act', *Eastern Africa Law Review*, vol. I, no. 1, 1968, p. 91; 'The Application of Commercial Law Doctrine in Prosecutions for Commercial Crimes', *Eastern Africa Law Review*, vol. I, no. 2, 1968, p. 161; 'Use of Marginal Notes in East Africa', *Eastern Africa Law Review*, vol. II, no. 1, 1969, p. 107.

and party officials, or they have little or no idea how such limits may be enforced ?[10]

CRIMINAL PROCEDURE CODE: CAP. 20

● 348.—(1) The High Court may, whenever it thinks fit, direct:

(a) that any person within the limits of Tanganyika be brought up before the court to be dealt with according to law;

(b) that any person illegally or improperly detained in public or private custody within such limits be set at liberty;

(c) that any prisoner detained in any prison situate within such limits be brought before the court to be there examined as a witness in any matter pending or to be inquired into in such court;

(d) that any prisoner detained as aforesaid be brought before a court-martial or any commissioners acting under the authority of any commission from the President for trial or be examined touching any matter pending before such court-martial or commissioners respectively;

(e) that any prisoner within such limits be removed from one custody to another for the purpose of trial; and

(f) that the body of a defendant within such limits be brought in on a return of *cepi corpus* to a writ of attachment.

(2) The High Court may from time to time make rules to regulate the
● procedure in cases under this section.

NOTE   The Habeas Corpus Rules, G.N. No. 150 of 1930, provide that an application under s. 348 shall first be made *ex parte* to a Judge in Chambers. If the application is not dismissed, a summons shall issue to the person having custody of the person detained ordering that person to appear to show cause why the person detained should not be released. The Judge may also order that the body of the person who is alleged to be improperly detained be produced before him in court. Pending the return of the summons, the court may also order that the person detained, if he is in public custody, be admitted to bail. If he is in private custody, the court may order his release on such terms and conditions as may be specified. On return of the summons, the court will inquire into the merits of the detention. The Register of the High Court in Dar es Salaam indicates that habeas corpus is, in fact, very seldom used. (It should be noted that the figures which follow do not give the complete picture, since there are also separate High Court Registries in Mwanza, Arusha, and Tanga, but it is suggested that they indicate a general pattern.) Of the twenty-two applications for habeas corpus between 1921 and 1969, twelve involved the alleged improper detention of an individual by a public authority, nine involved such detentions by private persons, and one application was not proceeded with. Of the twelve applications involving detentions by public authorities, five were withdrawn, six were granted, and one was refused. Of the five applications withdrawn, three were withdrawn

[10] See Nyerere, *Freedom and Development,* op. cit., p. 1.

because the detainees were released before the applications came on for hearing. Thus, although the remedy is seldom sought, it would appear that in cases of detentions by public authorities, habeas corpus is still a valuable weapon: six of the seven cases where a hearing proceeded, resulted in the persons detained being released. The applications in respect of private detentions, dealt mainly with the custody of children, and of these one was withdrawn, two were granted and six were refused.

Exhaustive judicial discussions of the nature of the remedy of habeas corpus and the procedure to be followed when seeking it, can be found in *Ibingira* v. *Uganda* (*No. 2*) [1966] E.A. 445 (CA); and *In Re Patel* (1956) 2 T.L.R. (R) 227. It appears that in addition to the remedy available under s. 348 of the Criminal Procedure Code, application may alternatively, or subsequently, be made to the High Court to grant an order of habeas corpus, in the exercise of its general common law jurisdiction. (*Re Shah* (*No. 2*) (1955) 22 E.A.C.A. 216.) The distinction is important because, if the High Court in the exercise of its criminal jurisdiction refuses to grant an order there may be no appeal to the Court of Appeal, while an appeal will lie from a refusal of the High Court when exercising its civil jurisdiction. (*Re Shah* (*No. 1*) (1955) 22 E.A.C.A. 381; *Ibingira* v. *Uganda* (*No. 2*).)

Habeas corpus does not, in practice, appear to be a very effective remedy whereby specifically political detainees may obtain their release. (See *Ibingira* v. *Uganda* (*No. 1*) [1966] E.A. 306 (CA); *Ibingira* v. *Uganda* (*No. 2*); *Uganda* v. *Commissioner of Prisons; ex parte Matovu* [1966] E.A. 514 (U). See also a comment by Professor Ghai on the *Matovu* case in *Eastern Africa Law Review*, vol. 1, no. 1, 1968, p. 68.) In fact, a recent Uganda case suggests that where a detention order is the result of a deliberate decision by a Minister, the courts will be very reluctant to issue habeas corpus. (*Re Ibrahim* [1970] E.A. 162 (U).)

The cases which follow indicate other judicial remedies available to the individual who alleges that statutory powers have been improperly exercised.

PATEL V. PLATEAU LICENSING COURT[11]

● O'CONNOR, C.J.: This is an application on the part of Ambalal Shankerbhai Patel to make absolute an Order nisi for 'a writ of certiorari and mandamus' to the Chairman and Members of the Plateau Liquor Licensing Court to restore and reissue to Ambalal Shankerbhai Patel the non-spiritous liquor licence cancelled by that court on 10th May, 1954.

The facts are not in dispute and are that the applicant, Ambalal Shankerbhai Patel was the holder, in respect of his business premises, of a non-spiritous liquor licence for the Uasin Gishu District of Kenya for the year 1954. On 27th January 1954, he was convicted by the Resident Magistrate, of allowing beer purchased on his premises to be consumed thereon, but no order was made by the Resident

---

11 Kenya, Supreme Court, 1954, 27 K.L.R. 147.

Magistrate disqualifying the applicant from holding a licence. On 10th May 1954, a sitting of the Plateau Liquor Licensing Court was held, of which no notice was given to the applicant and at which he was not present. At that meeting an application was made by the Inspector in charge of the Crime Branch that the applicant's licence be cancelled. That application was supported by a letter from the Superintendent of Police, Upper Rift Valley, asking for the cancellation of the applicant's licence on the grounds of his conviction already mentioned and stating that in addition to that conviction, there were two more convictions recorded against him under the Penal Code. Under section 50 (2) of the Ordinance, the holder of any retail liquor licence is liable (in addition to any other penalty provided by the Ordinance) to forfeit such licence if he is convicted of an offence under the Liquor Ordinance and a previous conviction within the preceding 12 months of the same or any other offence under that Ordinance is proved, or if three previous convictions within the preceding five years are proved. This section gives a clear indication of the view of the legislature as to the number of previous convictions which should cause a retail liquor licence to be liable to be forfeited in addition to the imposition of a penalty under the Ordinance. It will be observed that the previous convictions said to have been recorded against the applicant were two and not three, that they were said to be under the Penal Code not under the Liquor Ordinance, that the dates and descriptions of them were not given, and that they were not proved. However, the Plateau Liquor Licensing Court, apparently on the strength of the Superintendent's letter, cancelled the applicant's licence without giving any notice to him or giving him an opportunity to make any representations or to controvert the statements contained in the Superintendent's letter, or, if he desired to do so, to point out that, even if correct, those statements would not amount to grounds for forfeiture of a licence under section 50 (2) of the Ordinance.

A notice of the ruling of the Licensing Court was posted on the notice board outside the district commissioner's office between 10th and 17th May, 1954; but the applicant was not notified of the cancellation of his licence until 16th July 1954, when the district commissioner wrote to him informing him to send in the licence. Meanwhile, having seen the notice outside the district commissioner's office, the applicant had already launched these proceedings alleging that there had been a denial of natural justice in hearing other persons in support of the cancellation of his licence without giving him an opportunity of being heard.

The general principles which should guide quasi-judicial or administrative bodies to whom the decision of questions in dispute between parties has been entrusted are very well settled. Lord Loreburn, L.C., in *Board of Education* v. *Rice*, discussing the obligations of a tribunal of this character, said: 'They have no power to administer an oath and need not examine witnesses. They can obtain information in any way they think best, always giving a fair opportunity to those who are parties in the controversy for correcting or contradicting any relevant statement prejudicial to their view.' In 1915 in *Local Government Board* v. *Arlidge*, this statement of the law was reaffirmed by the House of Lords and it was held that a party to a dispute before a tribunal of this nature is not entitled to an oral hearing, but that the tribunal can act according to its own procedure and obtain its information in any way it thinks best, but that it must always give a fair opportunity to those who are parties to the controversy to correct or contradict any relevant statement prejudicial to their views. (Per Viscount Haldane, L.C.)

In *Rex* v. *Architects' Registration Tribunal*, it was held that not to give a party a real and effectual opportunity of meeting any relevant allegations made against him was contrary to natural justice. In *Stafford* v. *Minister of Health*, the *Board of Education* v. *Rice* case and the *Arlidge* case were followed and Charles, J. said, 'the appellant has, however, the inalienable right of every citizen to have his case considered before the adjudicating authority comes to a decision'. In *General Council of Medical Education* v. *Spackman*, Viscount Simon, L.C. said, 'unless Parliament otherwise enacts, the duty of considering the defence of a party accused, before pronouncing the accused to be rightly adjudged guilty, rests upon any tribunal, whether strictly judicial or not, which is given the duty of investigating his behaviour and taking disciplinary action against him. The form in which this duty is discharged—e.g. whether by hearing evidence viva voce or otherwise —is for the rules of the tribunal to decide. What matters is that the accused should not be condemned without being first given a fair chance of explanation'. And again the dictum of Lord Loreburn in *Board of Education* v. *Rice* was approved.

But it is argued by Mr O'Beirne for the Licensing Court that the Kenya legislature has otherwise enacted, and that the procedure followed by the Plateau Licensing Court was in accordance with section 23 (4) of the Liquor Ordinance, which Mr O'Beirne argues, allows a licence to be cancelled without giving the applicant a hearing of any kind. That sub-section reads:

(4)   A licensing court, when so sitting, may, at any time, without hearing the holder of the licence and without assigning any reason therefore, cancel a licence issued under the provisions of this Ordinance with effect from such date as the court may determine.

Mr. Couldrey, on the other hand, argues that the words 'without hearing the holder of the licence' mean 'without giving the holder of a licence an oral hearing'; but that they do not mean that his licence can be taken away without notice, upon the representations of the police, or of a hostile third party, and without giving the holder of the licence a fair (or any) opportunity to correct or contradict any relevant statement prejudicial to his view by making written representations for the consideration of the Licensing Court.

Mr Couldrey cites, in support of his proposition, *The King* v. *Tribunal of Appeal under the Housing Act*. In that case, a local authority acting under statutory powers, prohibited a company from carrying out certain building operations, on the grounds that these would interfere with the provision of dwelling houses. Under certain rules of procedure made by the Minister, a party prohibited was given a right of appeal to an Appeal Tribunal. These rules provided for notice of appeal to be filed by the appellant and for a statement in reply to be filed by the local authority stating to what extent they admitted the facts stated in the appellant's notice of appeal and including a concise statement of the grounds on which the order was based. The Appeal Tribunal was empowered to require either party 'to furnish in writing such further particulars as they think necessary'. Rule 7 (1) was as follows:

If, after considering the notice of appeal and the statement of the local authority in reply and any further particulars which may have been furnished by either party, the Appeal Tribunal are of opinion that the case is of such nature that it can properly be determined without a hearing, they may dispense with a hearing, and may determine the appeal summarily.

The Appeal Tribunal in that case decided the appeal against the company upon a consideration only of the appellant's notice of appeal and the local authority's statement in reply, without calling on the appellant company for further particulars or giving the appellant company any opportunity of controverting the statements contained in the local authority's reply. The company appealed to the court and the case was heard by the Lord Chief Justice and two Judges of the King's Bench.

Lord Reading, L.C.J. said:

The first question is: 'What is the meaning of that rule?' [i.e. rule 7]: I think it means that they may dispense with an oral hearing, that the decision in *Arlidge's* case is applicable to the present, and that a hearing by the consideration of the parties' cases as stated in writing would be sufficient. But there must be a hearing, although not necessarily an oral one.

The tribunal had the power under rule 6 to require either the appellants or the respondents to furnish further particulars, but they did not do so. Under those circumstances I cannot think that there has been a hearing of an appeal.

The principle of law applicable to such a case is well stated by Kelly, C.B., in *Wood* v. *Wood*. In a passage which is cited with approval by Lord Macnaghten in *Lapointe* v. *L'Association, etc. de Montreal*, where speaking of the committee of a mutual insurance society, the Chief Baron says: 'They are bound in the exercise of their functions by the rule expressed in the maxim, *audi alteram partem*, that no man should be condemned to consequences resulting from alleged misconduct unheard, and without having the opportunity of making his defence.' This rule is not confined to the conduct of strictly legal tribunals, but it is applicable to every tribunal or body of persons invested with authority to adjudicate upon matters involving civil consequences to individuals.

Sankey, J. said:

Now a hearing in my view need not be an oral one, it may be on written representations. But the party against whom it is sought to make an order must have an opportunity at least of stating his case in writing and so making his defence.

It was held that the meaning of Rule 7 was that the Appeal Tribunal might dispense with an oral hearing, not that they might dispense with a hearing of any kind, and that they were bound to give the appellants a hearing in the sense of an opportunity of making out their case. It was further held by the majority of the court that, in the circumstances, the Appeal Tribunal, not having given the appellant company any opportunity of correcting or explaining the statements in the local authority's reply which were prejudicial to their case, had not given the appellant company a hearing at all, and that the order dismissing the appeal must be set aside.

A provision such as section 23(4) of the Liquor Ordinance which purports to deprive the subject of an elementary right of natural justice of his property, should be construed strictly. In *Arlicge's* case, Lord Shaw described a procedure of hearing one side and refusing to hear the other as a 'defiance of elementary standards'. We should hesitate to impute to the legislature an intention to enact a provision in defiance of elementary standards of justice. Whenever the language of the legislature admits of two constructions, and if construed in one way would lead to obvious injustice, the courts act upon the view that such a result could not have been intended unless an intention has been manifest in plain words. A sense of the possible injustice of an interpretation ought not to induce Judges to do violence to a well-settled rule of construction, but it may properly lead to the selection of one rather than the other of two reasonable interpretations. We are of opinion that to construe the word 'hearing' in section 23(4) as an oral hearing is both reasonable and supported by authority and that, as it avoids manifest injustice, that construction should be preferred. Accordingly, following *The King* v. *Tribunal of Appeal Under the Housing Act* we construe the words 'without hearing the holder of the licence' in section 23(4) as meaning 'without giving the holder of the licence an oral hearing' and we hold that that sub-section does not exempt the Licensing Court from giving the holder of a licence a fair opportunity to correct or contradict in writing any relevant statement prejudicial to his views.

● *Certiorari and mandamus must go.*

NOTE In *de Souza* v. *Chairman and Members of the Tanga Town Council* ([1961] E.A. 377 (CA)), the rules of natural justice were summarized as follows:

1. If a statute prescribes, or statutory rules or regulations binding on the domestic tribunal prescribe, the procedure to be followed, that procedure must be observed.
2. If no procedure is laid down, there may be an obvious implication that some form of inquiry must be made such as will enable the tribunal fairly to determine the question at issue.
3. In such a case the tribunal, which should be properly constituted, must do its best to act justly and to reach just ends by just means. It must act in good faith and fairly listen to both sides. It is not bound, however, to treat the question as if it were a trial . . .
4. The person accused must know the nature of the accusation made.
5. A fair opportunity must be given to those who are parties to the controversy to contradict any statement prejudicial to their view, and to make any relevant statement they may desire to bring forward.
6. The tribunal should see that matter which has come into existence for the purpose of the [proceeding] is made available to both sides and, once the [proceeding] has started, if the tribunal receives a communication from one party or from a third party, it should give the other party an opportunity of commenting on it.

RE AN APPLICATION
BY BUKOBA GYMKHANA CLUB[12]

Summary

The Bukoba Gymkhana Club, which had held a liquor licence for about thirty-four years, applied for renewal for six months of its licence under s.9 of the Intoxicating Liquors Ordinance to the Bukoba Township Liquor Licensing Board. At its half-yearly meeting held under s.10 ibid., the board rejected the application and in its letter of 13 September 1962, informed the Club that the application was rejected on the ground that the Club's constitution was 'still largely discriminatory'. The Club was not represented at this meeting as the Ordinance did not require an applicant to be present, nor was there any suggestion that any recent changes had been made in the Club's rules. At a subsequent meeting of the board at

---

[12] Tanganyika, High Court, 1963 [1963] E.A. 478.

which members of the Club were present, it emerged that the board's objection to the issue of a licence was based largely on the fact that applicants for membership of the Club had to be proposed and seconded by a member. The president and trustees of the Club thereupon applied to the High Court for the issue of a writ of certiorari to bring up and quash the order of the board rejecting the Club's application for the grant of a Club licence and also for a writ of mandamus directing the board to hear and determine the application according to law.

● REIDE, J.: The writs of certiorari and mandamus are a means of controlling . . . bodies of persons having legal authority to determine questions affecting the rights of subjects and having the duty to act judicially . . . The degree of control which can be exercised is limited: provided that the Tribunal keeps within its jurisdiction and obeys the rules of natural justice, and refrains from setting out in its record the reasons for its decision, the court cannot interfere.

When the inferior tribunal has jurisdiction to decide a matter it cannot (merely because it incidentally misconstrues a statute, or admits illegal evidence, or rejects legal evidence, or misdirects itself as to the weight of the evidence, or convicts without evidence) be deemed to exceed or abuse its jurisdiction. If, however, an administrative body comes to a decision which no reasonable body could ever have come to, it will be deemed to have exceeded its jurisdiction, and the court can interfere.

In *Associated Provincial Picture Houses Ltd.* v. *Wednesbury Corporation* the plaintiffs appealed from a refusal of the High Court to grant a declaration that a condition attached to a permission for Sunday performances granted by the defendants, the licensing authority, was *ultra vires*. On the special facts of that case the appeal was dismissed, because, as Lord Greene, M.R., said:

It is perfectly clear that the local authority are entrusted by Parliament with the decision on a matter on which the knowledge and experience of the authority can best be trusted to be of value. The subject-matter with which the condition deals is one relevant for its consideration. It has considered it and come to a decision on it, and the courts were not prepared to find that the decision in that case was unreasonable.

In the course of his judgement, however, Lord Greene discussed the question of the principles on which a local authority must exercise its discretionary powers, and the circumstances in which the court will interfere with the exercise of those powers.

When an executive discretion is entrusted by Parliament to a local authority, what purports to be an exercise of that discretion can only be challenged in the courts in a very limited class of case. It must always be remembered that the court is not a court of appeal. The law recognizes certain principles on which the discretion must be exercised, but within the four corners of those principles the discretion is an absolute one and cannot be questioned in any court of law.

What, then, are those principles? They are perfectly well understood. The exercise of such discretion must be a real exercise of the discretion. If, in the statute conferring the discretion, there is to be found, expressly or by implication, matters to which the authority exercising the discretion, ought to have regard, then, in exercising the discretion, they must have regard to those matters. Conversely, if the nature of the subject-matter and the general interpretation of the Act makes it clear that certain matters would not be germane to the matter in question, they must disregard those matters. Expressions have been used in cases where the powers of local authorities came to be considered relating to the sort of thing that may give rise to interference by the court. Bad faith, dishonesty—those of course, stand by themselves—unreasonableness, attention given to extraneous circumstances, disregard of public policy and things like that have all been referred to as being matters which are relevant for consideration. In the present case we have heard a great deal about the meaning of the word 'unreasonable'. It is true the discretion must be exercised reasonably. What does that mean? Lawyers familiar with the phraseology commonly used in relation to the exercise of statutory discretions often use the word 'unreasonable' in a rather comprehensive sense. It is frequently used as a general description of the things that must not be done. For instance a person entrusted with a discretion must direct himself properly in law. He must call his own attention to the matters which he is bound to consider. He must exclude from his consideration matters which are irrelevant to the matter that he has to consider. If he does not obey those rules, he may truly be said, and often is said, to be acting 'unreasonably' . . . It might be useful to summarize once again the principle, which seems to me to be that the court is entitled to investigate the action of the local authority with a view to seeing whether it has taken into account matters which it ought not to take into account, or, conversely, has refused to take into account or neglected to take into account matters which it ought to take into account. Once that question is answered in favour of the local authority, it may still be possible to say that the local authority, nevertheless, have come to a conclusion so unreasonable that no reasonable authority could ever have come to it. In such a case, again, I think the court can interfere. The power of the court to interfere in each case is not that of an appellate authority to override a decision of a local authority, but is that of a judicial authority which is concerned, and concerned only, to see whether the local authority have contravened the law by acting in excess of the powers which the Parliament has confided in it.

Dealing with mandamus, Halsbury says:

The High Court will not question by mandamus the honest decision of the Tribunal, even though erroneous in matters of fact or law, on the matters within its jurisdiction. Where, however, a tribunal has in substance shut its ears to the application made to it and has determined on an application not made to it, it will be held to have refused to exercise its jurisdiction, and a mandamus will issue ordering it to hear and determine. Thus in the case where certiorari or prohibition may not lie, the proceedings being regular on their face and the tribunal having jurisdiction, mandamus to hear and determine may none the less issue to the tribunal on this ground, if the tribunal has been influenced by extraneous considerations or rejected legal evidence. In such a case even though they have purported to hear and determine the case, they will be deemed not to have exercised their jurisdiction.

The circumstances obtaining here were such that the application for both writs must succeed. There was both an excess of jurisdiction and a failure to exercise jurisdiction for which grants of certiorari and mandamus respectively were appropriate. The board is a body of persons having legal authority to determine questions affecting the rights of subjects and having a duty to act judicially. It rejected the licence application out of hand on the ground that 'the constitution is still largely discriminatory' where no discrimination in any ordinary sense existed at all, and certainly not in any pejorative sense, which could give rise to the exercise of a discretion. That was more than a failure properly to exercise an existing discretion, or a mistaken exercise of such a discretion: there was no matter before the board on which a discretion could be exercised. No opportunity was given to the licence applicants to present their case or to meet the board's objections. It has been suggested by the advocate for the applicants that the board, in rejecting the application as it did was not acting bona fide. I make no finding about that, but I do find that to reject the licence application for the reason which it gave and in the way that it did was clearly 'unreasonable' in the sense in which that word is used by Lord Greene in the *Associated Provincial Picture Houses* case, and the board's refusal of the licence application on these imaginary grounds was clearly a failure of natural justice. Further, although the board has no duty to hear a licence applicant against an intended refusal, yet, bearing in mind that the club had held a licence for thirty-four years, and had neither made any recent alteration in its rules nor, so far as is known, been notified of the board's intention to refuse a licence on this occasion, the out-of-hand refusal constituted another failure of natural justice.

Mr MacLeod (counsel for the respondent) submitted a number of arguments why the writs should not issue. I will deal first with those relating to certiorari. The first is that the board is 'an administrative rather than a judicial body' and that therefore the writs cannot issue against its determinations. Since no appeal lies to the court against its determinations, this would mean in effect that the club has no remedies at all. I should be most loth and unhappy to find that the decisions of liquor licensing boards were (I imagine, uniquely) subject to no control or review by the courts, but I am happily quite satisfied that that is not the case. Of course the board is an administrative body, but that does not preclude it from being as it is, a 'body of persons having legal authority to determine questions affecting the rights of subjects' as well, and so one amenable to the writs. As Halsbury says: 'The orders . . . will lie to bodies and persons other than courts *stricto sensu.*'

In *R.* v. *Woodhouse*, Vaughan-Williams, L.J. said:

I ask myself therefore, the question whether the licensing justices in granting or refusing a licence do a judicial act. In my opinion, the grant or refusal of such a licence is a judicial act, and the judgement of Lord Halsbury in *Sharp* v. *Wakefield*, seems to be an authority for this view; for he says that 'an extensive' power is confided to the justices in their capacity as justices to be exercised judicially, and discretion means, when it is said that something is to be done within the discretion of the authorities, that that something has to be done according to the rules of reason and justice, not according to private opinion; according to Law, and not humour; it is to be, not arbitrary, vague, and fanciful, but legal and regular. This view seems to me to be confirmed by old and recent decisions. It is impossible to read under the title 'certiorari' in the Burn's *Justice of the Peace* the list of the cases in which a writ of certiorari has been granted and the grounds for granting it without seeing that in practice a certiorari has issued in cases in which it is impossible to say that there was a court and a 'lis',

which is as clear an indication as one could look for that a liquor licensing board is a body amenable to the writs.

As regards mandamus, Mr MacLeod referred to *R.* v. *Port of London Authority* where Bankes, L. J. said:

There must be something in the nature of a refusal to exercise jurisdiction by the tribunal or authority to whom the writ is to be directed. A refusal may be conveyed in one of two ways: there may be an absolute refusal in terms, or there may be conduct amounting to a refusal.

and submitted that since there was no such refusal here,

the High Court will not question by mandamus the honest decision of a tribunal, even though erroneous in matters of fact or law, on matters within its jurisdiction.

The fallacy in that submission is that, as Halsbury goes on to say:

Where, however, a tribunal has in substance shut its ears to the application made to it and has determined on an application not made to it, it will be held to have refused to exercise its jurisdiction, and a mandamus will issue ordering it to hear and determine. Thus, in a case where certiorari or prohibition may not lie, the proceedings being regular on their face and the tribunal having jurisdiction, mandamus . . . may none the less issue to the tribunal on this ground, if the tribunal has been influenced by extraneous consideration;

and *R.* v. *Port of London Authority* is in fact authority also for that proposition. In that case Bankes, L. J. went on to say:

In the latter case (that is, where there is conduct amounting to a refusal) it is often difficult to draw the line between those cases where the tribunal or authority has heard and determined erroneously upon grounds which it was entitled to take into consideration and those cases where it has heard and determined upon grounds outside and beyond its jurisdiction, but this conclusion may be drawn from decided cases, that there is no refusal to hear and determine unless the tribunal or authority has in substance shut its ears to the application which was made to it, and has determined upon an application which was not made to it. On this point I would refer to the words of Farwell, L.J. in *R. v. Board of Education*: 'If the tribunal has exercised the discretion entrusted to it bona fide, not influenced by extraneous or irrelevant considerations, and not arbitrarily or illegally, the courts cannot interfere; they are not a court of appeal from the tribunal, but they have power to prevent the intentional usurpation or mistaken assumption of a jurisdiction beyond that given to the tribunal by law, and also the refusal of their true jurisdiction by the adoption of extraneous considerations in arriving at their conclusion or deciding a point other than that brought before them, in which cases the courts have regarded them as declining jurisdiction.' Again, in *R. v. Bowman*, where licensing justices had allowed their decision to be influenced by extraneous considerations, Willis, J. said: 'There has been no real hearing and the mandamus must therefore go'.

Those observations seem to me completely in point here. The board's decision was not only influenced by, but was indeed based on the fact that the club's rules provided that candidates for membership must be proposed and seconded by members. That fact was a consideration extraneous to the proper scope of the exercise of the board's discretion.

● *Order as prayed.*

On reading the cases above, one is struck by the irrationality and absurd complexity of the approach adopted by the courts. A brief excursus into the historical development of English administrative law may assist in clarifying the situation. While it is conceded by all commentators that modern administrative law is a response to the growth of the welfare state, the class pressures conditioning this response are generally ignored. Prior to the late nineteenth century, the state seldom impinged directly on the middle class. The working class, both industrial and agricultural, was kept in line through a rigid, brutal criminal law and a local and national state apparatus which was largely uncontrolled in its dealings with this class. Local administration was carried on by justices of the peace as representatives of the rural landowners. While a form of judicial review existed over the very wide powers given to these officials, it was the control of a superior court over a subordinate court, and was thus limited to the enforcement of procedural standards regarding the way the justices performed their 'judicial' functions. In other matters affecting the lives of the oppressed classes, judicial control was non-existent. Under the Poor Law Act, 1834 extraordinarily wide powers were given to the

Poor Law Commissioners to affect the lives of thousands of people, including, for example, the power to imprison people indefinitely in workhouses. No apparatus existed for the review of these powers. As the organized working class began to assert itself politically, concessions were made. A system of unemployment insurance was established, but no mechanism was created through which persons claiming such insurance could petition for the review of unfavourable administrative decisions. As working-class pressure increased, the bourgeoisie found itself compelled to grant greater concessions and, inevitably, contradictions began to develop between the state and the middle class. For example, if the state is forced to embark on a programme of slum clearance, it must, as a consequence, take away the property of slum landlords. As the welfare state began to impinge upon their property rights, the bourgeoisie turned to the courts for protection. The courts then began an *ad hoc* process of developing the existing rules of administrative law into some sort of system. No attempt was made, however, to articulate an overall approach to the problem of the legal control of public administration; rather, the judges relied on a random collection of rules from private law, which, heavily fortified by class prejudices, permitted them to guide the administrative process in directions which they thought fit.

Not surprisingly, the English judges seldom made explicit the nature of their function in cases involving judicial review. The claim was always advanced that the courts were not concerned with the substantive rightness or wrongness of the exercise of administrative powers, but simply with describing the limits within which those powers were to be exercised. In fact, the rules which were developed became so obscure that it was an easy matter for the courts to overrule administrative decisions of which they did not approve. Conversely, the courts could uphold any administrative action of which they did approve regardless of whatever injustices had been committed.[13]

This, briefly, was the system of judicial control of administrative action inherited in East Africa. Ironically, the English courts have in recent years attempted to rationalize their method of dealing with these problems. There are indications that a consistent approach to the exercise of all statutory powers is being formulated. This approach might, for example, reject the largely meaningless judicial/administrative dichotomy noted in the cases, and simply posit a general standard of 'fairness'. This would be the yardstick with which to measure the exercise of all statutory power. Where a power was

---

[13] A most instructive exercise is to compare the approach of the House of Lords in *Roberts* v. *Hopwood* [1925] A.C. 578 and *Liversidge* v. *Anderson* [1942] A.C. 206. As a recent example, see *Hall* v. *Shoreham-by-Sea U.D.C.* [1964] 1 W.L.R. 240. Very little has been written about specific class content of English law. See, however, D. N. Pritt, 'A Barrister', *Justice in England*, Gollancz, London, 1938; and by the same author, *The Apparatus of the Law*, Lawrence and Wishart, London, 1971.

exercised unfairly, the courts would be willing to interfere.[14] There is an indication in a recent Kenya case that the courts in East Africa may be moving gradually towards this new approach.[15]

Since Independence, there has, nonetheless, been little change in approach to the problem of judicial review by East African courts. Before the courts can break out of the contradictions of English administrative law, they must make a serious reappraisal of their stand on the enforcement of government policy. For example, a clear policy aim of government at all levels has been to eliminate the particular kind of racism imposed by colonialism. Yet the court in the *Bukoba Gymkhana* case reveals itself to be quite insensitive to this problem, while the effect of its decision is clearly to frustrate national policy. (This particular problem has not disappeared with the passage of time. Five years after the *Bukoba Gymkhana* case, the Kenya High Court on essentially similar facts reached a similar decision. See *Dent* v. *Kiambu Liquor Licensing Court* (1968) E.A. 80 (K).) If the courts in exercising their powers of review are seen to be frustrating the policies of the government (or the party) then their usefulness and effectiveness in the whole process of government will decline. A more useful approach might be for the courts to see their role as organs in the process of policy implementation, rather than as the protectors of bourgeois interests. They would have a special role to play in curbing anomalies or aberrations which arise in policy implementation through over-zealousness, misinterpretation of policy, lack of expertise, inefficiency, or, inevitably, bad faith. By so doing, not only would the courts guarantee their own future, but they would contribute significantly to the effectiveness of public administration. This point is easily demonstrable in respect of the procedural rules of natural justice as expounded in the *de Souza* case. An administrative authority following these rules is not only more likely to arrive at a 'just' decision in the context of the particular case, but, in the general context of sound public administration, is also more likely to arrive at a 'correct' decision.[16]

Certiorari and mandamus, the remedies sought in the *Patel* and *Bukoba Gymkhana* cases, arise historically from the exercise of the prerogatives of the English Crown.

Certiorari was developed as a device whereby the English superior courts exercised control over the local justices in the execution of their administrative functions. In modern times it has been used to control tribunals and court-

---

[14] See *Ridge* v. *Baldwin* [1964] A.C. 40; *Re K.* [1967] 1 All E.R. 226; *R.* v. *Gaming Board* [1970] 2 All E.R. 528; *R.* v. *Birmingham City Justices* [1970] 3 All E.R. 945.
[15] See *Re Maina*, unreported, Miscellaneous Case No. 7 of 1969; Noted in *East African Law Journal*, vol. VII, no. 2, 1971, p. 142.
[16] For a discussion of the technical aspects of this problem, see P. Bayne, 'Administrative Authorities and Government Policy', *Eastern Africa Law Review*, vol. II, no. 3, 1969, p. 343.

like bodies which either exceed their decision-making authority or fail to observe the rules of natural justice. The major defects of certiorari are first, that it has been held to be available only where the administrative authority in question is exercising a 'judicial' function, and second, it cannot be called in aid to invalidate substantively bad or incorrect administrative decisions which are given within the bounds of the power granted to the authority. The effect of certiorari is that the decision of the inferior tribunal is brought before the High Court which then has the power to quash that decision.[17]

Mandamus is a further order from the High Court, addressed to any public authority, whether exercising a 'judicial' function or not, directing that authority to perform a particular public duty according to law. Mandamus can only be granted where the authority has a clear duty to perform, and is not available to compel the exercise of a discretion.[18]

Prohibition and injunction are essentially the preventive complements to certiorari and mandamus. Prohibition issues to prevent an inferior tribunal acting in excess of its power or undertaking to adjudicate on a matter over which it does not have jurisdiction.[19] An injunction may be sought to prevent the commission of an unlawful act, but this remedy belongs largely to the field of private law and its usefulness against public authorities is somewhat limited. Of particular interest in recent times is the action for a declaration. The party seeking a declaratory judgement asks the court to declare his rights as against a specified authority in a particular set of circumstances. In order to obtain a declaration, the applicant must show both that the state has acted or intends to act unlawfully (as is the case with certiorari and prohibition), and that some direct interest of his has been, or will be, prejudiced by such act. Even if he is granted a favourable declaration, the aggrieved person may still find some difficulty in enforcing it. Nevertheless, the declaratory judgement does represent a great improvement over the rigidity of the older writs.[20]

These remedies suffer from one very serious deficiency in that they are all discretionary. Even where an applicant satisfies the court that an authority has acted unlawfully, the court may still refuse to grant a remedy where it feels the case is not an appropriate one.

Damages can be awarded without prejudice to the availability of any other remedy where a plaintiff can satisfy the court that he has suffered loss as a consequence of an unlawful act by the state or one of its servants.

One of the major defects of English administrative law has been its failure to develop a coherent system of remedies. A plaintiff cannot, as in civil

---

[17] See H. W. R. Wade, *Administrative Law*, 3rd ed., Oxford University Press, London, 1971, p. 128.
[18] See ibid., p. 158 et seq.
[19] ibid., p. 129.
[20] See *Opoloto* v. *A.G.* (*Uganda*) (*No. 2*) [1969] E.A. 631 (CA).

matters, simply plead the facts which he claims give rise to a legal liability on the part of the defendant; he must, in addition, satisfy the court that he is entitled to a particular remedy. Thus even though the plaintiff may convince the court that the state acted unlawfully, this may not be enough for him to obtain redress. If an aggrieved person applies for the 'wrong' remedy (e.g. he asks for a declaration when the appropriate remedy is certiorari) the court will not assist him even though he establishes clearly that he has been treated unlawfully. In this, as in so many other areas, the forms of action continue to rule us from their (English) graves.

It should be remembered that in most cases, judicial remedies against the state will only be sought after the whole range of administrative reviews and appeals has been exhausted. Often the first administrative decision taken in a particular case is far from final and a complex machinery including appeal tribunals and ministerial powers of review is available through which an aggrieved person can seek to present his case and have a decision reversed. On the other hand, exhaustion of administrative review is not considered to be a condition precedent to judicial review.

The practical significance of all these remedies may in fact be very limited. Between 1951 and 1969, there were nineteen applications in the High Court at Dar es Salaam for certiorari, mandamus, prohibition, or injunctions directed at public authorities. Of these applications, four were granted, ten were refused or dismissed, four were withdrawn, and one was settled. Finally, it should be noted that the 'prerogative writs' of certiorari, mandamus, and prohibition have been abolished in Tanzania. In practice, however, this represents only a change in terminology. The High Court is now empowered to make an order 'requiring any act' to be done, 'prohibiting any proceedings or matter', or, 'removing any proceedings or matter into the High Court for any purpose' in any case where it would previously have had jurisdiction to issue one of the three writs. (Law Reform (Fatal Accidents and Miscellaneous Provisions) Ordinance, Cap. 360, s.17 as added by Act No. 55 of 1968, s.2.)

Another important limit on the scope of judicial review is provided by the doctrine of the supremacy of Parliament. This theory gives that body the power by means of appropriate legislation, to overrule judicial decisions. (See the *Marealle* case in Chapter II.) This doctrine also permits the legislature to give retrospective validation to unlawful administrative or executive acts. In fact, this last power has only been used on one occasion, and then, merely to overcome a procedural defect.[21]

Although it is not strictly speaking a form of judicial review, the courts are given a further role in the control of possible abuses of state power by certain provisions of the Penal Code (Cap. 16). Sections 94 to 101 create a

[21] See Kigoma-Ujiji Town Council (Validation) Act, Cap. 516.

series of offences in respect of abuse of office. Section 96 provides that any person employed in the public service, who does, or directs to be done, in abuse of the authority of his office, any arbitrary act prejudicial to the rights of another, shall be guilty of a misdemeanor. If the particular act is for purposes of gain, it becomes a felony, and may be punished by up to three years imprisonment. A prosecution may only be undertaken, however, with the sanction of the Director of Public Prosecutions. The practical effect of this section may be somewhat limited, since all the normal protections of a criminal trial will be open to the accused. (See Chapter IV.) Further, there is the fact that many people may feel reluctant to report a senior official to the Police.[22]

NOTE   So far in this chapter we have looked at the powers given to the President, Regional Commissioners, Area Commissioners, and other public authorities. Yet these are quite remote figures in the day-to-day lives of most of the people of Tanzania. The figure who represents organized authority in the lives of the great majority of the people is the TANU cell leader. Although he is a party official, not a government official, this distinction at the level of the cell is so vague as to be meaningless. The cell, 'the basic organ of TANU', is composed of all TANU members in ten houses grouped together for this purpose. The cell leader is elected by all the TANU members living in the particular ten-house unit. The cell leader is a person to whom the members of the cell will often turn for assistance in settling disputes, and, more important, he is usually the person from whom people get their conceptions of their legal rights and duties. He is a person through whom the ideas of the masses can be transmitted upwards in the party hierarchy, but he will also keep watch on the attitudes and activities of people within his cell, and acts as an instrument through whom the Party can exercise control over the people. The cell system was established after the trauma of the 1964 Army Mutiny and, as the second Vice-President pointed out to a group of cell leaders in 1965, one of their responsibilities was to function as 'the eyes of the nation'. (*The Nationalist*, 6 January 1965.) The system was first introduced in Dar es Salaam, where one of its aims was to serve as a weapon in the struggle against vagrants, indigents, prostitutes, and petty criminals. The cell system was gradually introduced into the rural areas. Would it be possible, or desirable, to devise any kinds of controls over the activities of cell leaders ? For a discussion of the legal position of cell leaders, see *Isango* v. *R.* [1968] E.A. 140 (T). For the establishment of the cell system, see Bienen, 'National Security in Tanganyika After the Mutiny', op. cit.

In conclusion we shall examine briefly the problem of enforcing private legal claims against the government. Difficulties arise from the fact that the government is not in the same position as a private individual. For example,

---

[22] E. A. M. Mang'cnya, *The Permanent Commission of Enquiry (Ombudsman)*, Government Printer, Dar es Salaam, 1970, p. 3. See also ss. 120–124A of the Penal Code. For s.96 of the Penal Code see *Mzee s/o Selemani* v. *R.* [1968] H.C.D. n. 364, where a Divisional Executive Officer was found guilty as a result of unlawfully imprisoning a farmer.

if a farmer's goat is killed as a result of the negligence of the driver of a government landrover, he cannot sue for damages as of right. Under the existing legislation, which finds its roots in ancient English constitutional mythology about the divine nature of kingship, the Government may only be sued with the written consent of the minister responsible for legal affairs (Government Suits Ordinance, Cap. 5). In practice, the person who wants to enforce a claim against the Government applies to the Attorney-General, who may then make an *ex gratia* payment in whatever amount he sees fit. In April 1967, legislation was enacted which would, for most purposes, have made the government's liability in civil matters the same as that of a private individual. (Government Proceedings Act, 1967, Act No. 16 of 1967, especially s.3(1).) This legislation has not yet (December 1972) been brought into operation.[23]

---

[23] See J. S. Read, 'Tanzania' in N. Rubin and E. Cotran (eds.), *Annual Survey of African Law, 1967*, Cass Press, London, 1970, p. 167; A. W. Bradley, 'Legal Aspects of the Nationalizations in Tanzania', *East African Law Journal*, vol. III, no. 3, 1967, pp. 161–2.

CHAPTER FOUR

ASPECTS OF CRIMINAL PROCEDURE

This chapter attempts to investigate certain features of criminal procedure. In the broadest sense this involves an investigation of a particular set of techniques designed in order that organized society may enforce obedience to certain rules of behaviour. For the purposes of this investigation we are not concerned with the objective content of these rules, but with the procedures through which the rules are applied. However, consideration should be given to the kinds of objective standards which can best be enforced by means of these procedures. For example, while we might all agree that these techniques are a sound way of enforcing the rule of behaviour, 'Thou shalt not kill', there might be disagreement as to their appropriateness and effectiveness in enforcing standards of sexual conduct. As a brief illustration, let us look at the problem of what the nation's leaders generally refer to as 'idleness'. This term is used in respect of rural people who do not participate actively in development or self-help schemes, and civil servants who perform their functions either unenthusiastically or inefficiently. Section 89C of the Penal Code (Cap. 16) makes it an offence, carrying a maximum punishment of Sh. 1,000.00 and six months imprisonment, to dissuade or attempt to dissuade anyone from participating in an approved self-help scheme. It is not, however, an offence under this section to refuse to take part in a self-help scheme.[1] This apparent gap in the law was closed by the Ward Development Committees Act, 1969 (Act No. 6 of 1969) which gives to a Ward Development Committee the power to require all able-bodied citizens to participate in self-help schemes (s.6). A person may make a financial contribution in lieu of participation, but where a person refuses to participate or contribute, he may be ordered to contribute by an Area Commissioner, and such order may be executed as if it were the decree of a primary court (ss.6,9,10). The stated aim of this Act '. . . is not to suppress anyone but to curb the wave of idleness and idlers who might feel that they are above others and cannot participate in the activities of the masses; to stop idlers from exploiting others and to stop them from discouraging the masses'.[2] In the case of civil servants, s.121 of the Penal Code makes it an offence not to perform legal duties, unless, in the particular case, extraordinary courage would be required. A new s.284A of the Penal Code (added by Act No. 2 of 1970) makes it an offence for an employee of the Government or of a parastatal organization to

---

1   *Saidi Bakari Kionywaki* v. R. [1968] E.A. 195 (T).
2   *The Nationalist*, 10 October 1968.

cause pecuniary loss or damage to his employer through his failure either to take reasonable care or to discharge his duties in a reasonable manner. In addition the employee will be required to pay compensation in respect of any loss which he has caused.[2a]

Is criminal law an appropriate or effective technique for dealing with idleness ? (A useful comparison can be made between the Tanzanian approach to this problem and the 1971 Cuban Law on Loafing.[3]) One should, in fact, question generally whether the criminal law is necessarily a sound vehicle for the enforcement of legislated social change.

To repeat, then, although the materials in this chapter deal almost exclusively with procedural matters, the fact that these procedures are used to enforce a wide variety of substantive rules must always be borne in mind.[4]

The basic organizational approach used in this chapter is sequential. That is, it attempts to look at the operation of the criminal law as a continuous process from arrest, search, and pre-trial detention, to the trial, sentence, and appeal. At each stage we examine the powers which the state has over the individual who has become caught up in the process, the way in which these powers are exercised, and most important, the way in which the law says they should be exercised.

The process we are attempting to analyse is in many respects similar to those which were the subject of the last chapter. First, an objective standard of behaviour is assumed. The state at some point decides that a particular person has departed from that standard and determines to use its coercive powers against him. It investigates the matter, makes a decision, and either frees the individual or punishes him. In this chapter we will examine a highly developed set of rules which determine this process and which give certain important rights to the person who has become the object of it. Therefore, one should keep in mind the kinds of procedures outlined in Chapter III both to note the differences in technique involved, and to draw conclusions about the desirability and effectiveness of these varying methods.

Although the materials here tend to approach problems from the viewpoint of the individual rather than that of the state, we should not lose sight of two important and related considerations. First, in Tanzania, as in nearly every other part of the world, crime rates are increasing and becoming a social problem of major proportions. However, the fact that 'crime rates' go up does not necessarily mean that more people are doing more things which the average person regards as 'bad'. A crime is only that which the state has

---

[2a] *Haining* v. *R.* [1972] E.A. 133 (CA).
[3] See *Granma*, Havana, 28 March 1971.
[4] For substantive rules of criminal law, reference should be made to the Penal Code; Seidman, *A Sourcebook of the Criminal Law of Africa*, Sweet and Maxwell, London, 1966; and Collingwood, *Criminal Law of East and Central Africa*, Sweet and Maxwell, London, 1967.

chosen to call a crime and may, in fact, include acts of which the mass of the people in a given society would approve: this would be the case, for example, with acts of revolutionary violence committed by a people trying to free themselves from colonialism. Thus a high crime rate may not mean that a particular state is populated by a disproportionate number of 'bad' people, but that there is a sufficient degree of popular opposition to the ruling class for that opposition to be expressed through a large number of objective acts of resistance. The so-called crime wave sweeping the cities of the United States clearly falls into this category. Alternatively, an increasing crime rate may only reflect an improvement in police work and/or the gathering of crime statistics, rather than an absolute increase in the number of criminal acts. Although crime rates have levelled off somewhat since independence, there has been a fairly steady increase in Tanzania since 1945.[5] In such a situation, therefore, we should consider whether the techniques outlined in this chapter are appropriate and adequate to deal with such a problem.[6] Furthermore, the kind of economic development that Tanzania is now trying to undertake requires, among other things, a fairly high degree of social order. Thus, it may be that a high incidence of crime may militate against development.[7]

NOTE Unless otherwise stated, the rules of criminal procedure dealt with in this chapter are those which obtain in the High Court, and in District Courts exercising their original criminal jurisdiction. Primary Courts and District Courts in the exercise of their appellate or revisional jurisdiction follow considerably simplified rules. (See Magistrates Courts Act, ss.32 and 37, Third Schedule.) Should an accused person be allowed the benefit of different procedural safeguards depending on what court he is tried in?

A · CERTAINTY OF CRIMINAL LAW

The first step that the state takes in the criminal law process is to assume that everyone knows the law and that a person who commits a criminal act is doing so in more or less conscious defiance of the law. Thus, ignorance of the law is no defence to a criminal charge. It is highly questionable whether everyone in Tanzania knows the criminal law with sufficient particularity to be quite clear as to which acts are criminal and which are not, especially as the scope of the criminal law is constantly expanding. A further problem arises from the fact that the criminal law is foreign in origin, its

---

[5] See, for example, the Judiciary *Annual Reports*, Government Printer, Dar es Salaam, for 1945 to 1965.
[6] For some of the factors involved in such a consideration, see J. S. Read, 'Some Legal Problems in East Africa', *East African Law Journal*, vol. II, no. 1, 1966, pp. 46–51.
[7] See G. H. Boehringer, 'Social Defence Planning in the Context of Development with Special Reference to Tanzania', University of East Africa Social Sciences Council Conference, *Proceedings*, Nairobi, 1969.

basic principles and procedures being English. The Penal Code used to provide in s.4, that the Code was to be 'interpreted in accordance with the principles of legal interpretation obtaining in England'. This section now states that, in interpreting the Code, the courts are to be '. . . guided by the principles of natural justice'.[8] The state does attempt to balance the scales somewhat by the 'principle of legality'. Briefly stated, this means that if everyone is assumed to know the criminal law, then the criminal law should be knowable. That is, the criminal law should consist of clear, unequivocal, preferably statutory, rules of conduct and that no one should be subjected to the sanctions of the criminal law unless he has broken one of these known rules. Thus, the principle of legality comes to mean simply that no one should be punished unless he has broken the law. Consider the following two brief extracts in this context:

MAGISTRATES COURTS ACT, 1963: CAP. 537

● 66.—(1) No person shall be charged with, tried for or convicted of any offence contrary to customary law in respect of any act committed or
● omission on or after the appointed day.

PENAL CODE: CAP. 16

● 3. Nothing in this Code shall affect:
(1) the liability, trial or punishment of a person for an offence against the Common Law or against any other law in force in Tanganyika, other than
● this Code.

NOTE Section 3(1) of the Penal Code gives the courts the power to punish people for non-statutory or 'common law' crimes. Common law crime derives from the theory that the courts in England had a general duty to protect their society from mischief howsoever caused and regardless of whether the particular kind of mischief had ever been proscribed by the legislature. They were permitted to do so because they had '. . . never abandoned their function as *custodes mores* by surrendering to the legislature the right and duty to apply established principles to new combinations of circumstances'. (*Shaw* v. *D.P.P.* [1962] A.C. 220—a decision for which the House of Lords was severely criticized.) In Tanzania, the concept of the common law crime has been used to find people guilty of, for example, 'public mischief' in giving false information to a police officer. (*R.* v. *Patel*, High Court of Tanganyika at Dar es Salaam, Miscellaneous Criminal Case No. 4/44; *Hasham Hamir Juma* v. *R.* (1934) 1 T.L.R. (R) 195.) To what extent are the courts in Tanzania *custodes mores*? Can the purposes which appear to underlie s.66(1)

---

[8] Administration of Justice (Miscellaneous Amendments) Act, 1971, s.3. Assisting a wider number of people to 'know the law' and at the same time repatriating it are: N. E. R. Mwakasungula, *Jifunze Kisheria*, T. M. P. Book Department, Tabora, 1969; and, *Swahili Legal Terms*, Legal Research Centre and Faculty of Law, University College, Dar es Salaam, 1968.

of Cap. 537 and s.3(1) of Cap. 16 be reconciled? (See Eugene Cotran, 'The Position of Customary Criminal Law in African Countries' in *East Africa Law and Social Change*, op. cit.; and J. S. Read, 'Crime and Punishment in East Africa', *Howard Law Journal*, vol. X, no. 2, 1964, p. 164.)

A related problem concerns criminal legislation which is designed to operate retrospectively. Since there are no restrictions on the power of Parliament to legislate in respect of criminal law (except in so far as the liability of the President and the Head of the Executive for Zanzibar are concerned) it may pass legislation which, after the event, makes acts criminal which were lawful at the time they were committed. The courts have always been rather uneasy about legislation of this kind and they require an unequivocal statement that the legislature intends a particular statute to have retrospective application. Two 1970 amendments to the Penal Code are to have such application: first, the new ss. 39, 40, and 41 which change the law governing treason (a new s. 42 provides for retrospective application; see Act No. 2 of 1970) and, second, the new s. 284A to which reference has already been made in this chapter.

B · ARREST

The next step in the criminal law process as it affects the individual is an arrest.

CRIMINAL PROCEDURE CODE: CAP. 20

● 19.—(1) In making an arrest the police officer or other person making the same shall actually touch or confine the body of the person to be arrested, unless there be a submission to the custody by word or action.

(2) If such person forcibly resists the endeavour to arrest him, or attempts to evade the arrest, such police officer or other person may use all means necessary to effect the arrest.

20.—(1) If any person acting under a warrant of arrest, or any police officer having authority to arrest, has reason to believe that the person to be arrested has entered into or is within any place, the person residing in or being in charge of such place shall, on demand of such person acting as aforesaid or such police officer, allow him free ingress thereto and afford all reasonable facilities for a search therein.

(2) If ingress to such place cannot be obtained under the preceding subsection, it shall be lawful in any case for a person acting under a warrant, and in any case in which a warrant may issue, but cannot be obtained without affording the person to be arrested an opportunity

to escape, for a police officer to enter such place and search therein, and, in order to effect an entrance into such place, to break open any outer or inner door or window of any house or place, whether that of the person to be arrested or of any other person or otherwise effect entry into such house or place, if after notification of his authority and purpose, and demand of admittance duly made, he cannot otherwise obtain admittance:

Provided that if any such place is an apartment in the actual occupancy of a woman (not being the person to be arrested) who, according to custom, does not appear in public, such person or police officer shall, before entering such apartment, give notice to the woman that she is at liberty to withdraw and shall afford her every reasonable facility for withdrawing, and may then break open the apartment and enter it.

21. Any police officer or other person authorized to make an arrest may break out of any place in order to liberate himself or any other person who, having lawfully entered for the purpose of making an arrest, is detained therein.

22. The person arrested shall not be subjected to more restraint than is necessary to prevent his escape.

23. Whenever a person is arrested:
  (a) by a police officer under a warrant which does not provide for the taking of bail, or under a warrant which provides for the taking of bail but the person arrested cannot furnish bail; or
  (b) without warrant, or by a private person under a warrant, and the person arrested cannot legally be admitted to bail or cannot furnish bail,
the police officer making the arrest or, when the arrest is made by a private person, the police officer to whom he makes over the person arrested may search such person and place in safe custody all articles, other than necessary wearing apparel, found upon him.

24. Any police officer may stop, search and detain any vessel, boat, aircraft or vehicle in or upon which there shall be reason to suspect that anything stolen or unlawfully obtained may be found and also any person who may be reasonably suspected of having in his possession or conveying in any manner anything stolen or unlawfully obtained.

25. Whenever it is necessary to cause a woman to be searched, the search shall be made by another woman with strict regard to decency.

26. The officer or other person making any arrest may take from the person arrested any offensive weapons which he has about his person, and shall deliver all weapons so taken to the court or officer before

which or whom the officer or person making the arrest is required by law to produce the person arrested.

27. Any police officer may, without an order from a magistrate and without a warrant, arrest:

(a) any person whom he suspects upon reasonable grounds of having committed a cognizable offence;

(b) any person who commits a breach of the peace in his presence;

(c) any person who obstructs a police officer while in the execution of his duty, or who has escaped or attempts to escape from lawful custody;

(d) any person in whose possession anything is found which may reasonably be suspected to be stolen property or who may reasonably be suspected of having committed an offence with reference to such thing;

(e) (this subsection has been deleted);

(f) any person whom he finds in any highway, yard, or other place during the night and whom he suspects upon reasonable grounds of having committed or being about to commit a felony;

(g) any person whom he suspects upon reasonable grounds of having been concerned in any act committed at any place out of Tanganyika which, if committed in Tanganyika, would have been punishable as an offence, and for which he is, under the Fugitive Criminals Surrender Ordinance or the Fugitive Offenders Act, 1881, or otherwise, liable to be apprehended and detained in Tanganyika;

(h) any person having in his possession without lawful excuse, the burden of providing which excuse shall lie on such person, any implement of housebreaking;

(i) any person whom he suspects upon reasonable grounds of having committed an offence contrary to section 310;

(j) any person for whom he has reasonable cause to believe a warrant of arrest has been issued;

(k) any person whom he suspects upon reasonable grounds of designing to commit any cognizable offence if it appears to such police officer that the commission of the offence cannot otherwise be prevented.

28. Any officer in charge of a police station may in like manner arrest or cause to be arrested:

(a) any person found taking precautions to conceal his presence within the limits of such station under circumstances which afford reason to believe that he is taking such precautions with a view to committing a cognizable offence;

(b) any person within the limits of such station who has no ostensible means of subsistence or who cannot give a satisfactory account of himself;

(c) any person who is by repute an habitual robber, housebreaker, or thief or an habitual receiver of stolen property knowing it to be stolen, or who by repute habitually commits extortion or in order to commit extortion habitually puts or attempts to put persons in fear of injury.

29. When any officer in charge of a police station requires any officer subordinate to him to arrest without a warrant (otherwise than in such officer's presence) any person who may lawfully be arrested without a warrant under the provisions of section 28, he shall deliver to the officer required to make the arrest an order in writing specifying the person to be arrested and the offence or other cause for which the arrest is to be made.

30.—(1) When any person who in the presence of a police officer has committed or has been accused of committing a non-cognizable offence refuses on the demand of such officer to give his name and residence, or gives a name or residence which such officer has reason to believe to be false, he may be arrested by such officer in order that his name or residence may be ascertained.

(2) When the true name and residence of such person have been ascertained he shall be released on his executing a bond, with or without sureties, to appear before a court if so required:
Provided that if such person is not resident in Tanganyika the bond shall be secured by a surety or sureties resident in Tanganyika.

(3) Should the true name and residence of such person not be ascertained within twenty-four hours from the time of arrest, or should he fail to execute the bond or, if so required, to furnish sufficient sureties, he shall forthwith be taken before a court having jurisdiction.

31. Any police officer making an arrest without a warrant shall without unnecessary delay and subject to the provisions herein contained as to bail, take or send the person arrested before a court having jurisdiction in the case or before an officer in charge of a police station.

32.—(1) Any private person may arrest any person who in his view commits a cognizable offence, or whom he reasonably suspects of having committed a felony.

(2) Persons found committing any offence involving injury to property may be arrested without a warrant by the owner of the

property or his servants or persons authorized by him.

33.—(1) Any private person arresting any person without a warrant shall without unnecessary delay make over the person so arrested to a police officer or, in the absence of a police officer, shall take such person to the nearest police station.

(2) If there is reason to believe that such person comes under the provisions of section 27, a police officer shall rearrest him.

(3) If there is reason to believe that he has committed a non-cognizable offence, and he refuses on the demand of a police officer to give his name and residence, or gives a name or residence which such officer has reason to believe to be false, he shall be dealt with under the provisions of section 30. If there is no sufficient reason to believe that he has committed any offence he shall be at once released.

36. When any offence is committed in the presence of a magistrate within the local limits of his jurisdiction he may himself arrest or order any person to arrest the offender, and may thereupon, subject to the provisions herein contained as to bail, commit the offender to custody.

37. Any magistrate may at any time arrest or direct the arrest in his presence within the local limits of his jurisdiction of any person for whose arrest he is competent at the time and in the circumstances
● to issue a warrant.

NOTE The following are, *inter alia*, made cognizable offences within the meaning of s.27(a), by the First Schedule to Cap. 20:

Publishing false reports	Assault occasioning actual bodily harm
Unlawful assembly	
Treason	Theft
Administering or taking unlawful oaths	Robbery
	Housebreaking
Possession of prohibited publication	Criminal trespass
Rape	Attempting to set fire to crops or growing plants
Insulting the modesty of a woman	
Murder	Riotously interfering with railway
Manslaughter	Piracy
Wounding	Forgery
Attempted suicide	Counterfeiting coin

NOTE In connection with s.32 above, the then Inspector-General of Police, Mr Shaidi, made an appeal in July 1969 for greater public co-operation in the apprehension of criminals. 'The task of curbing criminal activity and of seeing that law and order is finally realized in our society is a total community responsibility . . . The powers of arresting are also extended to members of the public and they require no warrant of arrest whatsoever for that purpose. A private individual needs only to say that he reasonably suspects the person he has arrested as having committed an offence.' (*The Standard*, 5 July 1969.) What advantages are there in getting the general public more actively involved in law enforcement? What possible dangers are there? For police powers generally, see the Police Force Ordinance, Cap. 322, ss. 27-39. Compare the following statement of the Cuban Minister of the Interior, 'The task of preventing anti-social behaviour must be the responsibility of everyone.' (*Granma*, 6 April 1969.) For a similar statement by President Nyerere, see *Freedom and Development*, p. 4. For discussions of the relationship between the police and the public in dealing with crime, see C. Okonkwo, *The Police and the Public in Nigeria*, Sweet and Maxwell, London, 1966; and, a review by G. H. Boehringer in *Eastern Africa Law Review*, vol. I, no. 2, 1968, p. 214; and, generally, issues of the *Tanzania Police Journal*.

NOTE Party officials possess no special powers of arrest. See *Isango* v. *R.* [1968] E.A. 140 (T).

NOTE Sections 308 and 309 of the Criminal Procedure Code provide that a person who has twice been convicted of an offence punishable by upwards of three years imprisonment may be placed under police supervision for a period not exceeding five years after his release from prison. Such order will be made by the court having jurisdiction at the time it passes sentence. The order may also require that the individual concerned reside within a particular district during the period of police supervision. Section 310 referred to in s.27(i) above, creates an offence of failure to comply with such an order. It should be noted that an offence is committed only if the person placed under police supervision fails to comply with any of the terms of the order originally made by the court. Failure to comply with any additional terms or conditions imposed by the police themselves is not an offence. (*Wilbold* v. *R.* (1954) 2 T.L.R. (R) 95.)

NOTE An important issue involved in the state's power to detain people is the question of dealing with people who because of mental health problems constitute (or are believed to constitute) some danger to society. While this is not strictly a criminal law problem, it is included here because in most countries such people are dealt with by the same procedures as are used to deal with criminals. The procedures used in Tanzania are to be found in the Mental Diseases Ordinance (Cap. 98). A person believed to be of 'unsound mind' may be taken into custody by the order of a magistrate or of an officer in charge of a police station. Before such person can be committed to an institution, a hearing must be held in front of a magistrate. A medical officer must at this time certify that the particular person is 'of unsound mind and a proper person to be detained'. There is an appeal allowed from such proceedings. It is not clear whether the person whose mental health is the subject of the hearing has the right to be represented during the hearing. When a hearing as to a person's mental soundness is proposed to be held that person may be detained in custody on the order of a magistrate for a period of up to sixty days for medical examination prior to the hearing. Where no magistrate is available, an administrative officer may order that a person be held in custody for this purpose.

Other powers of arrest beyond those contained in Cap. 20 also exist. Most important among these are the powers granted to Justices of the Peace.

A GUIDE FOR JUSTICES OF THE PEACE[9]

● There are two main reasons for the appointment of Justices:

   (i)   to ensure that law and order is maintained throughout the rural areas of Tanganyika where there will often be neither magistrate nor police readily available to take appropriate action.

   (ii) to assist at court-houses presided over by magistrates who will often be peripatetic and absent on circuit. Justices will be able to give assistance to these magistrates by taking action to ensure that criminal and civil proceedings are ready for hearing and the parties duly summoned to attend Court
●   when the magistrate is next due at the Court-house.

MAGISTRATES COURTS ACT: CAP. 537

● 45.—(1) Every executive officer of a district council shall be a justice of the peace for the district in which such council has jurisdiction.

(2) The Minister may appoint any fit and proper person to be a justice of the peace for the district in which such person is ordinarily resident.

(3) Notwithstanding the provisions of subsection (1) or (2) of this section, the Minister may, by notice published in the Gazette, in any case in which he considers such an appointment to be desirable appoint an executive officer or person appointed a justice under subsection (2) to be a justice of the peace for more than one district.

(4) In this section 'executive officer' means the clerk to a district council and the clerk to a divisional committee of a district council, or such other person who is the chief executive of a district council or a divisional committee thereof, and any assistant executive officer of a district council or divisional committee thereof.

46. The appropriate judicial authority shall assign every justice to a primary or district court house in the district for which he is appointed.

47. A justice may arrest, or may order any person to arrest, any person who in his view commits a cognizable offence.

48.—(1) Where a complaint of facts which constitutes an offence is made, either orally or in writing, to a justice, he shall examine the complainant and, if satisfied that there are sufficient grounds for so doing, issue a summons or a warrant for the purpose of compelling

⁹ Government Printer, Dar es Salaam, 1963, p. 9.

the appearance of the person accused:

Provided that a justice shall not, in the first instance, issue a warrant for the arrest of the person accused, unless he is satisfied that it is proper that such person should be detained in custody pending his trial or should give security for his appearance, or that the circumstances of the case render it unlikely that such person will appear in answer to a summons.

(2) The power to issue a warrant under this section includes power to issue a warrant of arrest authorizing a police officer to whom it is directed to release the person accused on his executing a bond for a specified sum with or without sureties, for his appearance before the court.

(3) Every summons and warrant issued under this section shall be in the prescribed form and shall be returnable before a magistrate's court at a court house in accordance with the directions of the appropriate judicial authority.

(4) Where a justice considers a complaint under this section, he shall enter the same, together with his decision whether or not to issue process, in the records and registers of the court house to which he is assigned; and if he issues process, he shall enter the charge in the register.

49. Where any person is arrested by or on the orders of a justice under section 47, or any person otherwise arrested without warrant is brought before a justice, the justice shall, without unnecessary delay, either take him or cause him to be taken before a magistrate: Provided that where:

(a) the justice is assigned to a court house in the vicinity and, for the time being, there is no magistrate in attendance thereat; and

(b) in accordance with the arrangements made for the despatch of judicial business in the district by the appropriate judicial authority, the proceedings will be further prosecuted at such court house,

the justice may, instead, enter the matter in the registers of the court house and exercise the powers conferred by paragraph (a) or (b) of

● section 50.

NOTE Administrative officers working in regional or district offices normally receive appointments as Justices of the Peace as a matter of course.

Clearly, broad powers of arrest such as we have been investigating are open to abuse. We will look first at an example of such abuse and then attempt to see what sort of control the courts can exercise over the power to arrest.

G. Kanyeihamba
THE LAW AND THE CITIZEN IN UGANDA[10]

● The detention and subsequent punishment of a Makerere employee by the name of Andrew will illustrate the two points made above. Andrew is a law-abiding citizen. He has always paid his graduated tax and had never been to court before even as a spectator. On 30 October, Andrew went to market on the unfortunate hour when chiefs, accompanied by police officers, were checking everyone for graduated tax tickets. Unfortunately he did not have the tickets on his person that day. The chiefs questioned him and he honestly told them that he had paid all his taxes but had forgotten to carry with him the tickets they were after. He was subsequently arrested. Andrew begged the arresting officers to give him an escort so that he could go home to collect the tickets. This reasonable request was refused. He was led with other tax defaulters to prison at Makindye. At the prison, Andrew requested the officer in charge to allow him the use of the telephone so that he might alert his friends at Makerere who would be instructed to fetch his tickets from his house. The officer was not prepared to grant the request and to use Andrew's own words the said officer remarked, 'We do not allow prisoners to use government amenities here. Wait until you have seen a magistrate next week.' While Andrew sat in his cell, his friends at Makerere became anxious about his absence and began to make inquiries. He could not be found anywhere. It appeared to them that Andrew, a teetotaller and gentleman, had disappeared into thin air. After a week of intensive search the friends gathered that their mate had been taken to prison as a tax defaulter. Meanwhile, on the day of his friends' discovery, Andrew had been taken to a magistrate grade three and without ascertaining the circumstances under which Andrew was arrested, the magistrate adjourned the cases of all tax defaulters (no charges were read) for another week. That day Andrew's friends brought his tickets to the prison officials. The latter refused to release him with the explanation that they no longer had control over him since remand had been ordered by a court of law. He would have to wait until the next hearing. Two weeks after his arrest, Andrew appeared before the same magistrate who was satisfied that the prisoner had indeed paid his tax. However, 'for the trouble and inconvenience'
● caused, Andrew was found guilty and fined fifteen shillings.

---

[10] University of East Africa Social Sciences Council Conference, *Proceedings*, Kampala, 1968.

MWANGI s/o NJEROGE v. REGINAM[11]

Summary

The appellant was convicted of the possession of a home-made firearm without lawful authority or excuse contrary to regulation 8A(1)(a) Emergency Regulations, 1952. At about 8 p.m. on 2 August 1954, two police officers searched the appellant's quarters and arrested him. He was taken to a police station and 'handed over' to a police constable for questioning. After about twenty minutes, the police constable informed a police officer that the appellant would show them 'the gun'. This the appellant did at about 9.30 p.m. that night. He made the alleged statement next day at about 3.40 p.m. The Court of Appeal held that the weapon found had not been proven to be a 'firearm' within the meaning of the regulations, and also held that there had been an irregularity in the magistrate's treatment of a statement allegedly made by the accused.

● SIR NEWNHAM WORLEY, Ag.P.: A further point which calls for consideration is whether the police officers informed the appellant at the time of his arrest of the offence on suspicion of which he was being arrested. Mr Hardy, a member of the Kenya Police Reserve, said he thought that the appellant was asked before arrest whether he possessed a firearm; but Chief Inspector Bates, the senior officer present, denied that anyone questioned the appellant, except to ask his name, until he was at the police station. The appellant's own evidence confirmed this and so, we think, did the evidence of the constable who subsequently interrogated the appellant. The preponderance of evidence therefore is that nothing was said to the appellant at the time of his arrest which would indicate to him why he was being arrested. It is now well settled law that 'it is a condition of lawful arrest that the party arrested should know on what charge or on suspicion of what crime he is arrested', *Christie* v. *Leachinsky* ([1947] A.C. 573), and the omission to tell a person who is arrested at, or within a reasonable time of, the arrest with what offence he is charged cannot be regarded as a mere irregularity. This is an ancient rule of the Common Law and there is nothing which abrogates or supersedes it in any of the local enactments which give the police power to arrest without warrant on suspicion . . . . From our study of a great number of appeal records we have the impression, however, that this rule either is not generally known to police officers in Kenya or, if known, is too generally disregarded. We therefore take this opportunity of setting out the rule summarized by Viscount Simon in *Christie* v. *Leachinsky*:

11 Kenya, Court of Appeal for Eastern Africa, 1954, 21 E.A.C.A. 377.

1. If a policeman arrests without warrant upon reasonable suspicion of felony, or of other crime of a sort which does not require a warrant, he must in ordinary circumstances inform the person arrested of the ground of arrest. He is not entitled to keep the reason to himself or to give a reason which is not the true reason. In other words, a citizen is entitled to know on what charge or on suspicion of what crime he is seized.

2. If the citizen is not so informed but is nevertheless seized, the policeman, apart from certain exceptions, is liable for false imprisonment.

3. The requirement that the person arrested should be informed of the reason why he is seized naturally does not exist if the circumstances are such that he must know the general nature of the alleged offence for which he is detained.

4. The requirement that he should be so informed does not mean that technical or precise language need be used. The matter is matter of substance, and turns on the elementary proposition that in this country a person is, prima facie, entitled to his freedom and is only required to submit to restraints on his freedom if he knows in substance the reason why it is claimed that this restraint should be imposed.

5. The person arrested cannot complain that he has not been supplied with the above information as and when he should be, if he himself produces the situation which makes it practically impossible to inform him, e.g. by immediate counter-attack or by running away.

There may well be other exceptions to the general rule in addition to those I have indicated, and the above propositions are not intended to constitute a formal or complete code, but to indicate the general principles of our law on a very important matter.

By setting out Lord Simon's propositions, we hope to bring them effectively to the notice of local police officers and to provide an easy reference... It only remains for us to refer to the fact that the appellant himself led the police to the place where exhibit 1 was hidden and produced it...

The irregularities committed by the police in this case, that is to say, the failure to inform the appellant of the reason for his arrest and the failure to caution him before questioning would not necessarily render inadmissible the statements obtained from him; that would have been a matter of discretion for the learned trial Judge had his mind been directed to these points...

These irregularities, if they had stood alone, might not therefore have necessitated interference with this conviction unsatisfactory though they are. But in view of the misdirection as to the evidence relating to the 'firearm' exhibit 1, the majority of this Court has held ● that this conviction cannot stand. The appeal is allowed....

RASHID BIN ABDULLA *v.* MAJOR CARTWRIGHT[12]

● MURISON, J.: The plaintiff in this case sues the Governor of the

[12] Zanzibar, High Court, 1912 [1868–1918] 1 Z.L.R. 407.

Zanzibar jail for Rs. 300 damages for false imprisonment, and the return of eight pice belonging to the plaintiff.

It is admitted that the plaintiff was detained in jail for twenty-nine days beyond the date named in the warrant. He was imprisoned for three months for gambling.

It is further admitted, and it is settled law, that the defendant is liable for the excessive detention of the plaintiff, whether such detention is the result of his own or his subordinate's negligence. I am, therefore, spared any apportionment of balance between the parties concerned . . . .

Apart from the claim for the eight pice not returned to the plaintiff when he left the jail, the only question at issue is the amount of damages. The plaintiff's own evidence shows that he is a shopkeeper in a small way of business, and that his actual loss upon twenty-nine days' trading could not be more than Rs. 15 or 20. Mr Mead (counsel for the defendant) argues that it is not much more than Rs. 5, and that that amount is sufficient compensation.

I do not think Mr Mead's method of assessment is correct. If I hold that a jury in estimating the damages for false imprisonment are to be restrained to exactly the amount of the injury sustained by the plaintiff, it would in effect be placing the wrongdoer in the same position as if he had prevented the plaintiff from trading without having kept him in prison at all. Upon Mr Mead's principle, the damages for knocking off a man's hat in Piccadilly, and merely ruffling the nap, could not exceed the price of ironing it. There is, in fact, an English case wherein £500 was awarded as damages for knocking a man's hat off. In the cases of contract, and in cases of tort without aggravation, I agree that the damage should be restrained within the limits of compensation. But when the injury is to the person, character, and feelings, and the facts disclose cruelty or great negligence, or that the offence is of a grossly unconstitutional nature, the damages operate as a punishment for the benefit of the community and a restraint upon the transgressor.

Mr Framji (counsel for the plaintiff), in his argument for aggravation, has brought out some significant facts in cross-examination. The jailor admits that the jamadar twice complained to him at Prison Island that he was detained over time. The jailor says that he wrote to Dias, who was in Zanzibar, and was the clerk who kept the warrants and the Release Diary, to ask if this was so. Dias says that he never got the letter. The jailor says he did not bother about it any more as Dias had not answered. Major Cartwright says he went two or three times a week to Prison Island, but it does not appear that he ever made any direct enquiries from the prisoners there if they had any complaints to make, nor apparently were facilities given to them to complain. When the prisoners were transferred to Chukwani, the plaintiff seems to have continued his complaints, and at last, on 5 October, Major Cartwright made a note that the plaintiff had complained, but inasmuch as the complaint could not be looked into because all the books and warrants were in town, more delay occurred. In fact, it was not till the 12th of October, seven days after the Governor himself had noted the complaint, and twenty-nine days after the proper day, that the plaintiff was released.

Systematic negligence in the jail is relied upon by Mr Framji as a ground for exemplary damages, and in that connection it is admitted by the jail authorities, first that money and valuables are never handed to the Governor as required by Section 25 of the Prisons Decree; that there is no written record of the visits of the Governor as required by Section 20 of the decree; that there is no record in the jail or any writing to show whether a complaint is made or not; that the Governor does not examine the books every day; that he does not examine the warrants every day; that the books and warrants were habitually kept miles away from the prisoners; and, in short, that there are 'many things in the decree that it is impossible to carry out'.

Mr Mead replies that the advent of cholera was responsible, as no doubt in some degree it was, for the disorganization of the jail-work, and that Dias was overworked.

In my opinion, it is proved that there was considerable aggravation in the case, due to the gross neglect and slackness in the jail methods. Further, I believe the plaintiff's story about the eight pice. I think the claim would have been higher if it had been false.

In assessing the amount of damages one cannot overlook the fact that in England cases of this kind are regarded in a very serious light. Thus, where a plaintiff had been kept in custody for six hours without warrant, a verdict for £300 damages was upheld. Again, £200 damages were held not to be excessive where the plaintiff had been kept one night in custody on a charge of felony. And where the plaintiff in an action for false imprisonment was a native of Minorca and the defendant was the Governor, £3,000 damages were allowed. The circumstances in this case are widely different in many ways from the cases quoted, but these cases do indicate that the act of false imprisonment, wherever it takes place, is not a slight affair.

I assess the damages at Rs. 100, and give judgement for that amount and Court costs, and Rs. 20, counsel's costs.

Decree for plaintiff

SADRUDIN IBRAHIM *v.* R.[13]

● RUDD, Ag. C.J.: The appellant and his brother Sultan were charged in the court of the resident magistrate, Nanyuki at Meru, with assaulting a police officer in the due execution of his duty contrary to s. 248(b) of the Penal Code.

Sultan was acquitted but the appellant was convicted of common assault, contrary to s. 245 of the Penal Code and sentenced to six months imprisonment. The appellant appeals from this conviction and sentence.

The facts of the case are that a police officer having two summonses to be served on one Mohammed and on Sultan respectively, entered the shop of Mohammed for the purpose of serving one of the summonses on the said Mohammed and on being informed by Mohammed's son Ishmail that Mohammed was not there, tendered the summons for Mohammed to Ishmail and asked him to sign the duplicate in acknowledgement of service upon Mohammed.

Ismail called Sultan who was on the premises and the police officer then asked Sultan to explain to Ishmail that he wanted him to sign the duplicate of the summons, whereupon a protracted conversation took place between Sultan and Ishmail in a language which the police officer did not understand. The police officer concluded that Sultan was not assisting him to get the duplicate summons signed by Ishmail and told Sultan to 'shut up' as he wished to speak to Ishmail. Sultan took offence at this and became excited, shouting that the police officer had no right to go into other people's shops to serve summonses or to tell people to 'shut up'.

The police officer then asked Sultan to give his name and address but Sultan did not do so and asked what the police officer wanted his name and address for. The police officer then put his hand on Sultan and saying, 'I am arresting you for obstructing me during performance of my duty' and said further that until he gave his name and address he would arrest him.

Sultan resisted this arrest saying, 'I am not a thief, I have done nothing wrong. You cannot arrest me.' Sultan's shirt was torn in a struggle which ensued between him and the police officer during which the appellant came from behind and struck the police officer. The struggle then became a tripartite one in which the police officer ultimately succeeded in taking Sultan and the appellant into custody. No weapon had been used but the police officer suffered bruises and a slight cut. After the struggle had ended, the police officer produced the other summons and asked Sultan if he was the person named in

13 Kenya, Supreme Court, 1958, [1958] E.A. 518.

it and Sultan said that he was. Up to that time the police officer had not produced the other summons or realised that Sultan was the person named in it.

The learned trial magistrate acquitted Sultan because he was not satisfied that he had committed an offence in the presence of the police officer but he held that the appellant had no justification for his attack on the police officer.

It would be possible to dispose of this appeal quite shortly by pointing out that in effect both Sultan and the appellant were acquitted of assaulting the police officer in the execution of his duty from which it necessarily follows, on the facts of this case, that the magistrate did not consider that it had been established that the police officer was entitled to arrest Sultan and by pointing out that in law the appellant was entitled to prevent the police officer from arresting his brother, Sultan, unless that arrest was lawful and provided no undue or unreasonable force was used. In view of the fact that no weapon was used and that only superficial, trivial hurt was caused to the police officer and the further fact that Sultan and the appellant, notwithstanding their resistance, were unable to prevent the police officer from taking them into custody, it is impossible to hold that undue or unreasonable force was used and therefore appellant should not have been convicted of an offence under s.245 of the Penal Code.

We consider it desirable however to go into more detail.

In the first place the record does not show sufficient grounds to justify the police officer's demand that Ishmail should sign the duplicate summons for Mohammed. The relevant provision is s.93 of the Criminal Procedure Code which provides as follows:

Where a person summoned cannot by the exercise of due diligence be found, the summons may be served by leaving one of the duplicates for him with some adult member of his family or with his servant residing with him or with his employer; and the person with whom the summons is so left shall, if so required by the serving officer, sign a receipt therefor on the back of the other duplicate.

The evidence does not establish that Mohammed could not have been found by the exercise of due diligence. It only establishes that at the particular time in question he was not in his shop. The police officer should have made further enquiries before he attempted to take advantage of the provisions of s.93 of the Criminal Procedure Code, and he was not entitled to attempt to browbeat Ishmail into signing the duplicate of the summons.

In our opinion the appellant was entitled to advise Ishmail not to sign and the police officer was not correct in thinking that Sultan was obstructing him in the performance of his duty.

The power of arrest without warrant which applies to a person who is actually obstructing a policeman in the execution of his duty is provided by s.28(c) of the Criminal Procedure Code, which reads as follows:

Any police officer may, without an order from a magistrate and without a warrant, arrest:

(c) any person who obstructs a police officer while in the execution of his duty or who has escaped or attempts to escape from lawful custody.

In such a case arrest without warrant is not justified unless the police officer has actually been obstructed in the execution of his duty and it is not enough that the police officer should merely conceive that he has been obstructed in the execution of his duty.

In our opinion Sultan was entitled to refuse to give the police officer his name and address until he was satisfied that it was lawfully required of him and so the police officer was not entitled to put his hand upon Sultan to arrest him before he had established and communicated a good reason for insisting on demanding the name and address.

In our opinion the facts of this case as they appear from the record of the evidence are consistent with the fact that the police officer unfortunately and unjustifiably lost his temper because he conceived that Sultan was not advising Ishmail to sign the duplicate summons in accordance with the police officer's desire and that this fact led to the unfortunate mêlée which ensued in which all parties lost control of their tempers and we consider that it has not been established that the arrest of Sultan was lawful or that the appellant's intervention was unlawful.

For these reasons we allow the appeal and set aside the conviction
● and sentence.

NOTE The results of the three cases set out above should not be considered as typical of the administration of justice in colonial East Africa. They represent, rather, statements of an ideal.

The law regarding the torts of false arrest and false imprisonment in Tanzania is far from certain. From the above cases, we can extract two principles, neither of which precisely defines the limits within which the courts will attempt to control the power to arrest. First, under certain circumstances the courts will award damages to a person who has been falsely arrested or imprisoned and, secondly, there are other circumstances where an improper arrest will result in an acquittal.[13a]

[13a] See, also, the cases in Ch. VI of E. Veitch, *East African Cases on the Law of Tort*, Sweet and Maxwell, London, 1972.

Difficulties arise largely in those cases where a policeman, or private citizen, is exercising his power to arrest without warrant—an arrest under a valid warrant issued by a magistrate can generally not be impugned. (*Osman v. D.C. Hill* (1954) 2 T.L.R. (R) 183; affirmed (1955) 22 E.A.C.A. 169). The controlling legislation is s.27(a) of Cap. 20 which permits a police officer to arrest without warrant anyone whom he suspects on reasonable grounds of having committed a cognizable offence. An action for false arrest will only lie where there were no reasonable and probable grounds for the arrest. The decided cases vary widely on the question of how reasonableness, or lack of it, is to be proved. In some cases it has been decided that the plaintiff must merely establish the fact of detention or imprisonment, and the burden of showing that such detention or imprisonment was 'reasonably justifiable' shifts to the defendant. (*Ssekaddu* v. *Ssebaduka* [1968] E.A. 213 (U).) Other cases have suggested that the plaintiff must show that he resisted the arrest or did not submit voluntarily (*Clifton* v. *Hawley* [1966] E.A. 44 (K), and similar suggestions in *Sullivan* v. *Alimohamed Osman* [1959] E.A. 239 (CA)), or it may even be required that some degree of malice on the part of the person making the arrest be shown (*Osman* v. *D.C. Hill*). The question of reasonable and probable grounds must be related to the particular offence for which the person is arrested. For example, where the offence is clearly defined, reasonable and probable grounds will be correspondingly specific. However, where the offence is vaguely defined, it becomes difficult to limit the circumstances under which a suspect may be lawfuly arrested.

PENAL CODE: CAP. 16

- 176. The following persons:
    - (1) every common prostitute behaving in a disorderly or indecent manner in any public place, or loitering or soliciting in any public place for the purpose of prostitution;
    - (2) every person wandering or placing himself in any public place to beg or gather alms, or causing or procuring or encouraging any child or children so to do;
    - (3) every person playing at any game of chance for money or money's worth in any public place;
    - (4) every person wandering abroad and endeavouring by the exposure of wounds or deformation to obtain or gather alms;
    - (5) every person who publicly conducts himself in a manner likely to cause a breach of the peace;
    - (6) every person who without lawful excuse publicly does any indecent act; and
    - (7) every person who in any public place solicits for immoral purposes,

shall be deemed idle and disorderly persons, and shall be liable to a fine not exceeding five hundred shillings or to imprisonment for a period not exceeding three months or to both such fine and imprisonment.

177. The following persons:

(1) every person convicted of an offence unde s.176 after having been previously convicted as an idle and disorderly person;

(2) every person going about as gatherer or collector of alms, or endeavouring to procure charitable contributions of any nature or kind, under any false or fraudulent pretence;

(3) every suspected person or reputed thief who has no visible means of subsistence and cannot give a good account of himself; and

(4) every person found in or upon or near any premises or in any road or highway or any place adjacent thereto or in any public place at such time and under such circumstances as to lead to the conclusion that such person is there for an illegal or disorderly purpose;

(5) every person who, without the prior consent in writing in that behalf of the Area Commissioner, or, in the case of any municipality or township, the police officer in charge of the police in such municipality or township, collects, or makes any appeal for, subscriptions of money in any public place in such district, municipality or township, for any purpose,

shall be deemed to be a rogue and vagabond, and shall be guilty of a misdemeanour, and shall be liable for the first offence to imprisonment for three months, and for every subsequent offence to imprisonment for one year: Provided that paragraph (5) of this section shall not apply to:

(a) any person who, or the duly authorized representative of any organization which, has received the written consent of the Inspector-General of Police to collect, or make any appeal for, subscriptions of money for religious or charitable purposes, or

(b) any person authorized to collect, or make any appeal for, subscriptions of money under the provisions of any law, including any by-law, in force in Tanganyika:

Provided further that for the purposes of paragraph (5) of this section, the definition 'public place' in section 5 of this Code shall not be deemed to include any recognized place of religious worship.[14]

---

[14] The offences created in ss.176 and 177 are both cognizable offences. The introduction of legislation against 'rogues and vagabonds' represents one of the more sordid and brutal phases in the development of English capitalism. Beginning

ISSA s/o AMRI V. R.[15]

● BIRON, J.: The appellant was convicted on three counts, of conveying property reasonably suspected of having been stolen or unlawfully obtained, with being in possession of housebreaking implements by night and with being a rogue and a vagabond. He was sentenced to ... six months, twelve months and three months, all the terms of imprisonment to run concurrently. He is now appealing.

Evidence was given by a police corporal to the effect that at about three o'clock in the morning, whilst on patrol duty with a companion, he saw the appellant standing, or rather squatting, in the shadow of a building at a street corner. When the appellant saw the police he walked toward them whistling. They stopped him and asked him where he was going. The appellant replied that he was merely walking about as he had nowhere to sleep. He was wearing a vest and carrying a shirt and a pair of shoes. Inside one of the shoes was a receipt book. When searched there was found on him a bunch of six keys. The appellant claimed all the property found on him as his, as he did when he appeared in court, where he elaborated his defence. He said that he had come from Tanga to Dar es Salaam looking for work, apparently one and a half days previously. It should be noted that the record is somewhat defective, but it would appear that he had slept at the railway station on the previous night, and when found wandering about by the police he said he was looking for the railway station in order to sleep there again, but, being a stranger, he had not found his way to it when accosted by the police. He stated that he had bought the shoes at Kimamba, in Morogoro Region, for Sh. 15. The keys he had found on the road, and although he had tried to find the owner he had been unsuccessful. The shirt he had bought the previous year in Tanga, and as for the receipt book found on him, it had been given to him by a friend who had made a living selling local medicines. When this friend had obtained employment, he had given up his business and handed over the receipt book to him. The court had the appellant try on the shoes, and according to the magistrate they were too big for him.

In his judgement the magistrate directed himself, and properly so, that the appellant was found conveying the property in his possession. With regard to whether the property found on him could reasonably be suspected of having been stolen, he held that in view of the time when the appellant was found, the police had reason to suspect that the

---

in the sixteenth century, increasingly vicious sanctions were applied against destitute persons who had been forced off their land. See Karl Marx, *Capital*, vol. I, Random House, New York City, 1906, pp. 806-9.
[15] Tanzania, High Court, 1968, [1968] H.C.D. n. 195.

property in his possession was stolen. The magistrate, after taking into consideration that the shoes did not fit the appellant, found as a fact that they could not be his, as they were—and I quote—'over-size and extremely out of proportion'. The magistrate thereupon concluded that the appellant had not given a satisfactory account as to how he came to be in possession of the property described. With regard to the second count, that of being in possession of housebreaking instruments, the magistrate directed himself—as the direction is short, it can be set out in full:

In respect of Count 2, the only excuse accused gave is that he had found the keys in Kimamba and that he had tried to look for the owner whom he could not find at Kimamba Market. Accused said he did not bother to hand the keys to police because he did not care to do so. In my opinion accused had no lawful excuse of going about with a bunch of keys especially in the dead of the night even if in fact he had found them in Kimamba as he alleges.

With regard to the third count, that of being a rogue and vagabond, the magistrate directed himself that it was necessary for the prosecution to prove the following elements of the offence:

(i) That the accused was a suspected person or a reputed thief.
(ii) That the accused had no visible means of subsistence.
(iii) That the accused cannot give a good account of himself.

And he went on to state:

It is in evidence that accused was suspected by the arresting police officer. It is also in evidence that the accused had no visible means of subsistence. Accused himself admitted this fact when he told the court that he came to Dar es Salaam from Tanga to look for employment. Accused has failed to give a good account of himself. I am satisfied that the accused is a rogue and vagabond.

The magistrate accordingly convicted the appellant on all three counts as charged.

I propose to deal with the three convictions individually.

On this appeal first coming up for hearing before my brother Saidi, when the appellant appeared in person and insisted that the shoes were his, stating that the reason they appeared too large for him was that he had been asked to try them on without any laces, Saidi J. adjourned the hearing, directing that the shoes be transmitted to this Court, where the appellant should try them on. At the resumed hearing before me, the shoes were produced and the appellant tried them on laced. Although they appeared rather large for him, as conceded by learned State Attorney, they were not so unduly large as to be conclusive that the appellant could not have bought them for himself. Bearing in mind that the appellant said he had obtained them secondhand at an auction, when the size would be in inverse ratio to the price, I am very far from persuaded that the shoes are so outsize that they could not have been bought by the appellant for himself, as he asserted. With regard to the other property found . . . the shirt and receipt book, I fail to see how by any stretch they could reasonably be suspected of having been stolen or unlawfully obtained.

The conviction on the first count . . . cannot be sustained.

With regard to the second count, the position, it must be conceded at once, is by no means simple. The definition and meaning of 'house-breaking instruments' have in decided cases been given a very wide interpretation and cover a vast, if not unlimited, range of articles, which would include a bunch of keys, provided that the particular circumstances wherein they are found in an accused's possession justify the conclusion that he intended using them as housebreaking instruments. In this case all the suspicious circumstances were that the appellant was roaming the streets at night, being homeless, and had apparently stood, or squatted, in the shadow of a building, and when seen by the police he had walked towards them. Learned State Attorney concedes that in so far as this count is concerned it is a borderline case. To my mind, however, even if all the evidence is accepted in its entirety, it does not establish that the bunch of keys found in the appellant's possession was intended to be used by him for house-breaking purposes. The conviction . . . cannot therefore be sustained.

With regard to . . . the third count . . . the learned magistrate fully directed himself on the ingredients of the offence and also on the circumstances wherein the appellant was found . . . I am not persuaded that the Court would be justified in interfering with this last conviction as found.

NOTE Other decisions concerning the meaning of s.177 have tended to make its application somewhat stricter than *Issa s/o Amri* v. *R.* would indicate. (See, for example, *Rashidi* v. *R.* [1971] E.A. 112 (T), and *The Standard*, 30 September 1970.) All the cases agree that there are three elements which are necessary to the offence of being a rogue and a vagabond: (1) that the accused be a suspected person or a reputed thief, (2) that he have no visible means of subsistence, and (3) that he be unable to give a good account of himself. However, these three elements by themselves should not constitute the offence. A conviction should only result when the second and third elements together give rise to the suspicion that the accused is sustaining himself dishonestly. (*R.* v. *Godfrey s/o Siro* (1954) 2 T.L.R. (R) 40; *R.* v. *Mtambara bin Selemani* (1935) 1 T.L.R. (R) 29.) Thus, it has been stressed that as 'mere homelessness does not constitute roguishness' (*Hamisi Juma* v. *R.* [1968] H.C.D. n.469), it must be shown that the presence of the accused where found indicates an illegal or disorderly purpose. (*Juma s/o Abdallah* v. *R.* [1967] H.C.D. n.396.) The general impact of the decisions is that being a rogue and a vagabond is not to be used as a catchall charge and that this offence is not '. . . intended as a convenient method for supplying a hiatus in the evidence of felony'. (*Ramadhani* v. *R.* (1955) 2 T.L.R. (R) 118.)

Sections 176 and 177 are important means for dealing with the problem, referred to in Chapter III, of the large number of unemployable people who gravitate toward urban areas. The powers of arrest given by these two sections are often used in periodic roundups of 'undesirables'. Referring to one of these roundups, a police spokesman was quoted as saying that '. . . the people rounded up failed to satisfy the police when approached that they were out with reasonable cause . . . If enough evidence was established against any of them they would be charged'. (*The Standard*, 31 March 1969.) Does either s.176 or s.177 require that people going about in public should prove to the police on pain of being arrested that they are out with reasonable cause? What is 'reasonable cause' for being out in public? Is it lawful to arrest someone and hold him while evidence is established against him before charging him? How long may people who are rounded up be lawfully held in custody? (See *Njuguna s/o Kimani* v. *R.* (1954) 21 E.A.C.A. 316.)

A plaintiff may also obtain damages where the force used to carry out the arrest was more than was reasonably necessary. (*M'Ibui* v. *Dyer* [1967] E.A. 315 (K).)

An important policy consideration is the approach the courts should adopt when the police have acted illegally. The problem is fairly simple when the person who is arrested unlawfully is obviously guilty of no crime. Eventually, he will be released from custody and can then, in theory, collect damages from whoever arrested him. A more difficult problem arises where a person is unlawfully arrested but the state is nonetheless able to establish prima facie his guilt in respect of some offence. Should the court hold that as the police acted illegally in the first place, no conviction can result? Alternatively, should the court decide that since the accused was guilty of a crime, it does not matter how the police carried out their investigation? The court might justify the latter decision by reminding the accused that he can sue the arresting officer when he gets out of prison. In this respect, compare *Mwangi s/o Njeroge* v. *R.* (supra) and *Kuruma s/o Kaniu* v. *R.* (infra). This problem was raised in a particularly acute form in *Ochieng* v. *Uganda* ([1969] E.A. 1 (CA)). In that case the Court of Appeal accepted that the police had violated many of the procedural standards of the Criminal Procedure Code plus the fundamental rights provisions of Uganda's Constitution in conducting their investigation. On the other hand it was also quite clear that the accused had committed the acts with which he was charged. In the result, the court upheld the accused's conviction on a charge of murder. What is the purpose of procedural standards in the administration of the criminal law?[16]

16 On the difficult question of the permissibility of police 'traps', see J. S. Read, 'How to Set a Trap and When Not To', *Eastern Africa Law Review*, vol. III, no. 2, 1970, p. 103.

A final control over the power to arrest is provided by s. 253 of the Penal Code which creates the offence of wrongful confinement. For a conviction under this section, there must be proof of '. . . an unlawful and total restraint of the personal liberty of another, whether by detaining him against his will in a particular place or by constraining or compelling him to go to a particular place'. (*R.* v. *Sefu Said* [1964] E.A. 178 (T).) In one instance, a Justice of the Peace was found guilty of an offence under this section for remanding in custody a person who was unlawfully arrested. (*Oddov* v. *R.* [1970] E.A. 254 (T).) By way of contrast, it was held in *Kionywaki* v. *R.* ([1968] E.A. 195 (T)) that the immunity given judicial officers by s.60 (1)(b) of the Magistrates Courts Act, 1963 is sufficiently wide to protect a Divisional Executive Officer who, in his capacity as a Justice of the Peace, causes someone to be arrested wrongfully.

NOTE Information revealed in February 1970, concerning incidents at the Central Police Station in Dar es Salaam, gave rise to some concern about unlawful police practices. A Nigerian student doing unauthorized research in Tanzania was arrested and jailed for thirty-nine days. He alleged that he was held incommunicado and was at no time informed of the reasons for his detention. When released, he claimed that there were about thirty other people from various African countries being held under similar conditions in the so-called 'siasa' cells at Central Police Station. Later investigation revealed that these people had been arrested at the behest of the Special Branch, which itself has no powers of arrest, and that, with the exception of four men who were being detained under the Preventive Detention Act, they were not being held under any specific legislation. It was apparently the practice in such cases for the Special Branch to request arrests, not necessarily in writing, and then for the police to make the arrests without giving any reasons to those arrested, and to hold them in custody until the Special Branch decided they could go. Enquiries into these practices were launched by both the Ministry of Home Affairs and the Attorney-General's Chambers. A spokesman for the Attorney-General noted that unless a person is detained under the Preventive Detention Act or the Refugees (Control) Act, the law requires that he must be brought before a court as soon as possible, usually within forty-eight hours of his arrest. The Inspector-General of Police denied all knowledge of the matter. On 20 February, the Government released a statement confirming that the detentions had taken place, but noting the important requirements of national security. However, the Government politely chided the police, re-affirmed support for 'the liberty of the individual', and announced that '. . . appropriate procedures which will minimize the chances of innocent people getting caught up in situations such as this are . . . being instituted'. The non-Tanzanians who had been held at the Central Police Station were released and declared prohibited immigrants. (*The Standard*, 13, 14, 20, and 21 February 1970.)

While conducting the treason trial which began in Dar es Salaam in June 1970 and continued until February 1971, the then Chief Justice made a number of adverse comments on the disregard of rules of criminal procedure by various officials.

C · SEARCH

A search, which will normally be carried out by the police in an attempt to obtain information for a prosecution, may take place either prior to, or contemporaneously with, the arrest.

CRIMINAL PROCEDURE CODE: CAP. 20

● 118.   Where it is proved on oath to a court that in fact or according to reasonable suspicion anything upon, by or in respect of which an offence has been committed or anything which is necessary to the conduct of an investigation into any offence is in any building, vessel, carriage, box, receptacle or place, the court may by warrant (called a search warrant) authorize a police officer or other person therein named to search the building, vessel, carriage, box, receptacle or place (which shall be named or described in the warrant) for any such thing and, if anything searched for be found, to seize it and carry it before the court
● issuing the warrant or some other court to be dealt with according to law.

POLICE FORCE ORDINANCE: CAP. 322

● 34.—(1) Whenever a police officer not being lower in rank than a sub-inspector has reasonable grounds for believing that anything necessary for the purposes of an investigation into any alleged offence which he is authorized to investigate may be found in any place within the limits of any place or police station of which he is in charge, or to which he is attached, and that such thing cannot n his ʿpinion be otherwise obtained without undue delay, such officer after recording in writing the grounds of his belief and specifying in such writing, so far as possible, the thing for which search is to be made may, notwithstanding the provisions of section 118 of the Criminal Procedure Code, search, or cause to be searched, for such thing in any place within the limits of such police station.

(2) A police officer proceeding under subsection (1) shall, if practicable, conduct the search in person.

(3) If such police officer be unable to conduct the search in person, and there is no person competent to make the search present at the time, he may after recording in writing his reasons for so doing require any officer subordinate to him to make the search, and he shall deliver to such officer an order in writing specifying the place to be searched and so far as possible the thing for which search is to be made and such officer may thereupon search for such thing in such place.

(4) The provisions of sections 119, 120, and 121 of the Criminal Procedure Code as to search warrants shall, so far as may be, apply to a search made under this section.

(5) Copies of any record made under subsection (1) or subsection (3) shall forthwith be sent to the nearest magistrate empowered to take cognizance of the offence and the owner or occupier of the place searched shall on application be furnished with a copy of the same by the magistrate.

(6) The occupant of the place searched, or some other person in his behalf, shall, in every instance, be permitted to attend during the search.

KURUMA s/o KANIU v. REGINAM[17]

Summary

Accused was convicted under the Emergency Regulations of possessing two rounds of ammunition. He had been stopped and searched by a police constable as he was passing along the public road at a road block, the two rounds being found in his pocket. The prosecution argued that the arrest was lawful, either under the powers conferred by the Emergency Regulations, or under the section of the C.P.C. authorizing detention and search of persons suspected of conveying property reasonably suspected to have been stolen. As to the first point, there was a conflict in the evidence as to where the arrest occurred; this led the Court of Appeal to hold that since it was not clear that the area was one covered by the Regulations, the arrest could not be sanctioned on that ground. The Court continued as follows.

NIHILL, P., WORLEY, V.P. and BRIGGS, J.A.: We are of opinion that since the special power of search under Emergency Regulation 22(b)(2) cannot be invoked at this stage, the initial stopping and searching of the appellant was unlawful and irregular. It is quite plain from the evidence that he was stopped as a matter of routine in consequence of a general direction to the constables on duty at the road block to stop and search all or as many as they thought fit of the persons passing along the road. As the constable ran his hands over the appellant's person he felt in a trousers pocket 'what seemed to be a pocket knife and two rounds of ammunition'. From that moment he had a reasonable suspicion of the commission of a cognizable offence, and immediately seized the appellant, called for assistance, and a subsequent further search disclosed the two rounds of ammunition in question. But we agree with the second conclusion of the learned trial Judge that even if the original detention and search which led to the discovery of the ammunition and the arrest were unlawful and amounted to a trespass and an assault, this fact did not invalidate the production in Court of the incriminating articles which were found as a consequence of those irregular acts.

---

[17] Kenya, Court of Appeal for Eastern Africa, 1954, 21 E.A.C.A. 242.

It is well settled that an unlawful arrest does not affect the jurisdiction of a Court if it is otherwise competent to entertain the charge.

It seems to us, therefore, by parity of reasoning, that if a Court is not precluded, by the fact of the accused having been brought unlawfully before it, from adjudicating upon the charge made against him, there can be no good reason for holding that it is not entitled to receive evidence of articles found upon him or discovered in consequence of the search made at the time of that unlawful arrest. There is not much authority on the point, but the matter does seem to us to be concluded by the decision of Horridge, J. in *Elias and others* v. *Pasmore*, which was relied upon by the learned trial Judge . . . As Horridge, J. put it: 'In my opinion the seizure of these exhibits was justified, because they were capable of being and were used as evidence in this trial. If I am right in the above view, the original seizure of these exhibits, though improper at the time, would therefore be excused.' The learned Judge fortified his opinion by reference to the speeches of Lord Chelmsford and Lord Colonsay in the Scottish case of *Pringle* v. *Bremmer and Stirling*, and we may briefly cite the following from the speech of Lord Chelmsford in that case:

But supposing that in a search which might have been improper originally, there were matters discovered which showed the complicity of the pursuer in a crime, then I think the officers, I can hardly say would have been justified, but would have been excused by the result of their search. Then again, with regard to the arrest and imprisonment of the pursuer—as to that it is not alleged that there was any warrant at all; but then, it is said, the constable having discovered matters which, in his judgement, brought home to the pursuer complicity in the alleged crime, he was justified in exercising his discretion upon the subject, and in apprehending the pursuer and lodging him in prison. Again, I say . . . the result will either justify him or will not justify him . . .

● *Appeal dismissed.*

NOTE Under the provisions of the Emergency Regulations, Kuruma was sentenced to death for this offence. He appealed to the Privy Council, but his appeal was dismissed ([1955] A.C. 197), their Lordships holding that, ' . . . the test to be applied in considering whether evidence is admissible is whether it is relevant to the matters at issue. If it is, it is admissible and the Court is not concerned how it was obtained' (per Lord Goddard, at p. 203). The Judicial Committee was in fact saying to Kenya policemen that any method of obtaining evidence would be considered acceptable. In March 1955, a Kenya policeman was convicted of beating an African girl to death in an attempt to obtain evidence. He was sentenced to eighteen months imprisonment, the court apparently accepting that it was a general practice to use violence in such cases. (For the above and for a comment on the *Kuruma* case, see T. M. Franck in *Canadian Bar Review*, vol. XXXIII, 1955, p. 721; see also A. B. Kasunmu, 'Admissibility of Illegally Obtained

Evidence in Nigeria', *Nigeria Law Journal*, vol. III, 1969, p. 83. For a recent application of the *Kuruma* principle, see the decision of the Privy Council in a Jamaican case. *King* v. *R.* [1968] 2 All E.R. 610.)

QUESTION What is the purpose of s.118 of Cap. 20? What would be the effect of the *Kuruma* decision on the achievement of this purpose?

NOTE In connection with searches, it has been held that the general law of East Africa does not recognize a right to privacy. (*Thakkar* v. *The Vanik Mahajan* [1960] E.A. 208 (Z).)

D · PRE-TRIAL DETENTION

After a person has been arrested the law requires that he be brought before a court of competent jurisdiction and that the court decide whether he should be kept in custody.

CRIMINAL PROCEDURE CODE: CAP. 20

● 34.—(1) When any person has been taken into custody without a warrant for an offence other than an offence punishable with death, the officer in charge of the police station to which such person shall be brought may in any case and shall, if it does not appear practicable to bring such person before an appropriate court within twenty-four hours after he was so taken into custody, inquire into the case and, unless the offence appears to the officer to be of a serious nature, release the person on his executing a bond, with or without sureties, for a reasonable amount to appear before a court at a time and place to be named in the bond; but where such person is retained in custody he shall be brought before a court as soon as practicable.

(2) Where any person has been taken into custody without a warrant for an offence punishable with death, such person shall be brought before a court as soon as practicable.

(3) Where any person is arrested under a warrant of arrest such person shall be brought before a court as soon as practicable.

(4) Notwithstanding anything contained in subsections (1), (2), and (3) of this section an officer in charge of a police station may release a person arrested on suspicion on a charge of committing any offence when, after due police inquiry, insufficient evidence is, in his opinion, disclosed on which to proceed with the charge.

35. Officers in charge of police stations shall report to the nearest magistrate, within twenty-four hours or as soon as practicable, the cases of all persons arrested without warrant within the limits of

their respective stations, whether such persons have been admitted to bail or not.

123.—(1) When any person, other than a person accused of murder or treason, is arrested or detained without warrant by an officer in charge of a police station, or appears or is brought before a court, and is prepared at any time while in the custody of such officer or at any state of the proceedings before such court to give bail, such person may be admitted to bail:

Provided that such officer or court may, instead of taking bail from such person, release him on his executing a bond without sureties for his appearance as hereinafter provided.

(2) The amount of bail shall be fixed with due regard to the circumstances of the case and shall not be excessive.

(3) Notwithstanding anything contained in subsection (1) of this section the High Court may in any case direct that any person be admitted to bail or that the bail required by a subordinate court or
● police officer be reduced.

QUESTION Section 13 of the Official Secrets Ordinance (Cap. 45) reads as follows:

For the purposes of the *Criminal Procedure Code*, every offence under this Ordinance shall be deemed to be a cognizable and non-bailable offence.

What should be the result when a person charged with an offence under this ordinance applies to the High Court to be released on bail? (See *Mwambola* v. *R.* [1967] H.C.D. n. 441; for comments on this case, see *Eastern Africa Law Review*, vol. I, no. 1, 1968, p. 91 and ibid., no. 3, p. 300.)

PRIMARY COURTS MANUAL[18]

● Sometimes it may be possible to allow the person accused out on bail. This is a matter for the court to decide. If the court considers there are special reasons why the accused should not be allowed out on bail, e.g. that he may abscond, or is dangerous or may try and bribe some of the witnesses, it can refuse to release him—it is entirely for the court to say. If it decides to let him out on bail it can do so if he makes a deposit or signs a bond. The court may further require a trustworthy person or persons to make deposits or sign bonds, promising to pay into court certain sums of money if the accused runs away or does not appear in court when required. The amount to be paid should be about the same as the amount of the fine which would be imposed on the accused for the offence with which he is charged. Thus if he is accused of not taking out a pombe licence and the usual fine is Sh. 80.00 then

18 Government Printer, Dar es Salaam, 1964, p. 19.

the deposits or bonds should be for that sum. A bond should only be accepted from a person whom the court considers to be trustworthy;
● if it is in any doubt it should demand that a deposit be made.

MAGISTRATES' COURTS ACT, 1963: CAP. 537

● 50. A justice may, if there is no magistrate in attendance at a court house to which he is assigned, exercise at the court house any of the following powers of a magistrate exercising jurisdiction at such court house:

(a) to admit any person arrested, with or without warrant, for any offence, other than murder or treason, to bail either with or without security or release him in his own bond, and to issue a warrant of arrest for any person in breach of a bond for his appearance;

(b) to remand in custody any person arrested, with or without warrant, for a reasonable time, not exceeding seven days at any one time, to some prison, lock-up or other place of security:

Provided that:

(i) a justice shall not remand any person in custody unless a case file is, or shall have been, opened for the matter and a charge is, or shall have been, drawn up and signed by a magistrate, justice or police officer, containing such particulars as are reasonably necessary to identify the offence or offences, including the law and the section, or other division thereof, under which the accused person is charged; and

(ii) a justice shall not remand any person in custody for more than seven days at any one time, nor, save where normal means of access to the nearest magistrate are interrupted, for more than an aggregate of twenty-eight days, without taking him
● before a magistrate.

A GUIDE FOR JUSTICES OF THE PEACE[19]

● A person charged with murder or treason should always be remanded in custody. When deciding whether to issue a warrant of arrest or to summons a person, and similarly when deciding whether to remand an accused person in custody or to commit him to bail, a Justice should always bear in mind that to detain a person in custody is to deprive him of his freedom. He should, therefore, always satisfy himself that the accused is:

likely to run away; or

[19] p. 2.

    to refuse to attend court; or
    to commit a public nuisance; or
    to interfere with witnesses; or
    the charge is a serious one and investigation would be impaired were
●   the accused not in custody.

Douglas Brown
CRIMINAL PROCEDURE IN UGANDA AND KENYA[20]

(**NOTE**   The author is here outlining the factors which should be considered
in deciding to grant bail.)

● (1)   The nature of the accusation. Is the accused charged with a serious
    offence or not? Generally a magistrate should try to award bail in
    lesser offences and be cautious about awarding bail in serious offences.
    It would be unusual to award bail to a person charged with house-
    breaking.
    (2)   The severity of the punishment which conviction will entail . . .
    (3)   What sort of person is the accused? What is his social standing?
    Has he any property in the area? Is he an immigrant from a different
    tribe or country?
    (4)   When is the case going to be heard? How long would he be on
    remand if denied bail? . . .
    (5)   Will he or his sureties be able to pay if he fails to appear on the
    appointed day (assuming that the bail proposed is bond, rather than a
●   deposit in cash or property)?

QUESTION   Are the factors outlined above necessarily the correct ones
to be considered by the courts of a socialist state?

NOTE   Recent developments have considerably altered the practical
position of the courts in respect of bail. In September 1968, a District
Magistrate was placed in Preventive Detention for granting bail to an MP
who was allegedly involved in a spectacular murder case. Although the
magistrate was released after two days in detention, the effect of this affair
was to make other magistrates reluctant to grant bail. (See *The Standard*,
27 September, 28 September, 2 October, and 3 October 1968.) This reluc-
tance was increased by later policy statements of national leaders. Speaking
on 14 December 1969, the President explained why he had detained thirty-
nine people who were arrested as a result of an enquiry into alleged mal-
practice in the Immigration Division, rather than having normal criminal
proceedings launched against them. Had criminal proceedings been instituted,
the suspects would likely have been released on bail; their liberty, he believed,
would seriously interfere with the police investigation. 'When a magistrate

20 Sweet and Maxwell, London, 1965, p. 29.

knows that the people and the police are waging a war against corruption, why should he release [an accused person] when at the same time the police are pleading that his release might be a menace to their investigations.' (*The Standard*, 15 December 1969.) Speaking at the annual Judges' and Magistrates' Conference on 5 January 1970, the second Vice-President reminded his audience of the struggle being waged against the rising crime rate and criticized magistrates over the granting of bail. (*The Standard*, 6 January 1970.) The message appeared to have its desired effect: in a speech given six weeks later, the Minister for Home Affairs, Mr Maswanya (a former policeman) indicated that he had detected, since Mr Kawawa's speech, a satisfactory change in the attitude of magistrates towards the granting of bail. (*The Standard*, 24 February 1970.) By late 1970, it was extremely difficult for arrested persons to be released on bail.

If bail is not granted the accused person is remanded in custody until his case is finally disposed of. In Tanzania, it has been estimated that only twenty-five per cent of the people remanded in custody ever receive prison sentences. As a former Commissioner of Prisons has noted, the practice of detaining people before trial not only puts a severe strain on the resources of the Prisons Department, but it means that a number of people who are not criminals themselves are exposed to convicted lawbreakers for the period they are being held in custody. He recommended: first, a complete re-examination and re-organization of the bail system, and, second, ending 'the practice now prevailing of detaining persons suspected of crime, and then collecting evidence'.[21]

E · THE DECISION TO PROSECUTE

Before a trial can begin, the state must decide whether it wishes to prosecute the accused. Two factors are of consequence here. The first is the fact that there is always pressure on the police to obtain convictions, pressure which may lead to a practice known as plea-bargaining. Secondly, because of the issues or personalities involved in a particular prosecution, members of the legislative and executive branches of government may wish to interfere in the criminal process.

Plea-bargaining means essentially that the individual responsible for prosecuting a case agrees with the accused that if he pleads guilty, the prosecution will ask for a light or even a suspended sentence. Alternatively, the prosecution may agree to drop one charge against the accused if he pleads guilty to another. The supposed merit of this practice is that it satisfies

---

[21] O. K. Rugimbana, 'Various Aspects of the Imprisonment System in East Africa', *East African Law Journal*, vol. II, no. 1, 1966, pp. 21–3. For a general discussion of pre-trial detention supported by extensive statistics from one jurisdiction, see M. L. Friedland, *Detention Before Trial*, University of Toronto Press, Toronto, 1966.

everyone—the prosecutor gets his conviction and the accused is either unpunished or punished lightly. There is evidence that this practice exists in Tanzania.[22]

NOTE   In an article entitled 'Criminal Law in Tanzania' which appeared in *The Nationalist* of 23 and 25 November 1968, the author, Mr P. Msiska, a Resident Magistrate, said the following about discretion to prosecute:

> It is my view that the overriding factor that the police are concerned with here is what prosecutions will be able to further obedience to the social order, as laid down under the Criminal Law, by the individuals in society at large. The question whether there is enough evidence to prosecute or whether equality before the law is preserved is of secondary importance. No useful purpose is indeed served by prosecutions of every case of criminal misconduct.

NOTE   Criminal cases may arise where the interests or the prestige of the government are involved, as, for example, in deciding whether to prosecute a Minister for an alleged offence. The impartial administration of justice may demand a prosecution which is not, however, in the public interest. In this sort of situation, the crucial question is who should decide whether or not to prosecute. In Tanzania this job is performed by the Director of Public Prosecutions. The office was originally established under s.53 of the Independence Constitution, which provided that in the exercise of his powers, the D.P.P. was not to be subject to the direction or control of any person or authority. In the discussions which preceded the adoption of the Republican Constitution, the position of the D.P.P. was reviewed. It was deemed necessary to, 'provide for the exceptional case where the public interest is of overriding importance', and as the President was the person best qualified to judge the public interest, it was decided that he should be empowered to give directions to the D.P.P. (*Proposals for a Republic: Government Paper No. 1 of 1962*, op. cit.). The office of D.P.P. was not referred to in the Republican Constitution (or any of the subsequent constitutions), but was established by a new s.80A of the Criminal Procedure Code, which provided that he should be subject to the directions of the President, but of no other person. A number of political cases then arose, one of them involving the prosecution of a Regional Commissioner, but the President did not intervene and allowed the D.P.P. to function quite independently. (See Colin Leys, 'The Constitution of Tanganyika', *Journal of the Parliaments of the Commonwealth*, op. cit., p. 135.) The job of D.P.P. is presently performed by the Attorney-General.

F · THE TRIAL

In normal circumstances a trial must be held in open court. However, s. 76 of the Criminal Procedure Code does give the judge a discretion to hold certain portions of a particular trial *in camera* or to restrict the access of certain persons. This discretion ' . . . should only be used on the rarest

[22] Boehringer, 'Developments in Criminology in Tanzania', op. cit., fn. 330; see also *The Standard*, 16 April 1968.

of occasions and then only after [the judge is]... completely satisfied that it is necessary'. (*Musa* v. *R.* [1970] E.A. 42 (CA) at p. 45, per Newbold, P.) Generally, the superior courts will take account of the difficult conditions under which many magistrates have to operate in the rural areas and be willing to give a liberal definition of what physically constitutes an 'open court'. (See *Chungu* v. *R.* [1967] E.A. 68 (T).)

The trial begins with the accused being told, in a language which he understands, the precise nature of the accusations against him.

CRIMINAL PROCEDURE CODE: CAP. 20

● 135. Every charge or information shall contain, and shall be sufficient if it contains, a statement of the offences with which the accused person is charged, together with such particulars as may be necessary for
● giving reasonable information as to the nature of the offence charged.

The purpose of a charge is '... to inform an accused what it is that he is alleged to have done which contravenes the law. If the prosecution fails to prove that charge, although it might successfully prove another charge, the accused is entitled to be acquitted.' (*Sakila* v. *R.* [1967] E.A. 403 (T) at p. 404.) A charge will be sufficient if it informs the accused of the substance of the case he has to meet, despite any technical irregularities it may contain. (See *Seidi* v. *R.* [1969] E.A. 280 (T).)

After the charge is read, the accused will plead 'guilty' or 'not guilty' (or he may remain silent, in which case the court will normally enter a plea of not guilty). When an accused person pleads guilty, the magistrate should not automatically enter a conviction against him, but should record the facts presented by the prosecution and ask the accused if he admits these facts. If the accused agrees with and admits the facts, and the court is satisfied that a plea of guilty was correct, a conviction may then be entered.[23]

Where the accused is charged on two or more counts and he makes an apparently equivocal plea, such plea should be entered as not guilty on all counts. (See *Njani* v. *R.* [1970] E.A. 260 (T).)

If the accused pleads not guilty, it is then up to the state to prove beyond a reasonable doubt that he is guilty of the offence with which he is charged. (See *Mwihambi s/o Chinyeke* v. *R.* (1955) 2 T.L.R. (R) 128.)

SAIDI s/o MWAKAWANGA v. R.[24]

● WESTON, J.: It cannot too often be repeated that except in special circumstances which do not concern us here the accused in a criminal

---

[23] s. 203 Criminal Procedure Code; *R.* v. *Waiziri s/o Musa* (1954) 2 T.L.R. (R) 30; *R.* v. *Bison s/o Mwanga* (1954) 2 T.L.R. (R) 31.
[24] Tanganyika, High Court, 1962; [1963] E.A. 6.

trial is never to be put to the proof of any allegation he makes in his defence on pain of conviction if he fails—in other words, and shortly,
● the accused in any criminal trial does not have to prove his innocence.

NOTE In recent years the High Court of Tanzania has often stressed that the onus of proving the guilt of the accused is on the prosecution and that to be acquitted, the accused need only raise some doubt as to whether the prosecution has discharged this responsibility. Thus, the court need not accept the accused's side of the story, it has only to feel that his defence has raised a reasonable doubt as to his guilt. For example, '. . . where an accused sets up an alibi in defence, it is not on him to establish it, but it is sufficient if it succeeds in raising a reasonable doubt as to whether it was the accused who committed the offence with which he is charged'. (*Morrison s/o Shem v. R.* [1968] H.C.D. n.417. See also *Moshi d/o Rajabu v. R.* [1967] H.C.D. n.384; *Salehe s/o Kassim v. R.* [1968] H.C.D. n.251; *Fanuel s/o Kilua v. R.* [1967] H.C.D. n.369.)

NOTE Like all 'rights' arising under the common law, that which puts the burden of proving its case on the prosecution can be removed or altered by appropriate legislation. It is therefore possible for Parliament, if it wishes, to require the accused to prove his innocence. Under the Prevention of Corruption Act, 1971 (Act No. 16 of 1971. See also Act No. 1 of 1970), a police officer of the rank of superintendent or above, if so authorized by the President or the Attorney-General, may order a public officer to give an accounting of all or any class of his property and to give an account of how he acquired such property. If there is a reasonable suspicion that all or any such property was corruptly acquired, the public officer may be prosecuted and the burden of proving the contrary rests on him. Section 312 of the Penal Code creates the offence of possessing or conveying property reasonably suspected of being stolen or unlawfully obtained. In order to avoid conviction the accused must satisfy the court that the property came to his possession lawfully. (See K. Carey, 'Possession of Suspect Property', *Eastern Africa Law Review*, vol. II, no. 3, 1969, p. 358.) In cases where the burden of proof shifts to the accused, he is not required to prove his innocence beyond a reasonable doubt. He must simply convince the court that on a balance of probabilities, he is innocent. (See also the Stock Theft Ordinance, Cap. 422, especially s.3; the National Security Act, 1970, Act No. 3 of 1970, s.12; and the Protected Places and Areas Act, 1969, Act No. 38 of 1969.)

NOTE An important question at this stage concerns whether the accused is to be represented by a lawyer. This is a particular problem in a country where the criminal law is still to a large extent foreign, where there are few lawyers, and where most people cannot afford the services of a lawyer. In a socialist country two things must be considered. First, there is the clear desirability of providing every accused person with as full a defence as may be necessary. On the other hand is the equally clear need to prevent the economically privileged members of society from exploiting their position through a professionally prepared defence not available to the mass of the people. Tanzania has approached this problem from two directions. First, free legal aid is provided by the state in cases where a judge of the High

Court certifies that such legal aid is 'desirable in the interests of justice'. (Legal Aid (Criminal Proceedings) Act, 1969, Act No. 21 of 1969; for the position prior to this Act see the now repealed Poor Prisoners Defence Ordinance, Cap. 21 and *Mohamed s/o Salim* v. *R.* [1958] E.A. 202 (CA); for legal aid in East Africa generally, see Twining, 'Social Justice and the Law', *East African Law and Social Change*, op. cit.; for legal aid in Tanzania, see F. M. Kassam, 'Legal Aid and the Law Student', *Journal of the Denning Law Society*, vol. II, no. 2, 1969, p. 179, and Naijuka Kasiwaki, 'Legal Aid', *Sunday News*, 7 June 1970.) On the other hand, 'no advocate or public prosecutor as such may appear or act for any party in a primary court', which is, of course, where the bulk of the nation's judicial business is conducted. (Magistrates' Courts Act, 1963, Cap. 537, s.29(1); for a discussion of this provision, see J. P. W. B. McAuslan, 'The Problem of Representation in the Primary Courts', *East African Law Journal*, vol. II, no. 3, 1966, p. 179.) One should remember that this problem cannot be solved merely by instituting legal aid schemes. It will require a radical reappraisal of the role played by professional lawyers in the functioning of the legal system. Undoubtedly, one of the tasks of the Tanzania Legal Corporation will be to carry out such a reappraisal. (For background on this question, see Jackson, *Guide to the Legal Profession in East Africa*, op. cit.; and Ghai and McAuslan, *Public Law and Political Change in Kenya*, pp. 381-406. In 1958, Guinea abolished the private legal profession. When announcing this decree Sekou Touré stated that the legal profession was an expression of a 'legalistic formalism which is not only useless, but incompatible with the social realities of a young African nation', quoted in *Review of the International Commission of Jurists*, no. VII, 1971, p. 4.)

Of all other procedural issues which may arise during the course of the trial, the admissibility of a confession is probably the most important. Confessions are obviously crucial pieces of evidence in a criminal prosecution. In many cases a confession may be the only evidence against the accused. The basic point in the law concerning confessions is that they should be voluntary. That is, to put the principle in its most basic terms, the authorities should not arrest people and then torture them until they 'confess'. It is considered that the best way to prevent practices of this kind is to require that the state prove the voluntariness of any statement made by the accused before such statement can be introduced in evidence as a confession.

EVIDENCE ACT: ACT NO. 6 OF 1967

● 27. No confession made to a police officer shall be proved as against a person accused of an offence.

28. No confession made by any person whilst he is in the custody of a police officer, unless it be made in the immediate presence of a magistrate as defined in the Magistrates' Courts Act, 1963, or a justice of the peace under that Act, shall be proved as against such person.

29. No confession which is tendered in evidence shall be rejected on the ground that a promise or threat has been held out to the person confessing unless the court is of the opinion that the inducement was made in such circumstances and was of such a nature as was likely to cause an untrue admission of guilt to be made.

30. Where an inducement has been made to a person accused of an offence in such circumstances and of such a nature as are referred to in section 29 and a confession is made after the impression caused by the inducement has, in the opinion of the court, been fully removed, the confession is relevant and need not be rejected.

31. When any fact is deposed to as discovered in consequence of information received from a person accused of any offence in the custody of a police officer, so much of such information, whether it amounts to a confession or not, as relates distinctly to the fact thereby discovered, is relevant.

32. If such a confession is otherwise relevant, it does not become irrelevant merely because it was made under a promise of secrecy, or in consequence of a deception practised on the accused person for the purpose of obtaining it, or when he was drunk, or because it was made in answer to questions which he need not have answered, whatever may have been the form of those questions, or because he was not warned that he was not bound to make such confession, and that evidence of it might be given against him.

33.—(1) When two or more persons are being tried jointly for the same offence or for different offences arising out of the same transaction, and a confession made by one of such persons affecting himself and some other of such persons is proved, the Court may take into consideration such confession as against such other person.

(2) In this section 'offence' includes the abetment of, or attempt to commit, the offence.

NOTE   The original s. 33 (1) was amended by s. 19 of the Administration of Justice (Miscellaneous Amendments) Act, 1971 (Act no. 26 of 1971). This amendment marks a major departure from principle. Formerly s. 33(1) provided that a confession by one accused could *not* be 'taken into consideration' as against a co-accused. It is not clear exactly what is meant by taking a confession 'into consideration'. However, the side-note to the new section makes the purpose of the change quite evident. The side-note reads: 'Confession to be admissible as evidence against co-accused'. Most of the changes introduced by Act No. 26 of 1971 can be seen as responses to the 1970-71 treason trial.

QUESTIONS 1. If a man is 'guilty', is it necessarily wrong to beat a confession out of him?

2. What effect, if any, might ss.29, 30, and 32 have on the principle of voluntariness?

NOTE A crucial problem which the Evidence Act avoids is that of defining a confession. The definition most often used is that found in *Swami's* case (*Pakala Narayana Swami* v. *Emperor* [1939] 1 All E.R. 397 at p. 405 (PC).):

> In their Lordships' view no statement that contains self-exculpatory matter can amount to a confession, if the exculpatory statement is of some fact which, if true, would negative the offence alleged to be confessed. Moreover, a confession must either admit in terms the offence, or at any rate substantially all the facts which constitute the offence. An admission of a gravely incriminating fact, even a conclusively incriminating fact is not of itself a confession, e.g. an admission that the accused is the owner of and was in recent possession of the knife or revolver which caused a death with no explanation of any other man's possession.

(For a very full discussion of this whole area of the law, see P. Durand, 'Confessions in East Africa', *East African Law Journal*, vol. IV, no. 3, 1968, p. 70; see also H. F. Morris, *Evidence in East Africa*, Sweet and Maxwell, London, 1968, pp. 62-89.)

Our attitudes towards the foregoing will be determined by the way in which we view the nature of the judicial process. For example, the 'sporting theory of justice' would accept that every opportunity, whether substantive or procedural, must be given to the accused to avoid conviction. A more stringent attitude would be concerned solely with the question of whether the accused is innocent or guilty, and would overlook certain procedural niceties. Conflicting theories about the purpose of the criminal law process can be seen in the application of the privilege against self-incrimination. The privilege stems from the belief that no man should be condemned by his own words. Therefore, the accused cannot be compelled to testify at his own trial. In other words, the prosecution cannot make the accused person enter the witness box and give evidence against himself. However, the principle is somewhat compromised by the rule that if the accused chooses to testify, he will be required to answer all questions put to him, including ones which are definitely incriminating. (Evidence Act, ss. 127-130, s. 157.)

M. D. Bomani

MACHINERY OF JUSTICE IN A DEVELOPING SOCIETY

● What about the attorneys? What should they do? The prosecuting attorney must be interested in justice being done. His interest is not merely in seeing that the accused is convicted and sentenced. He is there to see that the truth is brought to the surface, all the facts are supplied to the Court and all aspects of the evidence are considered. In this country, for example, the language of the High Court and the R.M.'s Court is English. The vast majority of the people brought before the Court do not speak English. Questions put to them in English are translated into Swahili and very often further into some vernacular language. The accused's answers are likewise translated into English, or very often first into Swahili then into English. The person doing the translation isn't always an expert in languages. I have myself witnessed complete distortion of meaning in the process of translation.

It is the duty, therefore, of the prosecuting attorney to make sure the translation machinery is satisfactory and make sure himself that the accused person understands the questions being put to him. It is also his duty to tell the whole truth of the matter even if certain aspects of it may be damaging to the prosecution case. This he can do by asking all necessary questions. He should not leave it to the defence attorney to bring out everything favourable to the accused.

The defending attorney has a duty first to the accused, it is conceded; he also has a duty to the course of justice. He would, in my view, be failing in the latter if he concealed from the Court any facts that might influence the Court one way or another. The Anglo-Saxon tradition of leaving it solely to the prosecuting attorney to urge on the Court all points which are against the accused is, in my view, unsatisfactory. The defending attorney should not set out at all costs to get his client out; less still should he coach his client on what to say in Court.

At this point it may be valuable to question the validity of the classic adversary approach to a criminal trial. This theory holds that the trial is a contest between the totally opposed interests of prosecution and defence. The judge is a disinterested onlooker neither favouring nor assisting either side, and finally basing his decision only on those aspects of the controversy which have been illuminated by one or both of the combatants. It is clear that if the theory is to function properly in practice, both parties must be represented by experienced legal practitioners. Since this is rarely the case in Tanzania today, the adversary theory requires some modification. For example, it is recognized that the magistrate or judge may have to play a more active role in the conduct of the trial than a strict application of the theory might permit.[25] The degree to which the court holder should assist

---

[25] e.g. *Petro s/o Wanga* v. *R.* (1955) 2 T.L.R. (R) 121; this view has been supported by Chief Justice Georges, see 'Report on Judges' and Magistrates' Conferences', op. cit., p. 173.

either the prosecution or the defence is not clear, though it appears that the Government would like the courts to support the struggle against crime by being more helpful to inexperienced prosecutors. Mr Kawawa stated at the beginning of 1970 that he was, '... calling upon you [magistrates] to try and play the role of an inquiry officer more than merely that of a passive arbiter. You have the skills and the opportunity. Not all our prosecutors all over the country are possessed of these skills. You must not leave it all to the prosecutors even where you see clearly that something wrong is going on. You must guide them and help them just as you would guide the defence advocates. Of course, in doing this you must always have the interests of an innocent man in mind. *It may be about time you reappraised your own role in the administration of justice.*'[26]

On a superficial reading it might be felt that Mr Kawawa is suggesting that the courts do away with the traditional safeguards of the common law. Such a conclusion, however, would be based on the assumption that these safeguards are (or ever were) in general use. But the practical significance of these safeguards depends largely on the degree to which an adversary system of criminal justice is a functioning reality. In the most basic sense, this further depends on whether people plead 'not guilty' in criminal prosecutions, and although accused persons in the High Court may normally plead not guilty, in the great majority of Primary Court cases a guilty plea is accepted.

NOTE   Professor Gower has suggested that recourse to executive detention may often be occasioned by '... the extreme protection afforded the accused' in a criminal trial. See *Independent Africa: The Challenge to the Legal Profession*, Oxford University Press, London, 1967, pp. 86-7.

If the common law procedures are neither particularly appropriate nor widely used in Tanzania, the next question should be, as the Second Vice-President suggests, what procedures *are* appropriate?

The solution to this problem may become clearer not through a comparative examination of various types of procedures, but through an analysis of the overall aims of the administration of criminal justice. For example, traditional criminal law in Tanzania was concerned not so much with organized society punishing the individual transgressor, but with the maintenance of harmony in the community through reconciliation and compensation. Thus, certain procedures would develop appropriate to the achievement of this aim.[27]

---

[26] 'Speech to the Judges' and Magistrates' Conference, 5 January 1970', quoted in *The Standard*, 6 January 1970. Italics added.
[27] See, for example, J. S. Read, 'Some Legal Problems in East Africa', op. cit., pp. 46-51; Twining, *The Place of Customary Law in the National Legal Systems of East Africa*, University of Chicago Press, Chicago, 1963; Cotran, 'The Position of Customary Criminal Law in African Countries', op. cit.; and J. W. Katende, 'Why were Punishments in Pre-European East Africa mainly Compensative rather than Punitive', *Journal of the Denning Law Society*, vol. II, no. 1, 1967, p. 122.

On the other hand, Malawi appears to have decided that the purpose of the administration of criminal law is to punish criminals. A trial begins with the prosecution attempting to make out a prima facie case against the accused. If it succeeds in so doing, the accused is required, essentially, to prove his innocence. It should be noted that this instance is merely an example of a clear policy of returning to the colonial practice whereby in cases involving 'natives' the courts were to observe 'substantial justice without undue regard to technicalities'.[28] The point then, is that once the end purpose of criminal justice is clearly established, the means of achieving that end, that is, the procedures to be used, become clear.

One may usefully question the role which the public should play in a criminal trial. In England, the jury system is considered to be one of the fundamental protections the common law offers to the subject: in many criminal cases the final decision as to guilt or innocence is left not to the judge, but to twelve members of the community. Except for trials of white settlers in Kenya (where the jury was composed of other white settlers), the jury system was not considered 'appropriate' for introduction in colonial East Africa.[29] At present, the High Court is required to sit with at least two assessors in all criminal cases. (Criminal Procedure Code, s. 248.) The assessors merely deliver advisory opinions, and the final decision is left to the judge. This contrasts with the position in Primary Courts, where the assessors may overrule the magistrate. (Act No. 18 of 1969.) As a result of some extraordinary reasoning the Court of Appeal has decided that women may not sit as assessors in the High Court (*Kiwelesi* v. *R.* [1969] E.A. 227), though both men and women may act as assessors in Primary Courts. Sections 25 and 26 of Act No. 10 of 1969 overrule the *Kiwelesi* decision.

G · SENTENCE

If the court finds the accused not guilty, he should be released immediately and may not be tried again for the same offence. (Criminal Procedure Code, s. 139.) If the accused is found guilty, the court will then pass sentence on him. Depending on the offence, the court may choose from the following sentences or orders (given, of course, the different sentencing powers of the Primary Courts, District Courts, and the High Court): death, imprison-

---

[28] See V. G. Davidson, 'Reforms in Evidence and Criminal Procedure: The Malawi Experiment Considered', *East African Law Journal*, vol. IV, nos. 1 and 2, 1968, p. 31; Colin Baker, 'Criminal Justice in Malawi', *Journal of African Law*, vol. XI, no. 3, 1967, p. 147; Malawi, Presidential Commission on Criminal Justice, *Report*, Blantyre, 1967; and Ghai and McAuslan, *Public Law and Political Change in Kenya*, pp. 138–47.
[29] See J. H. Jearey, 'Trial by Jury and Trial with the Aid of Assessors in the Superior Courts of British African Territories', *Journal of African Law*, vol. IV, 1960, p. 133, and subsequent volumes.

ment up to a maximum term of life, corporal punishment, fine, forfeiture, payment of compensation, payment of costs, giving security for keeping the peace, absolute discharge, probation, probation with bond, police supervision, reconciliation, restitution. (Penal Code, ss. 25-38B.) While the legislature has limited the kinds of sentence that a court can award for a particular offence, and has specified a maximum sentence for each offence, it is generally considered that within these limits, sentence should be a matter of discretion for the presiding judge or magistrate.[30] This discretion has been restricted to some extent by the Minimum Sentences Act, 1972 (Act No. 1 of 1972) which provides for a minimum sentence of imprisonment in respect of scheduled offences. Judges of the High Court have been somewhat jealous of their prerogatives and have demonstrated great ingenuity in limiting the application of this Act.[31]

An important aspect of a sentence of imprisonment (clearly a very serious interference by the state with the liberty of the individual) is that it has a clear beginning and a clear ending. By way of contrast, an order made under the Preventive Detention Act or the Deportation Ordinance is open-ended and the person who is made subject to such an order has no idea when, if ever, he will regain his freedom.

NOTE The principle that a sentence of imprisonment imposed by a court should have a clear ending, has been changed somewhat by the Resettlement of Offenders Act, 1969 (Act No. 8 of 1969). Anyone convicted of an offence specified in the Schedule to this Act—essentially offences scheduled in the Minimum Sentences Act—may be given a 'resettlement order' by the Minister for Home Affairs. The order may be made either within thirty days of conviction if the person is not sentenced to imprisonment, or within thirty days of the end of any term of imprisonment (s.4). Furthermore, anyone convicted of any offence carrying with it a term of imprisonment of two years or more, may, subject to the conditions noted above, be given a resettlement order on the recommendation of the Commissioner for Social Welfare (s.5). Anyone who is subject to an existing order under the Deportation Ordinance or s.8 of the Witchcraft Ordinance, may receive a resettlement order (s.8). Finally, anyone who has been ordered to give security for good behaviour (ss. 45 and 60 of the Criminal Procedure Code) may, within thirty days of receiving such order, be made the subject of a resettlement order.

---

[30] For factors to be considered by the court in passing sentence, see P. T. Georges, 'The Judge's Role in Sentencing', *East African Law Journal*, vol. II, no. 1, 1966, p. 9. In respect of 'common law' crimes, the judge's discretion is complete: *Verrier* v. *D.P.P.* [1967] 2 A.C. 195. See B. Slattery, *A Handbook on Sentencing*, E. A. Literature Bureau, Nairobi, 1972.
[31] See J. S. Read, 'Minimum Sentences in Tanzania', *Journal of African Law*, vol. IX, no. 1, 1966, p. 20; and S. K. Huber, 'Statutory Interpretation and Judicial Discretion', op. cit.; on the question of the degree to which the legislature may interfere with the role of the courts, see *Liyanage* v. *The Queen* [1967] A.C. 259 (PC). Earlier legislation, the Minimum Sentences Act, 1963 (Cap. 526), provided for a mandatory twenty-four strokes of corporal punishment plus imprisonment. The 1972 Act repealed and replaced the 1963 Act, and in so doing, removed the requirement for the imposition of corporal punishment but increased the minimum sentence of imprisonment.

Any person who is the subject of a resettlement order must go to, and remain in, a 'resettlement centre' until released by order of the Minister, who has an unfettered discretion in this respect (s.15). The officer in charge of a resettlement centre will normally be a prisons officer, and most of the prisons regulations will be in effect. While the Minister is required to review resettlement orders from time to time, the courts are prohibited from reviewing any order made under the Act (ss. 15 and 16).

When the Act came into effect the Ministry of Home Affairs, in co-operation with the Social Welfare Division of the Ministry of Health and Social Welfare, 'rounded up' and 'screened' several hundred 'habitual offenders', and those who were believed to come within the ambit of the Act were 'distributed' to resettlement centres. (*The Standard*, Republic Day Supplement, 5 December 1969—the words in quotation marks are taken from a statement by the Minister for Home Affairs.) The Minister has referred to the centres as 'rehabilitation centres' and commentators have suggested that the Act is putting socialist principles into practice through re-integrating criminals into society as productive, self-reliant citizens. (G. Grohs, Note: 'The Resettlement of Offenders Act, 1969', *Eastern Africa Law Review*, vol. II, no. 3, 1969; and L. L. Kato 'Tanzania Innovation in Penology', Universities of East Africa Social Science Conference, *Proceedings*, Dar es Salaam, 1970.) A question arises, however, whether the Act is not an attempt to eliminate rather than rehabilitate habitual criminals. For example, the Minister for Home Affairs, in the statement referred to above, said that the offenders in resettlement centres will be joined by their families 'when appropriate' and that the centres will eventually be developed into ujamaa villages. This seems to imply that once a person goes to a resettlement centre he is to stay there permanently. (See, in this connection, the speech by the Cuban Minister of the Interior, in *Granma*, 6 April 1969, where he speaks of eliminating the repeater, the habitual criminal who is beyond all rehabilitation. See also G.N. No. 135 of 1969.)

By July of 1970 there were a total of four centres, located in Morogoro, West Lake and Mbeya Regions and altogether, 313 offenders had been resettled. (*The Standard*, 10 July 1970; G.N. No. 133 of 1969.) Does the fact that the courts have in recent years been criticized for not punishing criminals severely enough indicate anything about the possible reasons for the enactment of the Resettlement of Offenders Act?

NOTE Before leaving the question of sentence we might briefly consider the sentence which represents the ultimate form of interference by the state with the freedom of the individual—that is, the death penalty. Tanzania retains a death penalty for murder and a limited number of other offences, but it has not, as have Kenya and Uganda, extended its application. In fact, since independence, the annual number of executions has decreased in Tanzania. This is not because fewer people are being sentenced to death, but simply because President Nyerere has been more liberal than his predecessors in exercising the prerogative of mercy. The annual number of executions increased steadily throughout the colonial period, reaching a peak (pique?) of thirty-two in the year just before independence. By way of contrast, in 1965 eight people were hanged and forty death sentences were commuted to sentences of life imprisonment. (Judiciary, *Annual Reports*, 1961 and 1965.)

H · AFTER THE TRIAL

Once a convicted person enters prison there are rules governing the way he is to be treated, and even while in prison, a prisoner has certain 'rights'. The most important right a prisoner is given under the Prisons Act, 1967 (Act No. 43 of 1967) is that, depending on his behaviour and progress while in prison, he may have up to one third of his sentence remitted (s. 49 as amended by Act No. 29 of 1968). At the same time, however, the strongest weapon the authorities have over the prisoner is the ability to take away his remission and the salary he receives.[32] The prisoner is also subject to other punishments such as isolation or restricted diet. None of these disciplinary measures can be taken, however, until a hearing has been held and the prisoner has been given an opportunity to defend himself (ss.32-43). On the other hand, prisoners must perform all tasks and duties assigned to them and prison authorities may use such force as is reasonably necessary to ensure compliance with orders or to maintain discipline (ss. 13, 61). An important provision concerning imprisonment is that a person sentenced to a term not in excess of six months, may, with the consent of the administrative officer in charge of the area where he lives, elect to do extra-mural labour in lieu of imprisonment. The term of the extra-mural labour will coincide with the term of imprisonment and the administrative officer will supervise such work and set any terms and conditions surrounding it (s. 72; see also Penal Code, s. 116A).

I · APPEAL

The final step in our investigation of criminal procedure is a consideration of appeals. In most cases, if the accused person is convicted he will have the opportunity for at least one appeal. If he is originally convicted in a Primary Court, he may even be able to make three appeals—to a District Court, the High Court, and finally, to the Court of Appeal for East Africa.[33]

---

[32] See R. E. S. Tanner, 'The East African Experience of Imprisonment' in Alan Milner (ed.), *African Penal Systems*, Routledge and Kegan Paul, London, 1969.
[33] See Magistrates' Courts Act, 1963, Cap. 537, ss.16-20 for appeals from Primary Courts; Magistrates' Courts Act, 1963, ss.21-28 for appeals to the High Court; Interim Constitution of Tanzania, Act No. 43 of 1965, s.65(1); Treaty for East African Co-operation, Articles 81 and 82; Appellate Jurisdiction Ordinance, Cap. 451, ss.7-9; Court of Appeal for Eastern Africa Act, 1962, EACSO No. 13 of 1962 as amended by EACSO No. 5 of 1964, ss.3,3A, 4, 6 for appeals to the Court of Appeal. In 1971 s. 8 of the Appellate Jurisdiction Ordinance was amended to prohibit appeals to the Court of Appeal in respect of convictions for treason or offences of a seditious nature (Admininistration of Justice (Miscellaneous Amendments) Act, 1971, s. 14). A person convicted of such an offence may appeal to a full bench of the High Court (ibid., s. 17).

The person convicted may be able to appeal against conviction, or against sentence, or against both. Of course, it should also be noted that the state has roughly equal rights: it may be able to appeal against acquittal, or against sentence, or against both.

NOTE If a person is convicted and sentenced to imprisonment and decides to launch an appeal, he may apply to be released on bail pending the determination of his appeal. It is considerably more difficult for a convicted person to be granted bail than is the case when someone applies for bail prior to his trial. The rule is that, in such circumstances, bail should only be granted for exceptional and unusual reasons in a case where there is an 'overwhelming probability' that the appeal will be successful. (*In re R.* v. *Gangji* [1967] H.C.D. n.243.) What should be the position where a person is acquitted at his trial but the prosecution decides to appeal against the acquittal and asks that the individual in question be held in custody until the appeal is determined?

CHAPTER FIVE

THE PERMANENT COMMISSION OF ENQUIRY

In this chapter we look at a unique Tanzanian institution for protecting the rights and dignity of the individual. As we have seen, liberal-democratic constitutional theory sees this function being performed through the checks which the legislative and judicial branches of government are able to enforce on the executive. As we have also seen, the legislative and judicial branches in Tanzania have not been able to play this role effectively. It is indicative of TANU'S concern for human rights that the Permanent Commission of Enquiry was created to fill this constitutional void. It is also indicative of the nature of state administration in Tanzania that the most effective control on the executive is itself an arm of the executive.

The materials in this chapter concern the reasons for the establishment of the Permanent Commission of Enquiry, the nature and scope of its powers and responsibilities, and its methods of operation. These materials provide a basis for analysing the Permanent Commission's effectiveness, and also serve as a guide to the kinds of administrative misbehaviour which are prevalent and the areas where such behaviour is most often encountered. In this respect, the following words of President Nyerere are important:

> We must not forget that the Permanent Commission of Enquiry receives complaints only from the most literate, aware or energetic and courageous of our citizens; its Reports understate, rather than overstate the problem.[1]

A · THE ESTABLISHMENT OF THE PERMANENT COMMISSION OF ENQUIRY

The establishment of the Permanent Commission of Enquiry was among the recommendations made by the Presidential Commission on the Establishment of a Democratic One-Party State.

REPORT OF THE PRESIDENTIAL COMMISSION ON THE ESTABLISHMENT OF A DEMOCRATIC ONE-PARTY STATE[2]

A Safeguard against abuse of power
● In a rapidly developing country it is inevitable that many officials, both of Government and of the ruling Party, should be authorized to

[1] *Arusha Declaration Parliament*, op. cit., p. 8.
[2] p. 32.

exercise wide discretionary powers. Decisions taken by such officials can, however, have most serious consequences for the individual, and the Commission is aware that there is already a good deal of public concern about the danger of abuse of power. We have, therefore, given careful thought to the possibility of providing some safeguard for the ordinary citizen which will not have the effect of limiting the actions of Government and Party in a way which could hinder the task of nation building.

We are encouraged to note that this problem has already been faced in a most forthright fashion by the Annual Conference of TANU. By a resolution of the Conference, a Disciplinary Committee has been established to deal with allegations of misconduct by TANU officials. However, the Commission feels that this is not enough. Abuse of power is not confined to Party officials. Officials of Government at all levels of the Administration may also abuse the powers that have been entrusted to them. Moreover, in order to be really effective, such a Committee requires to be established by law and to enjoy certain powers and protection. We, therefore, recommend that the new constitution should provide for a permanent Commission to be appointed by the President, with a wide jurisdiction to enquire into allegations of abuse of power by officials of both Government and Party alike. We envisage a Commission of a broadly representative character under the chairmanship of someone of high standing in TANU. We suggest that apart from the Chairman, who should be a full time appointment, there should be five members of the Commission. This would enable the Commission to split up into two groups for the purpose of touring the Regions. The Chairman and other members should not be eligible to hold office as Commissioners for longer than two years, and, accordingly, we recommend that three Commissioners should retire annually. The Commission should be empowered to summon witnesses and call for papers, including papers in the custody of Government Officers. It should not, however, be bound by rules of evidence or required to disclose to the complainant information received from other sources. We do not suggest that the Commission should be invested with any executive power. At the conclusion of its enquiry into any complaint the Commission should submit a report of its findings to the President, together with its ● recommendations where appropriate.

President Nyerere warmly endorsed these recommendations when introducing the one-party state proposals to the National Assembly on 8 June 1965.

J. K. Nyerere

ADDRESS TO THE NATIONAL ASSEMBLY[3]

● Finally on these political developments, I wish to commend to you the proposal to establish a Permanent Commission on the Abuse of Power. The nature of our economic problems in Tanzania demands that many officers of the Government, the Party, and the law itself, should be entrusted with great powers over other individuals. At the same time our recent history, and the educational backwardness of the majority of our people, means that automatic checks on abuse of power are almost non-existent. To the people in the villages and scattered homesteads of our wide country, it is the policeman, the magistrate, the TANU official or the Government Officer, who represents government in their everyday life. And in the District and Regional Headquarters it is the Commissioner who wields direct and effective power in a manner which affects the life of our fellow citizens. This is inevitable and necessary. Only by entrusting real responsibility to such people can our nation be transformed. But we have to recognize that these powers can be—and have been—abused. And the sufferers are the people on whose behalf Government is, and should be, conducted.

It is intended that the Commission on the Abuse of Power should receive and investigate complaints by the people of this country, and that it should submit reports and make recommendations to the President. The people will have direct access to it. The Government believes that the operation of such a Commission should help to make a reality of the political equality of all our people, and of their individual
● freedom within the context of our socialist society.

The Interim Constitution then gave effect to these proposals.

INTERIM CONSTITUTION OF TANZANIA[4]

● 67.—(1) There shall be a Permanent Commission of Enquiry which shall have jurisdiction to enquire into the conduct of any person to whom this section applies in the exercise of his office or authority, or in abuse thereof.

(2) Subject to the provisions of this section, the Permanent Commission shall make an enquiry into the conduct of any such person aforesaid whenever so directed by the President, and may, unless the President otherwise directs, make such enquiry in any case in

---

3 8 June 1965.
  Act No. 43 of 1965.

which it considers that an allegation of misconduct or abuse of office or authority by any such person ought to be investigated.

(3) The Permanent Commission shall report the proceedings of every enquiry, and of its conclusions and recommendations thereon, to the President.

(4) This section applies to persons in the service of the United Republic, persons holding office in the Party, the members and persons in the service of local government authority, and the members and persons in the service of such Commissions, corporate bodies established by statute and public authorities or boards, as may be specified by Act of Parliament, but does not apply to the President or the head of the Executive for Zanzibar.

(5) Nothing in this section or in any Act of Parliament enacted for the purpose of this Chapter shall confer on the Permanent Commission any power to question or review any decision of any judge, magistrate or registrar in the exercise of his judicial functions or any decision of a tribunal established by law for the performance of judicial functions in the exercise of such functions.

68.—(1) The Permanent Commission shall comprise a chairman and two other members who shall be appointed by the President.

(2) A person appointed a member of the Permanent Commission shall forthwith vacate any office of Minister or junior minister, any office prescribed by Act of Parliament for the purpose of this section and any office in the Party.

(3) A person who vacates the office of a member of the Permanent Commission shall be eligible for reappointment: Provided that a person who has served as a member of the Permanent Commission for four consecutive years shall not, notwithstanding the provisions of subsection (3) of section 83 of this Constitution, be qualified to be reappointed as such member within two years of his last ceasing to hold such office. (Act No. 36 of 1968, s. 2.)

(4) Subject to the provisions of this section, the office of a member of the Permanent Commission shall become vacant:

(a) at the expiration of two years from the date of his appointment: Provided that one of the first members of the Permanent Commission, other than the chairman, shall vacate his office at the expiration of one year from the date of his appointment and, if no provision in that behalf is made in the instrument of appointment of one of such members, the member who shall so vacate his office shall be determined by lot; or

(b) if he accepts any office of a kind which he would be required to vacate on his being appointed a member of the Permanent Commission.

(5) A member of the Permanent Commission may be removed from office by the President only for inability to discharge the functions of his office (whether arising from infirmity of body or mind or from any other cause) or for misbehaviour.

(6) The Permanent Commission may act notwithstanding any vacancy or the absence of any member.[5]

69. Subject to this Constitution, the powers and immunities of the Permanent Commission for the discharge of its functions, and its procedure, shall be prescribed and regulated by Act of Parliament.

B · THE POWERS AND DUTIES OF THE PERMANENT COMMISSION OF ENQUIRY

The Bill for the Act referred to in s. 69 of the Interim Constitution was given its first reading in the National Assembly on 22 February 1966.

R. M. Kawawa
SPEECH INTRODUCING THE
PERMANENT COMMISSION OF ENQUIRY BILL[6]

● Mr Speaker, Sir, I beg to propose that the Bill as amended be read for the first time. I take great pleasure in presenting this Bill since I understand that the general public as well as the Government are waiting anxiously for it. This kind of Bill should be welcomed with both hands by any country that carries on its affairs in a just manner [cheers]. I think I am called to remind the honourable members of Parliament of the history and reasons of this Bill.

It is human nature sometimes to leave the right path of good conduct. This happens not only to leaders but others too. Leaders sometimes misuse their authority to the disadvantage of others. But also sometimes the common man can abuse the leaders with false allegations. This is something that our Party has opposed for a long time.

Among the principles of TANU there is a provision that all men are equal, and that every individual has a right to dignity. Also in the oath of membership is the undertaking, 'I shall never use my official position nor that of another person for my personal gain or private benefit.'

When a TANU member undertakes that, he takes on a heavy

---

[5] Section 68, as originally enacted, limited the tenure of the Commissioners to two years. The first Chairman, Chief E.A.M. Mang'enya served four years, left office, and was then re-appointed in accordance with s. 68 (3), after two years.
[6] National Assembly Debates (unofficial translation), 22 February 1966.

responsibility which must be discharged by conduct in his everyday life. In order to ensure the effectiveness of that undertaking, the Party established a committee on Discipline which has done its work well. And when our country was considering a new Constitution, this matter was not overlooked. The Presidential Commission on the Establishment of a Democratic One-Party State considered the matter and recommended that a Commission be established which will investigate and ensure the good conduct of leaders. Since there was to be a national party only, it did not make sense that the Commission should investigate or deal only with matters concerning party workers. So it was decided that its scope be wider to include different leaders, not just party leaders. And more, it should extend to all people whose conduct was questionable.

These recommendations were readily accepted by different sittings of the Party. We passed the Interim Constitution in July 1965 and it established the Permanent Commission of Enquiry. This Bill now seeks to specify the powers and duties of the Commission. It is a most important Commission, and one that will help to ensure that Democracy in this country is enhanced. Any person who feels he has been oppressed will have a chance to take his complaints to the Commission. And if any leader feels that some person or group of persons are following or propagating bad conduct, he too can petition the Commission.

I would, however, like to warn, Mr Speaker, that it will be against the whole purpose of the exercise for any person, leader or a common man, to make false allegations to the Commission. To do so would be to mislead and waste the valuable time of the Commission. I hope that such misuse of the Commission will not occur.

The things that the Commission will be concerned with will not be personal problems. For instance if a certain worker has not been given an increment or promotion, it is not for the Commission to look into that. For such matters there is existing administrative machinery and for things like assault there are courts of law. This is to say that everything that has an established machinery will follow that machinery. But we have no machinery for a leader who misuses his powers, insists on eggs and chicken and goats, fat goats already prepared, and who is so angry if he cannot get them. People are forced to give eggs and chicken. And they complain that these visitors want so much. Now we know this was a colonial practice. But if a leader follows that type of conduct, even if he does not obtain the eggs and chicken and goats by force, but he uses his influence to do so, then this is the kind of conduct that the Commission will investigate, things such as these which either are not against the law or where there is not sufficient evidence for a court of law to act.

Or sometimes a group of people take on a leader and start a campaign against him using malicious rumours or false allegations, the leader too can go to the Commission and seek an investigation so that the truth be established . . .

Before I explain the different sections of the Bill, may I point out an amendment which has been made and which appears in the National Assembly Order Paper issued today. After much thought, it was decided that it will be a very good thing if the National Assembly receives an annual report on the work of the Commission each year. This report will be a Government Report. It will detail how the Commission did its work in the year. The Report will not give names or in any other way compromise the confidential nature of its work. This report will be for the information of the Assembly. As a result of the amendment other small amendments had to be made in the Bill,

● and these appear on the Order Paper.

NOTE The Disciplinary Committee is established under the Constitution of TANU. It consists of three persons elected by the National Conference for a term of two years and its function is to '. . . investigate all allegations of improper conduct made against members of the Party and . . . report thereon to the N.E.C.' As the Disciplinary Committee does not make public reports, it is not possible to comment on its activities. At one period, at any rate, it appears to have been taken quite seriously as the then Inspector-General of Police, Mr M. N. E. Shaidi, was its chairman.

PERMANENT COMMISSION OF ENQUIRY ACT, 1966[7]

● 1. This Act may be cited as the Permanent Commission of Enquiry Act, 1966 and shall be read as one with the Constitution.

3. This Act shall extend to Zanzibar in relation to persons in the service of the United Republic and to Union matters as well as to Tanganyika.

4.—(1) In addition to the offices of Minister and junior Minister and any office in the Party (which, in accordance with section 68 of the Constitution, a person appointed a Commissioner is required to vacate), a person appointed a Commissioner shall forthwith vacate the following offices:

    (a)   the office of Speaker of the National Assembly;

    (b)   the office of judge and of a judicial officer;

    (c)   a Civil Service office;

[7] Act No. 25 of 1966.

(d)   the office of a member of the Electoral Commission;

(e)   the office of a member of a local government authority and any office in the service of a local government authority;

(f)   the office of a member of a scheduled organization and any office in the service of a scheduled organization,

and every such office is hereby prescribed for the purposes of section 68 of the Constitution.

(**NOTE**   See Act No. 2 of 1968, s.2.)

8. Subject to subsection (5) of section 67 of the Constitution, the jurisdiction and powers conferred on the Commission may be exercised notwithstanding any provision in written law to the effect that an act or omission shall be final, or that no appeal shall lie in respect thereof, or that no proceeding or decision shall be challenged, reviewed, quashed or called in question.

9.—(1) Subject to the provisions of this section, the Commission shall, before entering upon any enquiry:

(a)   record the nature and scope of the enquiry it proposes to make;

(b)   inform the appropriate authority of its intention to make the enquiry and furnish him with a copy of such record.

(2) If, in the course of any enquiry, the Commission considers that the nature or scope of the enquiry should be enlarged, the Commission shall cause a further record to be made to that effect and shall furnish the appropriate authority with a copy thereof.

(3) Where the Commission makes an enquiry, or the nature or scope of an enquiry is enlarged, on the direction of the President, such direction:

(a)   if in writing, shall constitute such record aforesaid;

(b)   if not in writing, shall be recorded by the Commission,

and if, in any such case, the President is the appropriate authority it shall not be necessary to inform him of the Commission's intention to make the enquiry or to furnish him with a copy of such record.

(4) A record and any further record made in accordance with this section shall form part of the proceedings of the enquiry.

(5) Nothing in this section shall be construed as precluding the Commission, before complying with subsection (1) or (2), from conducting an examination of any person who alleges that any misconduct or abuse of office or authority ought to be investigated, or from consulting the appropriate authority, in order that it may determine whether or not any enquiry should be made or whether or not the nature or scope of an enquiry should be enlarged.

10.—(1) Every enquiry shall be conducted in private.

(2) The Commission may hear or obtain information from such persons, and may carry out such investigations, as it thinks fit. It shall not be necessary for the Commission to hold any hearing, and no person shall be entitled as of right to be heard by the Commission: Provided that if at any time during the course of the enquiry it appears to the Commission that there may be sufficient grounds for its making any report or recommendation that may adversely affect any person or any department or scheduled organization, it shall inform such person or that department or scheduled organization, as the case may be, and shall give such person, department or organization an opportunity to be heard; and no comment that is adverse to any person, department or scheduled organization shall be contained in a report to the President unless such person, department or organization has been given an opportunity to be heard.

(3) Subject to sections 13 and 14, the Commission may hear and obtain information whether or not the same be evidence within the meaning of the law for the time being regulating the admissibility of evidence in courts of law.

11.—(1) Subject to the provisions of this Act, the Commission may require any person who, in its opinion, is able to give any information relating to any matter relevant to an enquiry to furnish it with any such information and to produce any documents, papers or things which may be in the possession or under the control of that person and may, by order under the hand of a Commissioner, require any such person to attend before the Commission at a time and place specified in such order and to be examined on oath or to produce any such document, paper or thing.

(2) Where the Commission orders any person to be examined on oath, any Commissioner may administer such oath.

(3) An order made under this section shall be served on the person to whom it is directed by a person holding office under the Commission or a police officer in the manner prescribed for the service of a summons on a witness in civil proceedings before a court of law.

(4) If a person to whom an order under this section is directed does not attend at the time and place mentioned therein, the Commission may, upon being satisfied that the order was duly served or that the person to whom the order is directed wilfully avoids service, issue a warrant under the hand of a Commissioner to apprehend such person and to bring him before the Commission at a time and place specified in the warrant. Every warrant issued under this section shall be executed by a police officer.

(5) Where a person is arrested in pursuance of a warrant issued under this section and is not brought before the Commission within twenty-four hours of his arrest or earlier released by order of the Commission on his undertaking to attend at a time and place specified by it, he shall forthwith be taken before a magistrate and such magistrate shall:

(a) if such person enters into a suitable recognizance for his appearance before the Commission, release him from custody; or

(b) order such person to be detained in custody until such time as he can be brought before the Commission.

(6) When any person is required by the Commission to attend before it for the purposes of this section, such person shall be entitled to the same fees, allowances and expenses as if he were a witness before a court of law and, for the purposes of this subsection, a Commissioner shall have the powers of a court to fix or disallow the amount of such fee, allowance or expenses.

(7) For the avoidance of doubts it is hereby declared that this section shall apply whether or not the person concerned is a person in respect of whose conduct the Commission has jurisdiction to enquire and whether or not such person is employed in any department or scheduled organization and whether or not such documents, papers or things are in the custody or under the control of any department or scheduled organization.

12.—(1) For the purposes of this Act, the Commission may at any time enter upon any premises occupied by a department or any scheduled organization and inspect the premises and thereon carry out any investigation for the purposes of an enquiry.

(2) Before entering upon any premises, the Commission shall notify the appropriate authority.

(3) The President may, from time to time, by notice to the Commission, exclude the application of subsection (1) in respect of any specified premises or class of premises if he is satisfied that the exercise of the power conferred by this section might prejudice the security, defence or international relations of Tanzania, including Tanzania's relations with the government of any other country or with any international organization.

13.—(1) Subject to section 14 of this Act, every person required to give any information by, or ordered to attend to give evidence or to produce any document, paper or thing before, the Commission shall be entitled in respect of such information, evidence, documents, papers or things to the same rights and privileges as witnesses have in a court of law.

(2) Except on the trial of any person for an offence contrary to sections 102, 103, 106, 108, or 109 of the Penal Code (which relate to perjury and similar offences) or section 19 of this Act, no statement made or answer given to the Commission by that or any other person in the course of an enquiry shall be admissible in evidence against any person in any court or in any other proceedings, and no evidence in respect of proceedings before the Commission shall be given against any person, other than in further proceedings before the Commission.

14.—(1) Where the President certifies that the giving of any information, the answering of any question or the production of any document, paper or thing:

(a) might prejudice the security, defence or international relations of Tanzania (including Tanzania's relations with the government of any other country or with any international organization), or the investigation or detection of offences; or

(b) might involve the disclosure of the deliberations of the Cabinet; or

(c) might involve the disclosure of proceedings of the Cabinet, or of any committee of the Cabinet, relating to matters of a secret or confidential nature, and would be injurious to the public interest,

the Commission shall not require the information or answer to be given or, as the case may be, the document, paper or thing to be produced.

(2) No person bound by the provisions of any written law, other than the National Security Act, the Judicial Service Act, or the Civil Service Act, to maintain secrecy in relation to, or not to disclose, any matter, shall be required to supply any information to or answer any question put by the Commission in relation to that matter, or to produce to the Commission any document, paper or thing relating to it, if compliance with that requirement would be in breach of the obligations of secrecy or non-disclosure:

Provided that, if an enquiry is made as a consequence of the complaint of any person and such complainant consents in writing to the disclosure, any person bound as aforesaid may be required by the Commission to supply information, to answer any question or to produce any document, paper or thing relating only to the complainant, and it shall be the duty of such first mentioned person to comply with that requirement.

(3) Save as provided by the foregoing provisions of this section but not withstanding the provisions of any other law:

(a) no person may refuse to disclose any information to, answer any question by, or produce any document, paper or other thing to, the Commission on account of any judicial, official, or State privilege or any privilege relating to information as to the commission of an offence;

(b)   the disclosure to the Commission of any matter in relation to which any person has taken an oath of secrecy shall be deemed to be a disclosure by such person in the course of his duties, for an authorized purpose, and with the authority of the person empowered to authorize the disclosure;

(c)   no person shall be liable to prosecution for an offence contrary to the National Security Act, the Judicial Service Act, the Civil Service Act, or any other written law, other than sections 102, 103, 106, 108 or 109 of the Penal Code or section 19 of this Act, by reason of his compliance with any requirement of the Commission under sections 10, 11, 13 or 14 of this Act.

15.—(1) In addition to any other matter required to be contained in a report to the President on an enquiry, the report shall contain a statement of any action that has been taken by any person whose conduct is under enquiry, or by the department or scheduled organization of which such person is a member or in which he is employed, to correct or ameliorate any conduct, procedure, act or omission that is adversely commented upon in the report.

(2) Where the Commissioners are not agreed on any report to the President, the report shall contain a statement of any matter which is the subject of disagreement signed by the Commissioner in disagreement.

16. Save as may be directed by the President, the Commission shall not disclose the contents of any report made to the President.

17.—(1) So soon as may be after the thirtieth of June in every year the President shall cause to be prepared and laid before the National Assembly a report of the Commission's operations and activities during the twelve months preceding the first of July in such year.

(2) A report required to be laid before the National Assembly shall not disclose the identity or contain any statement which may give an indication as to the identity of any person whose conduct the Commission may have enquired into or in respect of whose conduct any enquiry may be pending before the Commission.

18. No enquiry, proceeding or process of the Commission shall be held bad for any error or irregularity of form, and, except on the ground of lack of jurisdiction, no enquiry, proceeding, process or report of

the Commission shall be liable to be challenged, reviewed, quashed or called in question in any court.

19.—(1) Subject to subsection (3) of this section:

(a) no proceedings, civil or criminal, shall lie against any Commissioner, any person holding office under the Commission, or any police officer employed to serve or execute the orders or warrants of the Commission, for anything he may do or report or say in the course of the exercise or intended exercise of his functions under this Act, unless it is shown he acted in bad faith;

(b) no Commissioner or any such person as aforesaid shall be called to give evidence in any court or any other proceedings of a judicial nature in respect of the proceedings in any enquiry or anything coming to his knowledge in the exercise of his functions under this Act.

(2) Anything said, any information supplied, or any document, paper or thing produced by any person in the course of an enquiry shall be privileged in the same manner as if the enquiry were a proceeding in court, and a report of the Commission shall be privileged in the same manner as if it were the record and judgement of a proceeding in court.

(3) Nothing in subsection (1) shall apply in the case of any proceeding for an offence against the National Security Act, for an offence contrary to sections 102, 103, 106, 108 or 109 of the Penal Code in relation to an enquiry, or for an offence contrary to section 20 of this Act.

24. In addition to the persons specifically set out in subsection (4) of section 67 of the Constitution, the Commission shall have jurisdiction in respect of members and persons in the service of the commissions, corporate bodies, institutions, organizations and public authorities and boards set out in the First Schedule to this Act, and those organizations are hereby specified for the purposes of the said section 67.

THE FIRST SCHEDULE[8]

(1) The Civil Service Commission.
(2) The Judicial Service Commission.
(3) The Local Government Service Commission.
(4) The Police Service Commission.
(5) Every Board established under the Agricultural Products (Control and Marketing) Act, 1962.

---

[8] The First Schedule has not been amended since 1966.

(6)   Every Commission established under the Range Development and Management Act, 1964.

(7)   Every Regional Committee established under the Unified Teaching Service Act, 1964.

(8)   Every Co-operative Society registered under the Cooperative Societies Act, 1968.

(9)   The Lint and Seed Marketing Board.

(10) The Mwananchi Development Corporation Ltd.

(11) The National Co-operative and Development Bank, the National Co-operative Bank and the National Development Credit Agency.

(12) The National Development Corporation.

(13) The National Housing Corporation.

(14) The National Union of Tanganyika Workers.

(15) The Pyrethrum Board.

(16) The Tanganyika African Parents Association.

(17) The Tanganyika Coffee Board.

(19) The Tea Board.

(20) The Trustees of the Tanganyika National Parks.

(21) Umoja wa Wanawake wa Tanzania.

(22) Every waterworks authority established under the Waterworks Ordinance.

(23) The Workers Development Corporation Ltd. and every subsidiary of any of the foregoing.

NOTE   The phrase 'appropriate authority' in s.9 means the person having overall charge of the organization which is being investigated (s.2). Section 8 is very interesting because it presumably permits the Permanent Commission to investigate the exercise of powers which are specifically excluded from review by the courts. Thus, the first Chairman of the Permanent Commission, Chief Mang'enya, has suggested that a Preventive Detention Order might be investigated. While he notes that the order itself could not be reviewed, he argues that an enquiry could be made into the work of the Advisory Committee established under the Preventive Detention Act. If the Permanent Commission felt that the Advisory Committee had wrongly advised the President, it would then suggest to him that he review the detention order in question. (E. A. M. Mang'enya, *Permanent Commission of Enquiry (Ombudsman)*, op. cit., p. 6.)

J. P. W. B. McAuslan and Y. P. Ghai

CONSTITUTIONAL INNOVATION
AND POLITICAL STABILITY IN TANZANIA[9]

● We come now to the fourth and final institution of control—the Permanent Commission of Enquiry. The Presidential Commission

[9] pp. 501–7.

recognized that, in any modern state, officials have to be given considerable power and discretion, and that this inevitably leads occasionally to maladministration and abuse of power; it recognized further that this was especially likely to happen in a one-party state, where party as well as government officials take part in administration. It rejected a Bill of Rights because this might lead to clashes between the courts and the Government—a standard Tanzanian reason, but one which is somewhat overrated, if the effect of the Bills of Rights in neighbouring Kenya and Uganda on the process of government is borne in mind—and because the limitation imposed by such a Bill on legislative competence might clash with the implementation of socialist policies. Equally to the point is the fact that a Bill of Rights can only be adjudicated upon effectively in the High Court, and this means that such protection as it offers will rarely be invoked by the majority of the citizens in a poor country. In addition, many types of maladministration and abuse of power occur in situations where the courts have never attempted to exercise control, and a Bill of Rights could only alter that at the cost of making the judges the rulers of the country. What was required, and what the Presidential Commission proposed, was a new institution which could be within the reach of the ordinary citizen, would provide a possibility of redress, and would not at the same time antagonize too greatly the government and party bureaucracy. This last is an important point, for plans to increase surveillance and control of the bureaucracies must take into account their views, otherwise such institutions as are created will be stifled at birth.

This institution of control is new, is an attempt to increase the amount of control over the bureaucracy without antagonizing it, and provides a focal point for resentment and complaint against the bureaucracy, both government and party. It could not be allowed to become a rallying point for political opposition, yet it had to be effective enough to prevent such resentment and complaint turning into political opposition because nothing seemed to be done about them—a superhuman task both for the draftsmen of the Act and the members of the Commission.

We can see how these conflicting policies have been dealt with in the Act. Basically, they have been dealt with by the superficially simple but potentially dangerous expedient of leaving it to the President. Thus he is to take action or not on a report of the Commission; and he can prevent the Commission from making an investigation. Clearly, political factors will enter into decisions made in these situations and so it may be thought logical that the political head of the Government and the party should make decisions; but this does not dispose of the problems that have to be faced, and may ultimately result either in the Commission never feeling free to start an important investigation without getting the go-ahead from the President, or the President being constantly appealed to by persons, departments, and organizations to stop proposed investigations. Neither situation will help in establishing the authority of the Commission.

The fact is that, once an institution of control has been established —particularly where, as here, a good deal of publicity surrounds its establishment—if it is then prevented from being in any way effective because of the apprehension that it may be too effective, the end result may be much worse than if no such institution had been established in the first place. Expectations will have been aroused and disappointed; they are unlikely to disappear. It would not be unreasonable to suppose that this fact was present in the minds of the Presidential Commission, the N.E.C., and the Cabinet, and that power over tenure and the operations of the Commission has been given to the President because no way out of the dilemmas posed by the Commission could be thought of, other than to ensure that the Commission never became a threat to the government and party bureaucracy.

It is certainly true that the Commission is not as powerful as an Ombudsman; but, looked at from the reverse point of view, it provides the possibility of control in an area where there has hitherto been none, or at most the rather dubious chance of an MP taking the matter up; and this is a brave attempt to tackle a problem which many more stable governments have yet to deal with. If a prediction may be ventured, it is that the Commission will find government and party officials less than enthusiastic about its activities (the bureaucracy in Tanzania being for the most part still 'English' in their attitudes towards publicity and control) and that it may well need the authority of the President to make any headway; the Act may then turn out to have a very different effect from that which is feared. At any rate, its establishment does at the very least suggest that the party in Tanzania has not adopted the fallacy that, because it is the only lawful political party, there cannot be anything wrong with it or the Government that is formed from it.

Another point which must be mentioned is the Commission's possible effect on the National Assembly. Apart from an annual report, the two are not directly in touch, the Commission being responsible to the President and not to the National Assembly. Therefore, even if the latter gives full consideration to the annual report, MPs will have little contact with the work of the Commission. Yet they are or should be involved in the same work on behalf of their constituents, at all levels up to the parliamentary question to the Minister. There is a possibility of overlapping of functions here, and while any resulting competition might stimulate MPs to greater activity, it is also possible that this could lead to a further diminution of the role of the National Assembly in practice. Ministers may prefer the private if more thorough investigation of the Commission to the public questioning of the MP, and some MPs may even feel that if the Commission has not taken or will not take up a matter then it is not worth worrying about. Thus a practice might grow up that problems of maladministration would be excluded from the purview of the National Assembly. It seems hardly necessary to stress that such a development would be wholly bad and that the National Assembly must continue its function of calling Ministers to account for the administration of their departments.

Doubts about the effectiveness of the Commission may also arise from its dependence on the President. It appears that the Commission as now constituted is different from that originally conceived—it was perhaps intended to be an independent, quasi-judicial tribunal, even though its responsibility in the case of a complaint was to end with its recommendations to the President. Under the present rules, it becomes more of a presidential instrument. This leads us to a consideration of the President himself as an institution of control. Nyerere's own outstanding stature and abilities enable him to override departmental policies and overrule ministers and civil servants. The effect is one of self-restraint on the part of officials and party members, though of course sometimes things get done which would not meet with presidential approval. What we are here concerned with is not so much the 'control' effect of his personality as the institutions employed by him to control and check.

The presidential commission or committee is an instrument of policy increasingly used by the President, the outstanding example being of course that on the new Constitution. The basic purpose of these commissions is to recommend new policies, and often the result is to endorse the President's ideas. But the commissions also serve a secondary function—they enable the public to find out what is wrong with the organization and conduct of the affairs under consideration, and give the people concerned an opportunity to ventilate their grievances. A good example of this was the Committee on the Co-operative Movement and Marketing Boards (1966), which not only listed the complaints of the farmers but also criticized the officials of the co-operatives and the politicians who interfere in the running of them. There was considerable opposition to the report from those people—including MPs—who had a stake in the existing structure, but the President stood by the report.

A similar Commission is sitting on the National Union of Tanganyika Workers (NUTA), and it is possible that if there are adverse findings, the report may be used to discipline NUTA officials. The Permanent Commission of Enquiry may therefore be seen as a special type of the presidential commissions outlined above, whose emphasis is on control rather than on policy recommendations. If so, the Permanent Commission is not so much an independent institution of control as a presidential instrument, which he can use to discipline members of government and party when he wishes. This highlights the control functions of the President's position; but, since he has other means of discipline—e.g. his constitutional power to remove a Minister from office—his use of the Permanent Commission is
● likely to be rare.

NOTE   The power to create the *ad hoc* Commissions referred to above is found in the Commissions of Inquiry Ordinance, Cap. 32. The President may appoint a commission to enquire into: the conduct of any officer in the public service; the conduct of any local authority; the management of any department of the public service; or any other matter, into which an enquiry would, in his opinion, be in the public interest. Such commissions are, of course, temporary and the scope of their enquiry is limited by the instructions they receive from the President. The Commissions of Inquiry Ordinance was enacted roughly thirty years ago, indicating that, then as now, there was little agreement on the correct way to spell enquiry/inquiry.

C · THE OPERATIONS OF THE PERMANENT COMMISSION OF ENQUIRY

Now that we have reviewed the establishment of the Permanent Commission of Enquiry, and investigated briefly its jurisdiction and the procedures which it will follow, the important task of assessing the Permanent Commission's operation still remains. The best means for doing this is through the Annual Reports of the Permanent Commission itself.

ANNUAL REPORT OF THE PERMANENT COMMISSION OF ENQUIRY, 1966-7[10]

● 5. Immediately after taking the oath of Office, the Commission commenced its duties. As the institution was new, it was resolved to tour Regions, Districts, and Villages to explain to the Public what

[10] Government Printer, Dar es Salaam, 1968, pp. 4–13.

the Commission stands for, and to get members of the Commission acquainted with local conditions and circumstances and get an insight of the problems of the work, as well as some idea of the practical difficulties that would arise as a result of conditions peculiar to localities.

6. At first, members of the Commission travelled together as a group, but in January, this year, it was decided to make these tours in small groups. The Commission travelled 16,096 miles during 1966-7, visited 104 Divisions, 53 Districts, 14 Regions, addressed 64,065 people and received many complaints. In the last 12 months, the Commission has been on tour for a total of 215 days, in fact 7 months were spent on safari. Many witnesses have been called by the Commission and the cost of their fares and maintenance is met from the Commission votes. It must be noted that many and long tours were made during the dry season and not during the rainy season. The reasons are obvious, indeed, most of the safaris made during the wet season were those which were necessary.

7. When on such safaris, the Commission would hold a Public Meeting which is followed by question time which in turn is followed by a private session during which complaints are received from the public.

8. At Public Meetings, Commissioners explain to the people why the Permanent Commission of Enquiry was created, how it functions, what sort of complaints are receivable and what are not. During question time, the Public ask for further information or elucidation on a particular point, some of the questions have been academic or constitutional, for example, two questions have been asked almost everywhere we went—(1) Why are the President and First Vice-President excluded from your jurisdiction? (2) Why is the First Vice-President only excluded and not the Second?

9. Question time forms the second part of the programme. The questions are based on the speech. No complaints are allowed at this stage. The third part of the programme is the receiving of complaints. To avoid embarrassment, the meeting is closed and members of the Commission retire to a secluded place, e.g. School, Primary Court or Divisional Executive Officer's office etc., and receive complaints brought by the Public coming one at a time. It must be noted that neither Party nor Government Officials are allowed to be with the Commission when complaints are being heard. The Commission gives advice, notes serious complaints, settles on the spot some of the cases. The rest are dealt with at the Headquarters in Dar es Salaam.

10. In the early days, Public meetings were characterized by small attendance. This was mainly because leaders responsible for convening

the meetings were apprehensive as to what the Commission was doing. It is fair to state that some thought that the Permanent Commission of Enquiry was going to attack them in public and in order to avoid this, in some cases, only leaders of ten houses were called. The story does not end there, some leaders on hearing the approach of the Permanent Commission of Enquiry had unnecessary fevers, in some cases leaders were so apprehensive of what the Permanent Commission of Enquiry was doing in their areas that they planted some informers to report back to them what we were doing, [and] who have come to complain to the Commission. We are glad to state that all this is now very rare, and with time it will stop entirely.

11. To maintain its independence and in particular to make the Permanent Commission of Enquiry easily available to the Public who should come to complain without local fear, the Commission endeavours wherever possible to avoid being put up by officials especially of the Regional Administration. We therefore prefer to stay in hotels, and guest houses and only in the absence of these, we stay in, for example, the house of the Area Commissioner. There is a general tendency among members of the public to think that it is impossible to arrive objectively at an impartial decision against an official who gives you hospitality. Our aim is to dispel this fear and get the confidence of the Public. They regard the Commission, rightly too, as their weapon against misuse of power or office by those entrusted with Public Office and so expect the Commission not to identify itself too much with Public officials. It is of course impossible to satisfy the entire Public, of which Government officials and TANU leaders are part.

12. There are three methods by which complaints are received by the Commission:
Any person who thinks that he has suffered injustice as a result of maladministration can come to the Commission himself. This method is used mostly by people who live in Dar es Salaam where the offices of the Commission are. But some upcountry people no matter how far away they live, have travelled to Dar es Salaam to see the Commission personally. It must be pointed out that while the Commission is touring the regions, aggrieved members of the public have the opportunity of seeing the Commission in person.

13. The second method is for the complainant himself to write to the Commission. It must be realized that quite a big percentage of Tanzanians cannot read and write and under these circumstances those people who have this handicap can ask a friend to write for

them. The third method is applicable to the very old and the very sick. Such people can ask an honest friend or relative either to write to or to come and see the Commission. But in such cases, the Commission would endeavour to see the old or the sick man before an enquiry is commenced. This is done so as to avoid dealing with hypothetical cases of people who may not be in existence.

14. Whichever method is used, the emphasis is on direct touch between the Commission and the complainants. The most popular method is naturally by letters. The reasons are obvious.

19. Now, turning to the question of the type of complaints, the Commission has a mixed bag. Some complaints do not come under the Commission's purview. Others are frivolous. Many are groundless and a reasonable portion are justified. Between 1 July 1966 and 31 December 1966 the Commission received 666 cases. This indicates clearly that the first half of our year—Commission's year—saw a larger volume of complaints than the second half of the year. During the first half, the Commission travelled a lot because it was the dry season. The second half being the rainy season, there were very few tours.

20. Out of the 1,627 cases received, 290 cases had files opened. These were cases that warranted investigation. Up to 15 June 1967 our records show that out of 1,966 cases, 90 files have been closed. This sample reveals very useful and interesting information.

21. Complaints that did not fall under the Commission's purview formed 65.3 per cent of all the cases received. These were complaints that could be taken to other institutions, e.g. tribunals, Courts, Ministry's machinery, etc. Here the Commission is of the opinion that a campaign to educate the mass to lodge their complaints to proper venues is imperative.

22. Out of all the cases investigated, 52.6 per cent were found not justified. That is to say there was no justification whatsoever in the complaints, the Commission had to concur or confirm the former decision, be it Ministry's or Division's or Leaders', etc. So officials ought not to entertain any trepidation on the Commission's findings.

23. 47.4 per cent were complaints which were justified and were rectified wherever it was possible to do so. Ten cases were withdrawn by complainants themselves, or discontinued by the Commission for various reasons, e.g. death of complainant or death of the one complained against, loss of office of persons complained against, or lack of interest on the part of the complainant, etc.

24. There is a large group of cases which is termed miscellaneous. These are mainly personal, e.g. a father and his son have a difference or it is a complaint against Government or Party policy. The reduction of this group would be a joy to the Commission as it will show that the mass have learnt to separate the grain from the chaff.

25. The list of 1966-7 complaints shows that nearly every Ministry and Division has had its share of complaints. The State House, the Attorney-General's Chambers are also included. Private bodies such as Missions, Sisal Estates, Private Companies, large stores, etc., are also included.

26. However, the share of the load is not the same. Figures show that District Council takes the lead, followed by judiciary and Regional Administration. Then come other Ministries. The State House and the Attorney-General's Chambers boast for being at the bottom.

29. Out of the 1,060 cases declined, 439 were declined because the Commission had no jurisdiction. Complaints in this category include those against East African Common Services Organization, University College and following nationalization effected early this year Banks, and the nationalized establishments and decisions by Courts of law. It should be noted that the law establishing and governing the Permanent Commission of Enquiry was passed before nationalization. Inevitably nationalized and partially nationalized establishments were not included in the Schedule. As to Court decisions, the Commission as it has already been pointed out, has no jurisdiction but it can be said that the decisions which were referred to the Commission were those made mainly by Primary Court Magistrates. It must be pointed out that members of the Public, particularly in the Rural areas, are not conversant with Court rules and procedure. Time and again the Commission has received complaints to the effect that a person has been refused to appeal against a judicial decision or that judgement was given in his absence, etc. Such procedure is unknown to the people. The Commission feels that people lose their rights in this way. Something must be done to help the illiterate people.

30. The remaining 621 rejected cases were rejected although in fact they refer to departments or scheduled organizations which can be investigated by the Commission but for reasons explained in the Appendix itself, they were rejected. However the Commission found that it could in some cases advise the complainant to address the complaint to the appropriate authority. It is very much hoped that the number of cases rejected under these heads will in future be small as people get to know what and where to send their complaints,

and at what stage the Commission comes in. Most of the authors of rejected cases were referred to the appropriate authorities.

31. The second thing to note about the statistics is the fact that there are 443 cases still under consideration. The main reasons for this high number are, firstly the Commission was a new creation and had to start from scratch, staff and office accommodation had to be found before work could start. Secondly quite a considerable length of time, as it has already been pointed out earlier in this report, was spent holding Public Meetings and explaining to the people why the Commission was created. Thirdly some departments were reluctant or delayed in replying to letters of the Commission, thus keeping some of the cases unnecessarily long. In one case, a Ministry did not reply to our letter despite more than three reminders until well over two months had elapsed although their office and ours are both in Dar es Salaam. Under these circumstances therefore, the Commission found itself with 443 cases on the 'menu' still to be finalized.

32. 114 cases were dealt with to conclusion. Of these, 60 were found not justified and 54 found justified. Of the 'Not justified' cases, the Commission found that the Ministry, department or organization acted rightly the way it did. That is, the act, decision, direction or recommendation was right. It must, however, be pointed out that some of the cases which were brought to the Permanent Commission of Enquiry and which were later found to be not justified indicate that the particular Ministry, department or organization did not inform the complainant of its decision, or if it did inform the complainant about its decision, no reasons were stated for the decision or, at least in some cases, where the reasons were stated, the wrong ones were made. It is therefore suggested that in order to reduce the number of 'Not justified' cases, officials should state their reasons for acting or deciding this or the other way.

33. As it has been pointed out above that there were 54 justified cases, this represents about 46.4 per cent of the cases investigated. The line of action taken by the Permanent Commission of Enquiry when reporting to the President varies with the individual cases. The Commission is always conscious of the two sides of the coin, that is to say when considering what to recommend to the President the Commission has to consider in justifiable cases what could be done for the complainant—reversing the decision, cancelling the order, paying him compensation, etc., and then what could be done to the officials complained against—warning, dismissal, transfer, demotion, etc. In all these cases the recommendation to the President will depend

on the nature and gravity of the complaint.

34. In the category of 'justified cases' the Commission found that a particular official acted where he ought not to have acted, or omitted to act where he was supposed to. There are also decisions which were made contrary to law or recognized practice, rules, regulations, general orders, etc. This was more of misinterpretation than anything else. There were also cases in which decisions were obviously wrong because they lacked evidence to back them. Under this category, too, there are officials who are given discretionary powers, and they exercised these powers improperly. For example in exercising their discretionary powers, decisions were based on irrelevant grounds or that irrelevant considerations were taken into account. Included in this justified cases list also are decisions which are made with malice. Lastly, and this applies to many departments including Courts of Law, there were some unexplained and indeed unjustifiable delays in dealing with cases.

35. It is not within the jurisdiction of the Permanent Commission of Enquiry to point out defects in the law, but it is deemed incumbent at this juncture to state that in the course of our work obvious defects in some law were detected, for example under a certain act there is laid down a procedure to be followed if an employee is to be dismissed from work. It was discovered that there was no provision dealing with a situation where the employee follows the procedure, and a NUTA official does not discharge his duty, and the case becomes statute barred. Obviously here the fault is that of the NUTA official and not that of the employee and yet the employee is subsequently told that his case can no longer be entertained because time has expired.

51. The Permanent Commission of Enquiry has been accused of being too slow in its investigation. It must be admitted that some cases have taken long to investigate. This has been due to one or more of many factors. Firstly, Tanzania is a vast country and communication is not as good as one could want. This inevitably makes travelling difficult. Secondly, there is a tendency among many officials not to reply to our letters as soon as it is expected of them. In one case, for example, an official took two months to reply to our letter and he did ultimately reply after three reminders. Thirdly, there is an acute shortage of staff and all the investigations have to be shared by the very limited number now available. We appeal to members of the Public to be patient.

52. After working for a year, the Commission has been confronted with some problems and these include whether or not to continue

with an investigation after the person complained against retires or is dismissed or is promoted to a very high office; a complainant becomes more victimized by the person against whom he made the complaint; whether or not to provide joy ride transport to witnesses when they are in Dar es Salaam on top of the transport provided to and from the station; some officials neglect or fail to reply to Commission's letters despite many reminders.

53. The importance of having sufficient number of staff and sufficient office accommodation cannot be over-emphasized. As it has already been pointed out earlier in this report, shortage of staff has resulted in some delays in investigating cases, it has also meant that much of office routine work did not get the right attention. It should not be forgotten too that this has created some problems regarding leave since everyone in the Commission is required badly. Office accommodation is also another problem. The present one is certainly far too short of the irreduceable minimum and as such the Commission
● has suffered a lot.

NOTE Since the tabling of its first *Annual Report* in the National Assembly on 30 April 1968, the Permanent Commission has enjoyed an extremely good press. In that year, as in each succeeding year, both *The Nationalist* and *The Standard* carried lengthy extracts from the *Report* and had high words of praise for the Permanent Commission and its work. It is interesting that on the same day the first *Annual Report* was laid before Parliament, thirteen people died of suffocation near Mwanza after being locked up with nine others in a small cell. They had apparently been rounded up in a tax collection campaign directed at people who had failed to pay local rate. On 1 May 1968, *The Nationalist* noted emphatically that 'malicious misuse of power by bureaucrats accounted for the biggest number of justified cases received and processed by the Permanent Commission of Enquiry . . .' On the following day, an editorial in *The Nationalist* noted a connection between the kinds of conduct and attitudes criticized in the Permanent Commission's *Annual Report* and the tragedy which had occurred at Mwanza. The editorial asserted that it was ultimately up to the people themselves to resist any encroachments on their rights and called on the Permanent Commission of Enquiry to proceed further with its work of educating the people in this direction.

ANNUAL REPORT OF
THE PERMANENT COMMISSION OF ENQUIRY, 1967-8[11]

● 12. This year, like in the previous one, nearly every department was a subject of complaint. Following nationalization of a number of establishments, there were complaints against such organizations. At this juncture it is pertinent to mention that as regards complaints

[11] Government Printer, Dar es Salaam, 1969, pp. 5-16.

against the nationalized organizations, it was pathetic that a number of such complaints had to be rejected however justified or genuine the complaints might have been. The reason for this is that these are not included in the Schedule to the Act establishing the institution. In the proposed amendments of the law, it has been suggested that consideration should be given to the inclusion of such establishments in the list of scheduled bodies.

14. Primary Courts appear to be the origin of most of the complaints against judicial decisions as well as judicial officers. Perhaps it is because Primary Court Magistrates are in the main laymen. Further, although there is a system within the hierarchy of the courts whereby court files from Primary Courts can be scrutinized by a District Magistrate exercising his revisional jurisdiction powers; somehow most of the case files, civil and criminal, from Primary Court Magistrates manage to escape scrutiny. It can also be said that Primary Court Magistrates are in closer contact with the people and administration at local level. This, to some extent, accounts for the problem.

15. S. 67 (5) of the Interim Constitution 1965 precludes the Commission from questioning or reviewing any judicial decision made by judicial officers in the exercise of their judicial powers. In the course of the year, the Commission came across a number of cases in which it was not easy to decide whether or not the complaint was about a judicial decision. For example, a person complained that he appeared in court in a criminal case, and was remanded in custody between the 8th and 22nd of a particular month without any reason. The Commission could not plunge into the matter before ascertaining the facts properly because, on the face of it, the allegation involved a judicial decision. However, the Commission wishing to know what exactly the complainant meant, got hold of the appropriate criminal case file and discovered that it was true that complainant had been remanded in custody between the 8th and 22nd, but the case for which he was remanded had been concluded on the 15th. Therefore, the decision to keep the complainant in custody between the 15th and the 22nd did not seem to be justified. Supposedly this was a judicial decision exercised by a judicial officer in the course of judicial duties! The matter was referred to the Registrar for necessary action. This is pointed out merely to show how difficult sometimes it can be, to draw a line of demarcation between judicial and non-judicial decisions.

16. Sometimes it happens that a District Magistrate dismisses an application for an appeal from the decision of a Primary Court Magis-

trate on the grounds that it is time-barred. The complainant comes to the Commission and complains about this. The Commission under the law cannot challenge the decision of the District Magistrate not to allow the applicant to appeal. However, reading through the judgement of the Primary Court Magistrate, one discovers irregularities which could not be remedied by anyone else but by a higher Magistrate who as stated before, in practice, is supposed not only to scrutinize the files but has revision powers. The Commission rejects such cases.

17. It was alleged often by some of the complainants that there was clamour for local influence among the officials. Our clients went on contending that there is a tendency for officials over-stepping their fields of jurisdiction, and to act in a certain way just to show that, either they have authority or they are bosses in their own rights with unfettered limits. Quite a number of cases have been reported to the Commission on this point. For instance, a teacher complained of his arrest by a Magistrate for no reason. In another case a Magistrate was detained by a Regional Commissioner for no reason at all. In yet another case, an Area Commissioner unreservedly interfered with the day-to-day routine administration of a hospital. Investigation revealed that the complaints were founded. Closely connected with complaints in this category, is the interference by politicians or officials through a third person. For example, a Divisional Executive Officer, working through his Area Commissioner, who in turn influenced a District Magistrate to call for certain files from a Primary Court Magistrate with a view of reversing the decisions which were not satisfactory to the politicians! There was also a case where a politician ordered a Magistrate to convict an individual. In one case the man was convicted.

18. This is an unfortunate position because such interference or show of power, has the effect of creating an attitude of non-co-operation among officials and undermines the work which the various officials are supposed to do, apart from the fact that the rights of the individual are affected. Time and again, the Commission has received complaints that such and such an official had not done his duty, or has acted where he ought not to have acted. To illustrate these, a Police Officer did not take up a case because it involved a high official. In another case, a Police Officer arrested a person on the instructions of a high official, although he knew that the person should not, under the prevailing circumstances, have been arrested. In such cases, the Commission takes the cases.

19. The Commission also deals with some cases which technically

should have been taken to court but for one reason or another, they were not. The Commission of course advises the complainants to take legal action. In some cases our clients refuse, saying that if it involved going to court, they would rather sacrifice their rights than jeopardize their future and that in some cases to do so, would mean inviting troubles. Detention by Area and Regional Commissioners are not uncommon, but detained people refuse to take civil action. Also the police who effect the arrest on the instructions of the Area or Regional Commissioners usually do not take criminal action against them for unlawful detention. The Commission investigates the circumstances surrounding the administrative decision and reports accordingly.

21. Executive Officers and Divisional Executive Officers as Justices of the Peace, have power to arrest and lock up some individuals under certain circumstances. Some of these officials, like Area and Regional Commissioners, tend to use these powers wrongly. It appears that they use their powers in order to punish rivals or somebody they hate or just to demonstrate their power; for in some cases one does not see any reason why a person should have been locked up. There was a case, for example, when a Divisional Executive Officer, after a long session at a Bacchanalian feast, called upon every person present to stand up, and sing the National Anthem! When one of the 'disciples of Bacchus' refused to sing the National Anthem, perhaps he had acquired more propensities than the rest, he was locked up!!

22. Time and again, the Commission has received letters complaining that some individuals have been kept in custody without their cases being tried for a long time. Such cases are many. It is always difficult to find any reason as to why such cases have not been concluded, even if one allows a margin for the fact that courts of law are very busy, and also the fact that police officers have to make a thorough investigation. In one case, for example, a person was charged with an offence of stealing Sh. 90.00 yet our client was kept in custody for more than a year! The appropriate authorities were informed.

23. Conflicting cases were not uncommon during the year under review. An MP complained that he was locked up by a Regional Commissioner without any valid reason. Yet somewhere else in this report, there is an allegation that an MP, who was accompanied by a Woman Police Officer, went to a ceremony where he expected to find the former husband of his wife. Indeed, the former husband was present at the ceremony. Suspecting that the former husband would talk to his wife, the MP approached the former husband of

his wife and gave him a good beating. Then the MP ordered the Police Officer to take and lock up his antagonist!

24. Quite a number of cases have been received by the Commission regarding threats and the use of abusive language by officials. It is always difficult to find the circumstances under which an official could abuse a private individual. In so far as threats are concerned, if an individual is in breach of any code, the best thing to do is to take appropriate action against him.

25. Mention must be made of complaints received by the Commission as a result of different interpretation of some rule or law by different officials in different localities. In this category of cases, the safest way is for the appropriate authority to send circulars clarifying the matter in order to avoid peculiar or embarrassing results. The best example is a case which involved the interpretation of 'Medical Charges' in the Compendium of Medical Fees—whether or not 'charges' include accommodation, and in another instance the interpretation of dependants for the purpose of the Workmen's Compensation Ordinance raised a problem. Both were dealt with in the above suggested manner.

26. The law establishing and governing the Permanent Commission of Enquiry gives no executive powers to the Commission. It is not proposed here that the Commission should be given such powers. However, cases have been reported to the Commission about an injustice which is continuing. The Commission receives the complaint and starts making an investigation while the complainant continues to suffer the injustice. In the end it is found out that the decision by the officials concerned was wrong. There was a case, for example, when seven people were locked up and they reported the matter to the Commission. The person who locked them up had no power under any law to detain anyone for more than forty-eight hours, yet the Commission received the letter of complaint after the persons had been in custody for a week. The Commission could do nothing to get them out. They continued to be in the lock-up for a long time after. Surely something must be done to remedy this.

27. Once again this year, there have been cases of further victimization of people who have come to complain to the Commission by officials against whom they had complained. In one case, a person who had complained to the Commission was dismissed from work. The Commission takes a serious view of this. Certainly, revenge is unacceptable to the cherished principles of TANU in particular and the Tanzania society in general. This could also lead to even more serious conse-

quences. The Commission also received letters from people who had complained that they have been reprimanded by their superiors for complaining to the Commission. After all, high officials themselves could be subjected to maladministration.[12]

32. The first year of the Commission ended with many cases still to be investigated. The investigation of these cases was conducted. However, there still remain a few cases which for one reason or another have not yet been concluded. Firstly, it should be noted that, unlike in courts of law, certain cases are given priority; for example, a case of detention will get priority over that of promotion. The overriding or paramount factor in determining as to which case should get priority is the possibility of restoring the complainant to the position in which he would have been but for the administrative act or decision. Secondly, there are some cases which although they were received by the Commission very much later, were concluded because the officials concerned were prepared to rectify their acts or reverse their decisions immediately.

33. From the foregoing, it will be noted that some of the 1967/68 cases have been concluded while some of the 1966/67 have not. We try to deal with as many cases as we possibly can, but again we have experienced some practical problems in our work. It has already been mentioned earlier in this report, that the Commission does not have any branches in the regions or districts. This in turn means that whenever a case warrants an investigation, Members of the Commission have got to travel a long distance. We are having, as will be seen later, an acute shortage of staff. Apart from over-working the present staff, we always find that as a result of this shortage, some cases did not get the prompt attention which they should get had the strength been otherwise. Again, as pointed out earlier, some public servants do not reply to official letters immediately. This long delay has the effect of keeping a lot of cases pending.

34. As regards allegations, it will be noticed that the number of allegations received during the period under review has fallen from 1,627 to 783. These figures show a sharp decline, particularly in the number of rejected cases. Last year, 1,060 cases were rejected and only 567 were taken for consideration. Thus more than two-thirds of all the allegations received were rejected. This year the story is different, 419 cases have been taken for consideration, and only 364 have been rejected. It will be seen that more than half of the allegations

---

[12] On 18 July 1970, NUTA, through its official organ *Mfanya Kazi*, warned workers not to take complaints about the Union to the Permanent Commission. Although *The Standard* issued a sharp rebuke to NUTA on 17 August 1970, this incident indicates that the problem referred to is far from being solved.

received during the year 1967/68 were taken for consideration.

35. From the foregoing, it will therefore be seen that members of the public have realized or have now known what type of complaints the Commission deals with. They know now where to lodge their complaints. Hence, it is not surprising to find that the number of allegations in the first place has fallen down. In the second place, the number of rejected cases has also fallen down. In short, members of the public are beginning to hit the nail on the head. It may be that our advice to the individual has helped a great deal in this respect. As mentioned earlier, the Commission still received complaints against East African Community, judicial decisions, private persons, and non-scheduled organizations. However, we are still educating the public as to where they should lodge their complaints. In this aspect we are greatly indebted to members of the press who published our 1966/67 report, thereby making it possible for as many members of the public as possible to see what we can do and what we cannot do.

36. Like last year, every Ministry had a share. District Councils again take the lead with regard to allegations. Judiciary comes second. Home Affairs, however, jumped from a humble fifth to a noble third. Regional Administration was third last year. This year it boasts of being fourth.

37. Complaints were varied. Many were about work, decisions, payments, failure to discharge one's duty, land, threats, oppressions, detention, compensation and refunds, taxation, misinterpretation or misapplication of rules or regulations, licences, fees and fines, use of abusive language, corruption, interference by one official or another, misuse of government property, shortages, delays in doing work, etc., in that order.

38. During the period under review 783 complaints were lodged to the Commission. Out of these, 364 cases were declined even though they involved persons or institutions in respect of whom or which the Commission has power to investigate. The reasons for the rejections are to be found in the appropriate Appendix. To give an illustration of such rejected cases, one example here will be of some assistance. There are some people who seek the assistance of the Commission before they exhaust existing or available machinery. Others simply refer their complaints to the Commission before even the appropriate authority has made a decision. All in all, quite a number of cases in this category were rejected, simply because some members of the public were taking the Commission as an instrument to force a particular official to expedite matters. This type of client forgets completely

that such an official has a lot of work to do. However, the truth is that our clients are very impatient.

39. It has been mentioned earlier that investigation of cases received last year and during the period under review were conducted. During this period 585 cases were concluded of which 114 were found to be justified. 224 were found not justified; 244 were discontinued and 3 were withdrawn. These figures include cases which were received last year and this year. An allegation is deemed to be justified, when after an investigation the Commission comes to the conclusion that the client rightly lodged the complaint. This may mean promotion, return of his money wrongfully retained, getting his plot back, being reinstated, etc. In this case, the complainant gets something which he should have received but for the administrative decision. There are other allegations which though justified do not necessarily mean that something will be done for the complainant. This applies, for example, to cases of unwarranted detention and lock up. In such cases, something is done to the person complained against. In some cases nothing is done for the complainant, or to the person complained against. This is exemplified by cases which end in having circulars sent to various officials to clarify a point.

40. Appendix 'C' which is a table showing an analysis of justified cases, should be given particular attention. Compared to last year's figures, the 1967/68 table clearly shows that a large number of officials failed or ignored to do what they were supposed to do. The same applied to acts or decisions which were unjust or discriminatory. The percentage of unjustifiable delays has shot up by twelve per cent. This of course is the debit side. The credit side shows lower figures in malicious misuse of power—which should be a joy to everyone. Then comes wrong interpretation or application of laws, here the percentage is lower than last year's. Similarly, the percentage of discretionary or improper exercises of powers had a lower percentage. It is early to say whether the Commission is deterrent or not, but certainly its effectiveness is beginning to leave its mark in the Public Services.

51. We regret to have to state again in this report about the acute shortage of staff and office accommodation. This shortage hardly requires over-emphasis. It is evident that as long as this persists,
● the work of the Commission will continue to be greatly hampered.

NOTE Paragraph 26 above raises a very interesting problem. If someone complains to the Permanent Commission that his rights are being violated, there is no procedure through which such violation can be restrained until a determination of the position of all the parties to the dispute has been completed. Only the courts have the power to grant interlocutory relief of this kind. A possible solution might be for the Permanent Commission, in cases where it feels such action is necessary, to apply to the High Court, on behalf of the complainant, for interlocutory relief pending the final disposition of the complaint. Thus, in the case mentioned in Paragraph 26, the Permanent Commission might seek an order of habeas corpus ordering the release of the complainants while it conducted its investigation. Clearly, this is not a very satisfactory solution. Given, however, the practical limitations on the courts which have been discussed in other chapters, it is difficult to see in what other way this problem can be solved. The only real alternative would be to, in effect, turn the Permanent Commission of Enquiry itself into a court.

NOTE Inevitably, we must attempt a general comparison between the High Court and the Permanent Commission of Enquiry as institutions for controlling executive and administrative action. The starting point for such an enquiry is a consideration of the types of cases both bodies deal with. Once a matter is held to fall, prima facie, within the jurisdiction of the Permanent Commission, the decision as to whether an investigation will be carried out is up to the Commission itself. (Permanent Commission of Enquiry Act, s.10(2).) It has adopted the practice of not pursuing complaints which fall into any of the following categories:

(a) The complaint is frivolous, vexatious, trivial or not made in good faith; or

(b) having regard to the existing circumstances of the case any further investigation is unnecessary; or

(c) under the law or existing administrative practice, there is an adequate remedy or right of appeal and the complainant has not exhausted it; or

(d) the case is too old; or

(e) if after a preliminary investigation there is not a prima facie case against an official; or

(f) it is against Government Policy.

(*Annual Report*, 1966-67, p. 47.)

Clause (c) would seem to indicate that the Permanent Commission regards its jurisdiction as being *complementary* to, rather than *alternative* to, that of the courts. In fact, an examination of the case synopses contained in the Permanent Commission's *Annual Reports* shows many cases where a complainant was assisted by the Commission in circumstances where, at least in theory, he might have sought his remedy in the High Court. In the words of its first Chairman, the Permanent Commission can deal with, '. . . arbitrary decisions or arrests, omissions, improper use of discretionary powers, decisions made with bad or malicious motive or decisions that have been influenced by irrelevant considerations, unnecessary or unexplained delays, obvious wrong decisions, misapplication and misinterpretation of Laws, By-laws or Regulations'. (E. A. M. Mang'enya, *The Permanent Commission of Enquiry (Ombudsman)*, op. cit., p. 6; see also *Annual Report*, 1966-7, p. 48.) Thus the Permanent Commission has handled cases involving such clearly justiciable matters as wages, false imprisonment, ownership of, or rights of occupation in land, and workmen's compensation. Without repeating most of the discussion of the courts in Chapter II, it should be noted that in deciding to exercise this very broad jurisdiction, the Permanent Commission of Enquiry has become a forum for hearing a host of grievances which for the lack of an appropriate and accessible forum, previously went totally without redress.

The general approach and procedures adopted by the Permanent Commission are also interesting. As outlined in Chapter III, the courts are concerned essentially with a strict interpretation and delimitation of statutory powers, but not with substantive questions of the rightness or wrongness of the exercise of a power in a particular case. The Permanent Commission has concerned itself with such matters and has even gone beyond this to note and attempt to correct instances of maladministration. In this respect it is not only protecting the individual's rights, but is making a positive contribution to the quality of public administration. Restrained within the confines of the adversary system, the courts are unable to negotiate with either plaintiff or defendant in an attempt to extricate the controversy from its either/or impasse. It is clear that the Permanent Commission regularly negotiates between the parties to a dispute. (See Permanent Commission of Enquiry Act, s.15(1); and Mang'enya, *The Permanent Commission of Enquiry (Ombudsman)*, op. cit., pp. 7 and 9.) Similarly, a court hearing a case involving a public authority is generally concerned only with the question of whether or not to give a remedy to an aggrieved citizen. Because of English constitutional mythology about ministerial responsibility, the court cannot attach the blame for a particular abuse or misuse of power to the bureaucrat concerned. Here also, by singling out individual bureaucrats for censure, the Permanent Commission assists in the maintenance of sound public administration.

The Permanent Commission provides its services free of charge, and does not involve anyone in the formalities and intricate procedural rules of the courts. (Mang'enya, ibid., p. 3.) Thus, the Commission specifically recognizes that it is acting as a 'poor man's lawyer'. Conversely, it is not clear to what extent anyone involved in the investigation of a particular complaint may be represented by a lawyer. One court-like procedural tendency appears in the 1968-69 *Annual Report* of the Permanent Commission of Enquiry. (See *The Standard*, 15 July 1970, and 16 July 1970.) In its published case summaries, the Commission appears to be giving reasons for its decisions. Clearly, it is desirable that any decision-making body should give reasons for its decisions, but it is to be hoped that the Commission will resist any tendency toward developing a body of law on which complainants would have to base their petitions for redress. In this, as in many other respects discussed here, the development of the Commission's procedural rules with a former High Court Judge as its Chairman is interesting. Finally, it is evident that one of the reasons for the Commission's success has been that it holds its hearings in private. A great deal of potentially dangerous and embarrassing, and obviously extremely beneficial, investigations of administrative shortcomings have been conducted. That these investigations appear not to have been tampered with, must be due largely to the fact that they were not carried out in public.

The question of the enforcement of the Permanent Commission's recommendations has vexed several commentators. Such criticism seems to miss the essential point that decisions of the High Court depend, equally as much as those of the Permanent Commission, on the executive for their enforcement. It appears that the Commission only makes recommendations in justified cases when negotiations with the individual or organization complained against have broken down, but we do not have any knowledge of how the President reacts to such recommendations. (Mang'enya, ibid., p. 9.)

As a final point, it is clear that the Permanent Commission of Enquiry '. . . has demonstrated its greater relevance to the needs of Tanzanians than the High Court with its paraphernalia of prerogative writs and orders'. (J. P. W. B. McAuslan, 'The Evolution of Public Law in East Africa in the 60's', op. cit., p. 170; see also E. A. M. Mang'enya, *The Permanent Commission of Enquiry (Ombudsman)*, op. cit., p. 13, and his article in *The Standard*, Republic Day Supplement, 5 December 1969.)

NOTE Several years ago the *Journal of African Law* carried an interesting correspondence concerning the relevance of ombudsman-type institutions in African one-party states. T. Sargant suggested that an Ombudsman could serve two functions. First, he said, it would provide for '. . . an informal and friendly check on abuse of administrative power without the need to discredit the department or the individual concerned', and second, it would help to '. . . create a confidence between the administration and the ordinary humble citizen'. (*Journal of African Law*, vol. VIII, no. 3, 1964, p. 195.) E. V. Mittlebeeler replied that an Ombudsman was not an appropriate institution for an African one-party state as such institutions depended for their success on, *inter alia*, a strong and responsive legislature. Since such legislatures did not exist in African one-party states, an Ombudsman which was established in such a state would fail (ibid., vol. IX, no. 3, 1965, p. 184). N. M. Hunnings rejoined that a successful administrative watchdog did not necessarily need to be an arm of the legislature, but could also be responsible to the executive (ibid., vol. X, no. 2, 1966, p. 138). This discussion is interesting because it does raise the question of the relationship of the Permanent Commission of Enquiry with other institutions, particularly those which are supposed to be exercising some control over the executive. In a thoughtful article, Professor Albert Abel has argued that Ombudsmen are not appropriate institutions in nations with Westminster-model constitutions. In such countries, he notes two important institutions which are already occupying the Ombudsman's prospective field. These are a supreme Parliament with an organized opposition, and a system of courts which act as a powerful monitor of the administration. A newly-established Ombudsman will discover that his role is so circumscribed by these existing institutions, that he will have little or no useful function to fulfil. ('Commonwealth Constitutional Complications' in D. C. Rowat (ed.), *The Ombudsman*, George Allen and Unwin, London, 1965, p. 281.) This argument may assist in explaining the success of the Permanent Commission of Enquiry. As we have seen, Parliament and the courts in Tanzania do not perform the functions that the Westminster-model theory assigns to them. If we stand Professor Abel's analysis on its head, we may conclude that the practical absence of these institutions in Tanzania may have had an important effect in creating the conditions for the Permanent Commission's success.

Y. P. Ghai
OMBUDSMEN AND OTHERS[13]

● The Commission's initial problems were similar to those of parallel institutions elsewhere. The bureaucracy appeared to receive it rather coldly; there was marked distrust of its function, so much so that 'some leaders on hearing the approach of the Permanent Commission of Enquiry had unnecessary fears, in some cases leaders were so apprehensive of what the Permanent Commission of Enquiry was doing in their areas that they planted some informers to report back to them what we were doing'. There was, further, victimization in some cases where a complainant had referred the conduct of an official to the Commission. The Commission was in a dilemma here; it seemed anxious to placate and reassure the bureaucracy but was sensitive to the fact that too close an association with it might damage its own image as a protector against the arbitrary acts of the latter. To an extent, the Commission has been helped out of the dilemma by the rule requiring the submission of a report to the President; once the report is submitted, the Commission's function ends; it is not required or expected to pursue further the question of remedies or to mobilize public opinion against particular administrative acts or trends which it may have condemned in its private report to the President.

Another of the Commission's initial problems has been that, apart from general ignorance of its existence and functions, there was much confusion about its jurisdiction and a large number of cases had to be declined because they did not fall within its competence. Of the 1,060 cases declined, 439 were outside its jurisdiction. What to do with such cases was another of the Commission's difficulties; it ended up in most instances by giving advice to the complainant as to his rights and the proper procedure for him to enforce those rights. There was also another problem of jurisdiction—the law does not define clearly what kind of complaints which are otherwise admissible should be disregarded for certain procedural defects, such as the complainant having insufficient personal interest in the dispute or that he should pursue his redress elsewhere. Some working rules about admissibility are necessary for various reasons—to protect the Commission against a flood of complaints and to prevent a waste of resources on frivolous complaints, to give the aggrieved citizen some guidelines about the acceptability, and therefore the value, of a complaint, and to maintain the integrity and consistency of the general administrative

---

[13] *East Africa Journal*, vol. VI, no. 8, 1969, pp. 34–6.

machine by minimizing and defining the instances when the Commission would interfere with the normal provisions for administrative decision making and the appellate system.

We now turn to the role the Commission sees itself performing. We discussed earlier the twin purposes that a watchdog on the administration can serve—it can help to protect the individual against the wrong or high-handed conduct of officials, and it can try to ensure integrity and competence in the bureaucracy and so promote the effectiveness of the government. In its conception, the Commission was envisaged as serving the former, and the conduct of the Commission has underlined that purpose strongly (there are constant references in the report to its 'noble task' as a 'defender of people's rights'). It has a marked humanitarian outlook and has apparently devoted much time and care to the cases of poor helpless people whose complaints were clearly outside the scope of its authority. We have seen that it acted as the 'poor man's lawyer or adviser' in cases outside its own jurisdiction. In some other instances it was concerned to promote a settlement, even though the official action was unimpeachable on legal grounds. While its concern for justice in the broad sense is generally unobjectionable, it is possible that sometimes it may come into conflict with its other function of ensuring conformity with established procedures and regulations; civil servants may be encouraged to ignore or gloss over rules and procedures if their application should lead to 'unjust' results. If so, the Commission will not only not have served the second purpose mentioned above, but may actually retard it; and the advantages to the Commission of this approach in winning popular support will probably be more than offset by the distortion of the administrative process. There is no evidence so far to indicate that the Commission's conduct has produced such a tendency—and indeed one of its general recommendations that officials should state the reasons for their decisions may have a wholly beneficial effect in this respect—but the Commission may need to be on its guard against too lax an application of the procedural requirements.

What of the success or otherwise of the Commission? It is clearly too early to reach any conclusions; much more time and experience are necessary before a proper evaluation of its work can be made. On the evidence available, however—the number of complaints received and the volume of work transacted—it is possible to state that a promising start has been made. There is some value in a political system for machinery where complaints against bureaucrats can be taken and investigated; it may help to counteract a sense of desperation

and helplessness in the community in the face of bureaucratic omni-
potence and tyranny. Quite apart from this psychological advantage,
the Commission's work has other benefits. It has considered itself
competent, though without a statutory mandate, to comment on the
defects in the law that have come to its attention in the course of its
investigations. This is a welcome development, and in a country
which has inherited so much law which is archaic in the context of
its new policies, the Commission's initiative can help considerably
to highlight anomalies and injustices in the legal system, and hopefully
lead to reform. Further, its overview of the administrative process
and personnel should have helped to engender greater attention
to detail and conformity with the requirements of the law on the part
of the officials. It may also have reduced instances of arbitrary or
capricious acts. It is obvious from the Report that on various occasions
the Commission was able to prevail upon an official to treat a complainant more fairly or leniently and obtained a better deal for him,
when it is equally obvious that the complainant would have had no
other help. Moreover, the Commission has pinpointed several undesirable trends in the administration, which the relevant authorities
can attempt to check.

The exact impact and effect of the Commission's work, however,
may remain difficult to evaluate as, apart from its annual report,
which gives only a bare outline of its actual investigations, its investigations and recommendations remain strictly confidential. Nor does
one know what action the President has taken on the reports and
recommendations made to him. Ultimately, the President's own
attitude is decisive; were he to take vigorous action against officials
adversely reported on, or to give serious consideration to the recommendations, the Commission's standing would be considerably
enhanced. Another factor which affects the success of the Commission
is the unduly restrictive rules of the exercise of its jurisdiction which
it has adopted. An additional restrictive rule, though not listed by
the Commission but which it applied in at least one case, is that the
complainant must have a personal interest in the matter, otherwise
he has no standing and the Commission will not accept jurisdiction.
Many of these rules appear to be inspired by the law or practice of
ombudsmen elsewhere; some are unnecessarily prohibitive in conditions
of illiteracy and the ignorance of citizen's rights and normal appellate
procedures. While it is important not to alienate the bureaucracy—
and restrictive rules help in this respect—the Commission ought not
to adopt too rigid a position on issues of *locus standi*. One of the
great attractions of an ombudsman-type institution is its easy access,

informality and flexibility. The care with which the Commission has perused difficult and almost illegible letters of complaint is commendable, and it is to be hoped that it will show the same concern for justice in its interpretation of its jurisdiction.

A final comment may be made in the evaluation of the Commission's effectiveness. Its function is to ensure conformity with the law and procedures, and so to investigate allegations of abuse of power and unfair administration. It has already declared in one of the principles for the exercise of jurisdiction that it is not concerned with complaints about official policy. The Commission's work therefore depends in large part on the laws and procedures provided. We have seen that Parliament, and in some cases the government, are free to determine what procedures have to be followed by the officials, how much discretion they are to be vested with and what safeguards are to be provided. While the Commission can achieve results of value by its vigilance and thoroughness, its effectiveness will suffer so long as the law itself does not set out in detail the procedures to be followed by the administrators. What is needed is some general legislation laying down minimum and fundamental principles and rules to be followed in any administrative regulation or decision. Armed with such legislation, the Commission could play an infinitely more positive and useful part in ensuring both fairness to the individual and efficiency in the administration.

The foregoing discussion of the Report of the Commission has perhaps demonstrated the need for a body of this kind. Suitable modifications of the traditional models may be necessary as in Tanzania (it may be of interest to mention that while the Commission is very conscious of the need to be a Tanzanian institution, it is also anxious to be seen as a valid instance of an ombudsman), but there is little reason to doubt that it can serve a most useful function, given a genuine desire to ensure fairness, openness and efficiency in administration. The bureaucracy has a key role to play in the development of new societies and it is no exaggeration to say that unless there is adequate administrative support, the projects for development have no chance of success. The developing countries therefore need to give much greater thought than they appear to have done so far to the problems of establishing and maintaining honest and efficient administration and administrators. Tanzania, which in addition to the establishment of the Commission, has enacted constitutional rules to prevent excessive property ownership and commercial enterprise or participation by its leaders, has shown evidence of its determination to tackle some of the most fundamental problems of socialism and development. The

outcome of its experiments has great relevance for many other develop-
● ing countries and will no doubt be watched with interest.

NOTE   For further comments on the Permanent Commission of Enquiry,
see A. Kiapi in *Eastern Africa Law Review*, vol. I, no. 2, 1968, p. 204;
R. Martin in *Journal of Modern African Studies*, vol. VII, no. 1, 1969, p. 178;
H. Kjekshus in Universities of East Africa Social Science Conference,
Proceedings, Dar es Salaam, 1970 and M. Kimicha (former Chairman)
in *Journal of Administration Overseas*, vol. XII, no. 1, 1973, p. 46. For
Ombudsmen, see D. C. Rowat, *The Ombudsman*, op. cit.; Walter Gelhorn,
Ombudsmen and Others, Harvard University Press, 1967; and 'The Ombuds-
man or Citizen's Defender', *Annal of the American Academy of Political and
Social Science*, vol. CCCLXXVII, 1968. For a comment on the abortive
attempt to establish an Ombudsman in Ghana, see Josiah Hagan, 'Whatever
Happened to Ghana's Ombudsman', *Transition*. no. 41, 1971, p. 28.

NOTE   As a final comment on the Permanent Commission of Enquiry,
the Commission was extremely fortunate to have as its Chairman during its
first years a man possessed of as much ability, energy, and humanity as
Chief E. A. M. Mang'enya.

INDEX

Abel, Professor A., 215
Act of State, 7; definition of, 7
ad hoc commissions, 198
Advisory Committee (preventive detention), 194
African Independence Party of Guinea and Cape Verde Islands (PAIGC), 21, 31, 98
Afro-Shirazi Party (A.S.P.), 45, 51
Anangisye, M.P., 52, 92
appeal, right of 179–80
Appeals Tribunal, 24
Arbitration Tribunals, 70
arrest 137ff, 160–1, 163; powers of, 137–42, 144–7, 153; false arrest, 150–3, 158–9, 162; use of unreasonable force, 158
Arusha Declaration, 17, 18, 26, 34, 49, 51, 67, 95
assembly, control of, 105–7
assessors, 60, 70, 176
Attorney–General, 2, 5, 72, 159, 168, 170

bail, 163–7, 180
Bills of Rights, 8, 38–45, 113, 195; Nigerian Bill of Rights, 39
Boards, District, 65, 71; Regional, 65
Bolsheviks, 12, 16

Canada, 44
Castro, Fidel, 21
Chief Justice, 60, 64–5, 69, 73, 159; appointment of, 60
chiefs, 57–8, 110
China (Chinese), 19, 27, 31, 32, 96–7; Communist Party of, 53; Great Proletarian Cultural Revolution, 21, 32
Chirwa, O.E.C., 4
class, 11–20, 23, 25, 27–8, 31, 43, 111, 126–7, 135; class structure in Tanzania, 17–18; class struggle, 11–20, 25, 31; ruling class, 25, 43, 55, 111, 135
Cliffe, L., 47–8
colonialism, xxi, 21, 55, 79, 96, 98, 128, 135; Colonial Office, 38; colonial

rule, 55, 84, 86, 94, 105, 109–11, 152, 176, 178
Commissioner, Area, 103–4, 106–7, 109–10, 131, 133, powers of, 100–110; District, 77, 100, 109–10; for Social Welfare, 104, 177; of Prisons, 167; Provincial, 77, 100, 109–10; Regional, 52, 65, 69, 96, 106–7, 109–10, 131, 168; powers of 105–6
confessions, 171–3; definition of, 173
Congo, 26
courts, 53, 54–81, 110–15, 126–32, 137, 145, 152, 158, 162, 166, 169, 174–6, 178, 194, 213–15; language of, 174; role of, 56–7; Court of Appeal for E. Africa, 55–6, 65, 73, 116, 158, 176, 179; District Courts, 135, 176, 179; High Court of Tanganyika, 55–6, 60–65, 73, 111, 115–16, 129–30, 135, 164, 170–1, 174–7, 179, 213–15; Primary Courts, 64–5, 68–71, 110, 135, 171, 175–6, 179
crime rate, 134–5, 167
Cuba, 20, 34, 96, 142

death penalty, 176, 178
decision to prosecute, 167–8
Denmark, 26
detention, pre-trial, 163–7; preventive, 8, 87–92, 166, 194; *see also* Advisory Committee
deportation, 8–9, 83–4

Devlin, Lord, 16
Director of Public Prosecutions, 168

Engels, F., 11, 13–16, 25
executive, 55–6, 72, 74–5, 110–15, 181

freedom, concepts of, xix, 1–5, 19, 33–5, 39, 58–9; of individual, 38, 40–41, 43, 112, 159, 177–8; of expression, 94, 96; of press, 93–6

general elections, 53
Georges, P. T., former Chief Justice, 38, 71, 92

Typeset by Kenya Litho Ltd., P.O. Box 40775, Changamwe Road,
Nairobi, Kenya. Prepared for press, designed and published by
Oxford University Press, Eastern Africa Branch, Harambee Avenue,
P.O. Box 72532, Nairobi, Kenya.

Printed by Kenya Litho Ltd., P.O. Box 40775, Changamwe Road, Nairobi, Kenya. Prepared for press, designed and published by Oxford University Press, Electricity House, Harambee Avenue, P.O. Box 72532, Nairobi, Kenya.